ANIMAL RIGHTS

Also by Mark Rowlands

SUPERVENIENCE AND MATERIALISM

Animal Rights

A Philosophical Defence

Mark Rowlands
Lecturer
Department of Philosophy
University College
Cork
Ireland

Consultant Editor: Jo Campling

palgrave
macmillan

Published by PALGRAVE MACMILLAN
Houndmills, Basingstoke, Hampshire RG21 6XS and
175 Fifth Avenue, New York, N. Y. 10010
Companies and representatives throughout the world

PALGRAVE MACMILLAN is the global academic imprint of the Palgrave
Macmillan division of St. Martin's Press, LLC and of Palgrave Macmillan Ltd.
Macmillan® is a registered trademark in the United States, United Kingdom
and other countries. Palgrave is a registered trademark in the European
Union and other countries.

Outside North America
ISBN 0–333–71131–9

In North America
ISBN 0–312–21720–X

This book is printed on paper suitable for recycling and
made from fully managed and sustained forest sources.

A catalogue record for this book is available from the British Library.

Library of Congress Catalog Card Number: 98–23544

Transferred to digital printing 2002

Printed and bound in Great Britain by
Antony Rowe Ltd, Chippenham and Eastbourne

Contents

Preface and Acknowledgements

SEE HIS WOLF BOOK

I started thinking seriously about the idea of animal rights a couple of years ago following a rather unfortunate incident involving a car, a domesticated wolf, and a ferry journey. The incident, and subsequent exchange of views with the ferry's car-deck attendant, dovetailed quite nicely with some thinking I had been doing about Rawls, and this book emerged fairly quickly and easily from that. My thanks to both parties.

My thanks also to University College Cork (or the National University of Ireland, Cork, as I think we now are – or might be – called) and to the Department of Philosophy in particular for providing a pleasant working environment in which this book could be completed. A timely sabbatical greatly aided in the completion of this work as did a research grant from the Faculty of Arts. Many thanks also to Jo Campling.

Finally, my thanks to Aurore Degez for waking me up.

1 Animal Rights: a Contractarian Defence

The contemporary philosophical arm of the animal rights or liberation movement effectively began in 1975 with Peter Singer's book *Animal Liberation*.[1] In this work, and in subsequent development of its ideas,[2] Singer argues that the moral theory known as *utilitarianism* can be used to justify and defend the moral claims of non-human animals. According to utilitarianism, a morally good action is one which promotes or produces the greatest amount of pleasure, happiness, or satisfaction of desires, and Singer argues, quite forcibly, that such promotion requires abandoning such practices as animal husbandry, and experimentation upon animals for scientific or commercial purposes. Singer's case for animal liberation, then, is anchored in his adoption of a utilitarian moral theory.

In 1983, Tom Regan published his important work *The Case for Animal Rights*.[3] Rejecting Singer's utilitarianism, Regan argued that many sorts of non-human animals possess moral rights because they possess what he referred to as *inherent value*. In virtue of this, Regan argued, we are morally obligated to treat them in ways that respect this value. And, for Regan as for Singer, this requires us to abandon such practices as animal husbandry, vivisection, and so on. Inherent value for Regan is an objective property, and whether or not an individual possesses it does not in any way depend on whether he, she, or it is valued by others. Whether or not a person possesses inherent value depends only on their *nature* as the type of thing they are. And this places Regan, at least in one important respect, in the tradition constituted by the doctrine of *natural rights*. Or, at least, it makes him an important intellectual inheritor of this doctrine.

To claim that Singer's *Animal Liberation* and Regan's *The Case for Animal Rights* are the two seminal works of the contemporary philosophical literature on animals would not, I think, be inaccurate. This, of course, is not to deny that there have been other important contributions. Philosophical analysis of the moral issues raised by non-human animals is a burgeoning field, and some of the contributions to this field have been quite excellent.[4] However, I think it is true to say that, in terms of the widespread circulation and recognition of

1

their work, by both philosophers and non-philosophers, by both friends of animal liberation and its foes, the work of Singer and Regan has been the most influential. And this means that any attempt to adjudicate the moral claims of animals, or on the moral issues raised by animals, must, effectively, define itself in relation to the work of Singer and Regan. This book is no exception.

While the defender of the moral claims of animals can only be indebted to the work of Singer and Regan, the inordinate influence of this work has, in effect, left a large and glaring hiatus in the philosophical defence of such claims. While Singer bases his argument on utilitarianism, and while Regan operates from within a framework established by natural rights doctrine, there is another, equally influential, type of moral theory that is widely thought to be inimical to the moral claims of non-humans. This theory is known as *contractarianism*, and is historically at least as important as utilitarianism or natural rights doctrine. Therefore, if a philosophical defence of the moral claims of animals is to be secure, it must be shown that such claims are derivable not only from a utilitarian approach, and not only from a natural rights approach, but also from a contractarian approach. It is widely thought that this latter task cannot be achieved. The principal aim of this book is to argue that it can be achieved, and to show exactly how this can be done.

The immediate impetus for the writing of this book, then, stems from an assumption shared by both friends and foes of the concept of animal rights. The assumption is that a contractarian, or contractualist, account of our moral commitments can find no room for the claims of non-human animals. Contractarian moral theories, it is thought, view one's moral rights and duties as deriving from the terms of an agreement reached by contractors in a hypothetical bargaining situation. Non-human animals, being non-rational, cannot plausibly be regarded as contractors in such a situation. And, therefore, it is argued, non-human animals cannot be the bearers of moral rights or entitlements, and, conversely, we have no duties towards them.

This view of contractarianism is shared by both opponents and proponents of animal rights. Peter Carruthers, an opponent, has developed this argument quite forcefully in his book, *The Animals Issue*.[5] Carruthers accepts that contractarianism provides the most adequate basis for a moral theory, and this provides the framework for his case against non-humans. Because animals are not rational agents of the sort who can plausibly be regarded as framers of a contract, they lack moral status. On the other hand, Tom Regan, perhaps the staunchest supporter of the concept of animal rights, and certainly one of its most important intellectual progenitors, has attacked contractarian moral theories on precisely these grounds.[6] Regan, too, believes that contractarianism is incompatible with the attribution, to non-human animals, of moral rights.

The view that contractarianism is incompatible with animal rights, then, is both widespread and tenacious. In this book, however, I shall argue that this view is simply false. Firstly, contractarian moral theories are certainly compatible with possession of moral rights by non-human animals, and by non-rational humans. Secondly, contractarianism, properly understood, provides the most satisfactory theoretical basis for the attribution of moral rights to non-human and non-rational individuals. Far from being a thorn in the side of the friend of animal rights, then, contractarianism is, in fact, possibly her greatest ally.

The widespread failure to realize this is due to another, possibly even more widespread, failure to adequately distinguish two crucially distinct forms of contractarian moral theory. On the one hand, there is the form of contractarianism which derives, in a fairly direct way, from Hobbes. This form emphasizes the benefits, in terms of protection of life, limb, and property, which a contract affords. We might refer to this as *Hobbesian contractarianism*, and interpreted in this way, the contract is an essentially prudential device, its purpose consisting in the security it provides.[7] Hobbesian contractarianism will be discussed more fully later on (Chapter 3). At the outset, however, it should be clear that this view is going to have a very difficult time accounting for our moral commitments to certain sorts of human beings, let alone non-human animals. If the point of the contract derives from the protection it affords us, and if we only need protection from those individuals who are a threat, or possible threat, to us, then there is simply no point in contracting with those individuals who are sufficiently weaker than oneself that they pose no real threat. For the Hobbesian contractarian, morality reduces to rational self-interest. And rational self-interest will extend the scope of one's contractual commitments only as far as those individuals who in some way constitute a threat, or to those individuals with whom contracting might yield some advantage. It is, I think, the Hobbesian interpretation of contractarianism which leads to the supposition that contractarian moral theory is incompatible with the attribution of moral rights to non-humans. Animals, in general, pose very little threat to us. And, more importantly, not being rational agents, they cannot coherently be regarded as contractors. Therefore, we cannot contract with them, and have nothing to gain from attempting to do so. Therefore, we should not contract with them. And, therefore, they lack moral status. The same argument, presumably, can be applied to any non-rational individual, including, notoriously, certain categories of humans. Thus, if Hobbesian contractarianism is incompatible with the attribution of moral status to non-humans, it is, without further argument, equally incompatible with the attribution of moral status to certain sorts of human being.

There is, however, another, very different, way of developing the idea of the contract, a way that has its roots in the work of Kant, and receives its most influential recent formulation in the work of John Rawls.[8] We can refer to this interpretation of the contract idea as *Kantian contractarianism.*[9] The central concept underpinning this interpretation is that of the moral equality of all individuals, and the resulting ideal of *impartiality* as constitutive of moral deliberation. In Rawls's work, impartiality in moral deliberation is safeguarded by an imaginative, and purely heuristic, device known as the *original position*. The contractors in the original position find themselves behind a *veil of ignorance*. That is, each contractor has no knowledge of his or her natural talents and characteristics – his or her intelligence, gender, physical appearance, athletic aptitudes, etc. Nor do they know their position in society. In fact, each contractor does not even know his or her conception of the good, the things they value, the things they despise, etc. From behind this veil of ignorance, then, each contractor is, in effect, forced to be impartial in their deliberations. One can be partial towards oneself only if one knows who, and what, one is. This book argues that *Kantian contractarianism* provides a theoretically viable framework for the attribution of moral rights to non-human animals. In fact, I shall argue that the framework it provides in this regard is demonstrably superior to those of its traditional competitors. Kantian contractarianism, then, provides the first plank in the central argument of this book.

In the preceding paragraph, I described Kantian contractarianism as providing a *framework* for the attribution of moral rights to non-human animals. A framework, however, is not the same as a *foundation*. One of the distinctive features of Kantian contractarianism, as a moral theory, is that it does not attempt to provide a foundation, or foundational justification, for the moral principles derivable from it. It cannot do so. Kantian contractarianism provides an expression of the idea that individuals have equal moral status whatever their physical or intellectual capacities, whatever their socio-economic status, and whatever their conception of the good. And it uses the device of the original position to identify what is involved in treating individuals as moral equals. It does not, however, provide, nor does it purport to provide, a *defence* of any particular idea of moral equality. Rawls, for example, is quite clear that there are many possible variations in the description of the original position, for example, many different assumptions about the dispositions of the contractors, so that 'for each traditional conception of justice there exists an interpretation on the initial situation in which its principles are the preferred solution.'[10] Given that this is so, then, the only way we can identify which interpretation of the original position is preferable is to determine which interpretation yields principles that match our intuitive convictions of justice. If the principles chosen on one interpretation of the original position do not match our intuitive convictions, or considered opinions as Rawls puts it, then we move to another interpretation which yields principles more in line with those convictions.

This is the reason why Kantian contractarianism cannot be thought of as providing a foundation for morality. Which principles of morality are derivable from the contracting situation depends essentially on which description we give of that situation. And which description we give of this situation will depend essentially on our prior acceptance of certain moral principles. It would, therefore, beg the question to attempt to use a Kantian contractarian approach in any sort of foundational way. If one is a Kantian contractarian, then one's use of the contract idea must be anti-foundationalist through and through. The correct role for the contract device in this context is not one of grounding or justifying certain moral principles but, rather, of *elucidating* them.

This anti-foundationalist approach to moral argument and deliberation, an approach derivable from Kantian contractarianism, provides the second plank in the central argument of this book. Foundationalist conceptions of ethics claim, of course, that morality has a foundation of some kind. According to some versions, this foundation is normative in character. According to these versions, the foundations of ethics consist in some set of principles, rules or judgements in terms of which all other ethical principles, rules, or judgements may be justified. Other versions of foundationalism assert that ethics has a meta-ethical foundation; that is, that there are non-moral facts that make particular ethical principles rationally necessary. A foundationalist approach to the question of animal rights sees the issue as depending essentially upon whether such rights can be derived from foundational moral norms, or from non-moral facts.

The approach adopted by this book, however, is anti-foundationalist, and this is necessitated by its reliance on a Kantian contractarian approach to moral deliberation and argument. The strategy to be adopted, then, looks, roughly, like this. Firstly, it will be argued that morality, at least as understood today, rests on a certain principle, which we can call the principle of *equal consideration*. Very roughly, this principle claims that all relevantly similar individuals should be accorded equal consideration and respect. This principle is effectively constitutive of moral argument as it is presently understood, and, in turn, derives, given certain relatively uncontroversial assumptions, from the more basic principle of *universalizability*: there can be no moral difference without a relevant natural difference. While the principle of equal consideration is essential to our understanding of what it means to think or reason morally, it cannot, by itself, significantly advance the case for animal rights. The problem is not simply that the principle is so vague, but also that it is, in an important sense, *theory-dependent*. Different moral and political theories will have very different understandings of what it means to treat distinct individuals with equal consideration and respect. This leads us to the second step of the strategy. If different moral theories and political ideologies embody distinct conceptions of what it means to treat individuals with equal consideration, then it would make sense to work from a currently dominant political ideology. That is, the second step of the strategy consists in identifying a currently dominant political ideology and working off the concept of equal consideration embodied therein. And there can scarcely be any doubt that a currently dominant political ideology, indeed, *the* currently dominant political ideology in most of the Western world and increasing amounts of the rest of the world is liberalism, with, of course, a small 'l'. To speak of *liberalism* with a small 'l' is to allude not to any particular political party, but to a set of presuppositions or sentiments of a broadly universalist and neutral order which span the ideological divide between various particular democratic parties, and thus provide the underpinning for political debate and argument. And it is these presuppositions and sentiments that play a central role in the argument of this book.

Accordingly, the argumentative framework adopted in this book is of the following form: liberalism, a dominant political ideology of today, embodies a certain conception of what it is to treat distinct individuals with equal consideration and respect. And once we understand this conception, and the basis of it, we will realize that the according of equal consideration and respect must, logically, be extended beyond the human circle to incorporate at least some kinds of non-human animals. That is, the very *content* of the concept of equal consideration embodied in the liberal political tradition logically requires that the principle of equal consideration be extended beyond the human sphere.

The restriction of focus to liberalism, and to the conception of equal consideration embodied therein, does not, and is not intended, to imply that liberalism is the only political ideology that could underwrite the attribution of moral rights to non-human animals. Far from it. As Dworkin has shown, every plausible political theory has the same ultimate value: equal consideration. Any plausible political theory, just like any plausible moral theory, will, in this sense, be an egalitarian one. And the basic idea of equal consideration is to be found in Nozick's libertarianism, for example, as much as in Marx's communism. And this makes it likely that the same sort of arguments as those developed in the following pages could be applied, *mutatis mutandis*, to other ideologies also. I will not, however, argue for this claim here.

The central argument of this book, then, is that embodied in a, or *the*, dominant political ideology of today is a certain conception of what it means to treat relevant individuals with equal consideration, and that this conception, when properly understood, entails that the class of relevant individuals includes at least some kinds of non-human animals. The content of the concept of equal consideration, as embodied in liberal ideology, requires that such consideration be extended beyond the human sphere. But how are we to identify the content of this concept of equal consideration? To answer this question, it is, first, important to remember that there are three distinct strands of liberal thought corresponding to three distinct ways in which basic liberal ideology has been motivated. And the specific content of the concept of equal consideration embodied in liberal thought is not independent of its motivation. Therefore, to examine the content of this concept it is necessary to examine these distinct motivations for liberal ideology.

The three motivations are: (i) the doctrine of natural rights, (ii) utilitarianism, and (iii) contractarianism. The doctrine of natural rights is represented in the writings of liberals such as John Locke.

The principal liberal defender of utilitarianism was, of course, John Stuart Mill. And the work of John Rawls provides a good example of a defence of liberalism based on contractarian ideas. Interestingly, the two truly seminal defences of the moral claims of non-human animals are based on the first two strands of liberal thought. Peter Singer's case for animal liberation was based on an application of utilitarian ideas to the case of animals. And Tom Regan's case for animal rights, I shall argue, is, in effect, based on precisely the sort of reasoning employed by those liberal thinkers in the natural rights tradition. In future chapters, I shall examine the arguments of Singer and Regan, and try to show that they are deficient in several important respects. Then I shall argue that contractarianism, in its Kantian incarnation, provides the best framework for understanding not only liberal thought in general, but also for the attribution of moral rights to non-human animals in particular. The argument, then, will be that liberal contractarianism, as developed by, for example, Rawls, employs a certain conception of what it means to treat distinct individuals with equal consideration and that the very content of this conception requires that such consideration be extended to at least some sorts of non-human animals. The device of the contract, in this context, becomes a means not of *defending* the concept of equal consideration as embodied in liberal ideology, but of *identifying* the specific content of this concept.

In broad outline, then, the book looks something like this. The following chapter, Chapter 2, examines the nature of the arguments typically employed by supporters of animal rights. The chapter highlights the role played by (i) the ethical principle of according equal consideration to all relevantly similar individuals, and (ii) by the meta-ethical principle that there can be no moral difference without a relevant natural difference, the principle upon which (i) is based. Chapter 3 further examines the principle of equal consideration, and focuses upon how this principle is embodied in liberal ideology. In this chapter, the various motivations for liberalism – natural rights doctrine, utilitarianism, and contractarianism – will be examined in some detail, with particular reference to John Locke, John Stuart Mill, and John Rawls respectively. Chapter 4 critically evaluates Peter Singer's attempt to ground the moral claims of non-humans in preference utilitarianism. It will be argued that Singer's attempt fails because utilitarianism, by its very nature, is committed to an inadequate understanding of the concept of equal consideration. Chapter 5 examines Tom Regan's case for animal rights. It is argued that

Regan's case is best understood as belonging quite centrally in the natural rights tradition, both in terms of the type of argument it employs, and in its view of the basis of moral evaluation and commitment. Regan's view, it will be argued also fails, but not, or not primarily, because it utilizes an inadequate conception of equal consideration (as in the case of Singer) but, rather, because it relies upon an inadequate understanding of the basis of equal consideration. Regan's position, it will be argued, rests on metaphysical assumptions that are unnecessary, ad hoc, and dubiously coherent. One of the results of this is a rather unwieldy conception of equal consideration that cannot do the work Regan requires of it. Chapter 6 develops the contractarian case for animal rights. It will be argued that a proper understanding of the nature of Kantian contractarianism, as developed by its most influential recent exponent, John Rawls, requires attributing to at least some sorts of non-human animals a substantial set of moral rights; a set of rights far more hefty and robust than such individuals have hitherto been accorded. This conflicts with a widespread understanding of the nature and implications of contractarian moral theory, most notably an understanding that seems to be evident in certain remarks of Rawls. This conflict, too, will be examined. Finally, the contractarian theory developed in Chapter 6 will be applied to one concrete case central to the debate over the rights of non-humans: vegetarianism. Chapter 7, the final chapter, continues the defence of the claims of Chapter 6. One of the principal implications of contractarian theory is that the limits of moral considerability are set by the limits of those things one could rationally worry about being from the perspective of the original position. The final chapter considers one, currently popular, argument for the claim that one could not rationally worry about being a non-human animal. The argument derives from the work of Donald Davidson in particular, and leads to the claim that non-humans do not possess preferences that one could rationally worry about satisfying, since they do not possess beliefs, desires, and other so-called propositional attitudes. Chapter 7 argues that once the nature of propositional attitude ascription is properly understood, there are no valid reasons for thinking that non-human animals lack beliefs and desires, and plenty of reasons for thinking that they do possess such states.

There are two further points worth making. Firstly, this book argues that at least some sorts of non-human animals are bearers of moral *rights*. The concept of a right employed here, however, is fairly minimalist in character, and bears little relation to, for example, the sort of conception that will be seen to be employed by Regan in Chapter 5. Throughout this book, moral rights will simply be understood as entailments of moral theories, or of the various principles which make up such theories. Thus, to use a rather simplistic example, if one adopts a moral theory that contains as one of its constitutive principles, 'Thou shalt not kill', then, on the present understanding of a moral right, this entails that all those individuals who fall under the scope of the principle have at least a *prima facie* right not to be killed. Rights, that is, will be understood here as simply moral entitlements. And entitlements are understood as entailments of moral theories. One of the advantages of this understanding of the concept of a right is that it removes any puzzles concerning the ontological status of rights, a problem, which, as we shall see, dogs Regan's case for animal rights. On the present view, then, whether or not an individual possesses a given moral right R is essentially a theory-relative matter: an individual I possesses a moral right R, relative to theory T, if among the entailments of T is the proposition that I is entitled to the treatment, or the freedom, prescribed by R. It is in this fairly unencumbered sense that, I shall argue, many sorts of non-human animals possess moral rights. The theory, of course, is liberal – with a small 'l' – theory, and relevant principle is the principle of equal consideration constitutive of this theory as such. That many sorts of non-human animals possess moral rights is, I shall argue, a genuine entailment of this theory. And this is true even though it is an entailment that the vast majority of us liberal human beings fail to grasp. There is nothing new in this sort of failure of course; essentially the same failure lay behind past generations' (and, no doubt, some of the present generation's) treatment of blacks and women.

Secondly, this book is fairly critical of the arguments of Peter Singer and Tom Regan. Part of what is involved in being a philosopher, I suppose, is criticizing the arguments of other philosophers. And, even, perhaps especially, for issues about which one cares deeply, there can, as a philosopher, be no legitimate case for abrogating this general approach. Nonetheless, anyone who cares about the moral claims of non-humans must acknowledge an enormous intellectual debt to both Singer and Regan. And, notwithstanding the criticisms of Singer and Regan to follow, there is another way of looking at the role of this book. And this brings us back to the opening remarks of this chapter. Personally speaking, perhaps the greatest psychological impetus for writing this book was provided by a tendency amongst certain sections of the philosophical population to assume that while the arguments of Singer and Regan were quite reasonable taken in themselves, they should be rejected on the grounds that the most adequate moral theory is contractarianism, and this is incompatible with the attribution of rights to non-humans. Peter Carruthers' book, *The Animals Issue*, is simply a codification of this view that, personal experience suggests quite strongly, is extremely pervasive among philosophers. The present book attempts to close off this avenue of escape for those who, for whatever reason, do not believe, or perhaps even want to believe, that non-humans possess substantially more valid moral entitlements than most of us are prepared to countenance. Contractarianism, at least in its most plausible form, is not only compatible with, but actually requires, the attribution of moral rights to non-human animals. Given that just about any moral theory can be seen to have its roots in either natural rights doctrine, utilitarianism, or contractarianism, this book, if correct, closes off an important hiatus in the philosophical defence of the moral entitlements of animals. If the arguments of this book are correct, and the hiatus successfully closed, then we can say that (i) either Singer is correct, in which case, the moral claims of non-humans can successfully be supported by way of utilitarian arguments, or (ii) Regan is correct, in which case, the concept of animal rights can be successfully underwritten by arguments deriving, in essentials, from the natural rights tradition, or (iii) I am correct, in which case the attribution of moral rights to non-humans is justified by appeal to contractarian moral theory. And this seems, just about, to exhaust the possibilities.

2 Arguing for One's Species

> Who speaks for wolf?
>
> Cheyenne invitation

'The rich man had exceeding many flocks and herds. But the poor man had nothing save one little ewe lamb, which he had bought and nourished up: and it grew up together with him, and with his children; it did eat of his own meat, and drink of his own cup, and lay in his bosom, and was unto him as a daughter. And there came a traveller unto the rich man, and he spared to take of his own flock and of his own herd to dress for the wayfaring man that was come unto him; but took the poor man's lamb, and dressed it for the man that was come unto him.' And David's anger was greatly kindled against the man; and he said to Nathan ... 'the man that hath done this thing shall surely die ... because he had no pity.' And Nathan said to David, 'Thou art the man.'

> Samuel 12: 2–7

1. THE INDEPENDENCE DAY SCENARIO

Suppose the earth were to be invaded by a species of powerful aliens. These aliens, for reasons which will no doubt become almost immediately clear in the embarrassingly unsubtle and thinly veiled story to follow, we can call *namuhs*. The intentions of these creatures are in no way benevolent, at least not towards us. In fact, they make it very clear that their primary purpose in invading this planet has to do with food. They plan to cultivate and farm the earth's planetary fauna, which has a galaxy-wide reputation as being of excellent nutritional value. In particular, at the top of their list of desirable food species is the human race, the meat from which is regarded as one of the tastiest in this part of the galaxy. We might call this the *independence day* scenario, after the rather successful film with a similar story line. Actually, in the film, it is not clear if the aliens intend to eat humans; simply killing us seems to cohere better with the overall story line. (Therefore, it might have been better to have called it the *lifeforce*

12

scenario, after Tobe Hooper's significantly lower budget, less successful, but still cult 1983 movie, although even here the aliens didn't plan
to eat us exactly, but only appropriate our lifeforce. In the end, the
wider circulation of the former won out, and the independence day
scenario it is.)[1] Let's suppose that in our independence day scenario,
the plan of the aliens is to engage in what we might call *human
husbandry*: they plan to raise, kill, and eat us. This sort of scenario is,
of course, a common science-fiction theme. Let us suppose also that
there are certain features which the aliens possess.

Firstly, their intelligence is vastly superior to ours. In fact, so much
is this so that they regard us in much the same way as we regard other
higher mammals. They think of us in much the same way as we think
of dogs and cats, pigs and cows, sheep and poultry. And let us suppose
that they are largely correct in this estimation of our relative intelligence. That is, the difference in intelligence between us and, say, dogs,
is roughly the same as the difference in intelligence between the aliens
and us. This difference in intelligence results in them having a vastly
superior technology which allows them to subdue us quite easily.

Secondly, although they take great pleasure in eating meat, especially human meat, they do not require meat in order to survive. They
can survive, indeed flourish, on a purely vegetable diet. Their roving
the galaxy in search of fresh supplies of meat stems only from the fact
that they enjoy eating meat much more than vegetables, and from the
fact that meat eating is their traditional diet, adopted by their fathers
and their fathers before them, etc.

Third, with regard to the interactions between themselves, the
aliens adhere to a strict moral code. In fact, they have evolved a
democratic culture and society in many ways similar to our own. The
conceptual centrepiece of this democratic culture is a principle of
equality: roughly the idea that each of the namuh is to be treated
with equal consideration and respect. Of course, it is not clear, even
to themselves, what treating namuhs with equal consideration and
respect amounts to. And their philosophers spend a good deal of
time arguing over this. Some, regarded by the aliens as being on the
left wing of their political culture, emphasize equality of welfare: at
the very minimum, the welfare needs of everyone are to be taken
care of. Others, of a more-right wing alien political persuasion, put
much more emphasis on equality of opportunity: everyone is to be
given equal opportunity to make whatever they can of their lives.
Nevertheless, while, in their culture, there are different and competing interpretations of the idea of treating everyone with equal

consideration and respect, the aliens all agree that, whatever the best interpretation of this idea turns out to be, everyone should be treated with equal consideration and respect. Furthermore, they recognize that this principle of equality is not a *description* of an actual equality that holds between them. They recognize that some of them are more intelligent than others, that some of them are physically more powerful than others, that some of them have skills and aptitudes that others do not possess, and so on. So, they recognize that if the principle were to be interpreted as a description of an actual equality that existed between each of them, then the principle would almost certainly be false. But this is not, in fact, the case. The principle is not a description of an actual equality, but a *prescription* for how each of them is to be treated. The principle claims that each alien is to be treated with equal consideration and respect, whatever their level of intelligence, whatever their physical strength, whatever their skills and aptitudes might be. This is, in many ways, the fundamental moral principle of their society; the principle from which all others stem. And the aliens take it very seriously, or at least profess to do so.

Finally, their adherence to a moral code means that the aliens are not morally blind. They recognize moral considerations and moral arguments when they see them, and they can be swayed by these considerations and arguments.

Let us suppose then that the alien invasion of earth is proceeding apace, and more and more humans are finding themselves on what are essentially factory farms. Unfortunately, in our independence day scenario there is no heroic American president (played heroically by Bill Pullman) to save humanity. Nor is there a feisty US air force pilot (played feistily by Will Smith) to force the aliens to think again. In fact, the fate of humanity lies in the hands of a few philosophers who have hitherto escaped capture. Curtains for humanity, one might think. However, the philosophers, heartened by the fact that the aliens recognize moral considerations and arguments, and can be swayed by these considerations and arguments, decide to try and convince the aliens that what they are doing is wrong. If you were one of these philosophers, how would you go about this? How would you attempt to convince the aliens that the practice of human husbandry was wrong?

2. THE OPENING GAMBIT: HOW TO ARGUE (MORALLY) WITH ALIENS

This is how to argue with aliens. First of all, we examine in more detail their conception of morality in general, and the principle of equality in particular. The principle of equality, of course, is a moral or ethical principle; that is, it is a principle which states what sort of behaviour is required if the demands of morality are to be met. In examining their conception of morality, however, we find that this moral principle rests on a further meta-ethical principle. A meta-ethical principle, in this sense, is one which is not a moral principle as such, but which provides a justification for a particular moral principle. So, when we examine the alien morality, we find, first, a moral principle:

Each namuh should be treated with equal consideration and respect (whatever that amounts to)

and, secondly, a meta-ethical principle:

No moral difference without a relevant natural difference.

A natural difference, here, is simply a non-moral difference. The second principle, then, claims that there can be no moral difference without a non-moral difference. The moral principle, the principle of equality, holds in virtue of the meta-ethical principle.

The meta-ethical principle provides, for the aliens, a constraint on the way they think about morality and the way they use moral language. And this principle applies to all things that can be the subject of moral evaluation: persons, actions, events, rules, institutions, and so on. Consider two aliens whom we can call 'Worf' and 'Schworf'. Suppose Worf and Schworf are very similar. In fact, they have pretty much the same qualities and features. Both are honest, courageous, and benevolent (at least by namuh lights), and both tend to be a little rash and belligerent. In short, with respect to any features that might conceivably go into making a moral evaluation of them, Worf and Schworf are identical. Then, by the meta-ethical principle that there is no moral difference without a relevant natural difference, Worf and Schworf must be given the same moral evaluation. That is, either both must be good or neither is. Given that there is no difference in their relevant natural properties, it would make no sense to say that Worf is good but Schworf is not, or that Schworf is good but Worf not. A difference in moral evaluation would be justifiable only if there is a relevant natural difference between the two, and, *ex hypothesi*, in our example, there is not. The same sorts of considerations apply to all other things that can be the subject of moral evaluation. Thus, if both Worf and Schworf help distinct elderly female namuh across the road, and assuming there is no natural difference between their actions (e.g. both elderly female namuhs want to cross the road, etc.) then if Worf's action is good, Schworf's must be good also. Conversely, if Schworf's action is bad, Worf's must be also. A difference in the moral evaluation one makes of two actions can only be justified if there is a relevant natural difference between those actions and, *ex hypothesi*, in our case there is not.

Notice that there is nothing in the claim that there can be no moral difference without a relevant natural difference which requires that moral evaluations are logically entailed by natural properties. The claim, for example, is not that because Worf has certain natural properties, this entails that he is good. Rather the claim is that if Worf has certain natural properties and he is also good, then any other individual – Schworf, or whoever – who has precisely the same natural properties as Worf, must also be good. Unless there is a relevant natural difference between two individuals, both must be given the same moral evaluation: either both are good, or neither are.

In the interests of precision, and when the fate of the human race lies in your hands it might pay to be precise, we might formulate the meta-ethical principle in the following way:

(S) For the set of all moral properties M, and the set of all natural properties N, necessarily, for any objects x and y, if x and y share all properties in N then x and y share all properties in M – that is, indiscernibility with respect to N entails indiscernibility with respect to M.

Once again, a natural property is to be understood simply as a non-moral property. (S) states that any two objects – where an object can be understood broadly as including persons, actions, events, institutions, and the like – that are identical with respect to the natural properties they possess must also be identical with respect to the moral properties they possess. This is often put by saying that moral properties *supervene* on natural ones. And namuh moral philosophy is based on the idea that moral properties are supervenient upon natural ones in this sense.

The fundamental ethical (as opposed to meta-ethical) principle held by the namuhs is that all namuhs – whatever their intellect, strength, skill, and aptitude – should be treated with equal consideration and respect. As we have seen, namuhs disagree about what exactly treating individuals with equal consideration and respect amounts to, but they still agree on the fundamental idea. The reason they believe this can now be explained by the meta-ethical principle that moral properties supervene on natural ones. If we are to justify treating one individual differently from how we treat another individual, we must be able to cite a relevant natural difference between those two individuals. Sometimes differential treatment of two individuals, or between groups of individuals, can be justified in this way. Suppose, for example, that a certain segment of the namuh population is, because of slight genetic differences from the remainder of the population, susceptible to a certain disease against which the remainder of the population is immune. Suppose, further, that this disease can be prevented or controlled through an early screening procedure. This difference between the two sections of the population is sufficient to justify a certain sort of differential treatment. In particular, the namuhs could justifiably deny the screening procedure to members of one section of the population while making it available to members of the other. In this case, there does seem to be a relevant natural difference between the members of each section; a natural difference which justifies, or could justify, this sort of differential treatment. When the namuhs deny certain members of their popu-lation access to the screening procedure, it is not true that they are thereby failing to treat them with equal respect. Since those members of the population are not susceptible to the disease, treating them with respect does not require making the screening procedure available to them.

On the other hand, according to the namuhs, the fundamental idea of treating individuals with consideration and respect is of a different order. If we are to treat one individual with consideration and respect, then we can only, justifiably, not treat another individual in the same way if there is a relevant natural difference between the two. In other words, the moral entitlements of individuals – what an individual is morally entitled to – supervene on natural properties. Therefore, there can be no difference in the moral entitlements possessed by two individuals unless there is some relevant natural difference between them. And, according to the namuhs, with respect to the entitlement to be treated with consideration and respect, there is no relevant natural difference between individual namuhs. While individual namuhs may differ with respect to their intelligence, physical strength, skills, aptitudes, and so on, none of these, according to accepted namuh morality, constitute relevant natural differences that could justify treating one sort of namuh with consideration and respect while denying that treatment to another. Therefore, because there are no relevant natural differences between namuh, all must be treated with equal consideration and respect. Thus says the namuh moral law.

So far, we have identified the fundamental ethical principle of namuh morality, and the fundamental meta-ethical principle from which the former derives. We have seen also how the ethical principle derives from the meta-ethical principle. This gives us a bridgehead; a platform from which to engage the namuhs in moral dialogue.

One way of arguing in ethics goes like this. You identify what your opponent believes, call it X, and then try to show that if she believes X, then she is also logically committed to another claim Y. And Y is hopefully the claim that you yourself endorse. This, for me, is the best way to engage in ethical argument. The alternative is to try to derive your own view from *first principles*. First principles are principles which, so it is thought, nobody could reasonably contest. The basic problem with invoking principles that nobody could reasonably contest is that such principles are typically contested, and often quite reasonably. Now, when the future of humanity is at stake, it is probably best not to rely on first principles since it would be somewhat disappointing, to say the least, to find that one's alien interrogators do not share your apparently uncontestable principles. Far better, far safer, to rely on principles you know your interrogators share. Whether you agree with those principles or not is not really relevant. What is relevant is that the namuhs believe them. That is all we need.

In other words, the strategy we can now adopt is this: we have identified the fundamental ethical and meta-ethical principles on which namuh morality is based. Now what we need to show is that these principles commit the namuhs to the claim that the practice of human husbandry is morally wrong.

Given the adherence of the namuhs to the meta-ethical principle that there can be no moral difference – including a difference in one's moral entitlements – without a relevant natural difference, the following strategy is clearly the one to adopt. We try to show that there is no relevant difference between us and the namuhs. While there are, of course, clear differences between us and them, none of these differences are morally relevant ones. Therefore, if namuhs are morally entitled to be treated with consideration and respect, so too are humans. If we can show this, then we have shown that the namuhs, by their own moral principles, are committed to treating humans with consideration and respect equal to that they show to their own.

This task, however, can only be achieved by finally engaging the namuhs in the dispute. We can only show that there is no morally relevant difference between us and them if we consider, assess, and finally demolish whatever proposals they put forward for the relevant difference, or differences, between them and us.

3. THE ALIEN RESPONSE

The namuhs are likely to have several proposals for what constitutes the morally relevant difference between them and us. The first of these is the most obvious.

A. Species Membership

According to this suggestion, the relevant natural difference between namuhs and humans, the difference which accounts for the fact that the former are entitled to be treated with consideration and respect, while the latter are not, is simply that the former but not the latter, are members of the namuh species, or the namuh *race*, as they prefer it to be called. Namuhs are all entitled to be treated with (equal) consideration and respect simply because they are namuh. Humans do not deserve to be so treated because they are not namuh. Thus, species membership provides the criterion of what is known as *moral considerability*, where an individual is morally considerable if it is morally entitled to consideration and respect. Even with our vastly inferior human intellectual capacities, however, it is easy to see that there are formidable problems with this suggestion. We might put the matter to our namuh disputants in this way. Suppose it were to be discovered that a certain substantial proportion of the namuh population were not really namuhs at all. Whether or not one is a namuh is, after all, a question of one's genetic structure, since the category of a species is ultimately a genetic one. Let us suppose that these deviant inhabitants of the planet *htrae* (you've guessed it! and pronounced 'hut-ray-eh', by the way) are of extra-htraen origin, coming from another planet in the htraen solar system. However, by the sort of logically possible coincidence for which philosophers will be eternally grateful, these non-htraens exactly resemble the namuhs. There are no phenotypic differences between the two, and while the genetic differences are significant enough to constitute the non-htraens as a distinct species from the namuhs, the namuhs, for religious reasons, banned any form of genetic research early in their development, and so are unable to detect these differences. As a result, the non-htraens became useful and much loved members of namuh society. Neither the namuhs nor the non-htraens were aware of the fact that they belonged to different species. Intermarriage was common between the two groups, though, of course, no one realized that this is what it was. And no one seemed to be perturbed by the fact that many of the marriages on htrae were childless, or resulted in sterile children. Such a situation was thought of as quite natural. Now, the question to put to the namuhs is quite obviously this. If such a state of affairs were in fact to be the case, what would you say about the moral status of the non-htraens? Do they in fact have no moral entitlements, simply because of these genetic differences? Would one be willing to deny one's husband, or wife or (albeit sterile) children any moral entitlements, simply because of this genetic difference? Indeed, the point can be pushed further. How do you know that you, my supposedly namuh interlocutor, are not yourself one of these non-htraens? For all you know, you could be one also. So think carefully before you deny moral entitlements to the non-htraens, you may also be denying them to yourself.

On the basis of this, I think we might have reasonable confidence in the namuhs abandoning the claim that species membership is the criterion of moral considerability. What reason do we have for this confidence? Simply that in a similar situation – a situation in which what was thought to be the class of human beings is in fact made up of two genetically distinct species – we would do the same. Our reasons for this would, of course, be partly self-interested ones. If you do not know whether you will turn out to be a member of the deviant group, it would not be wise to endorse a rule which, by stripping members of that group of their entitlements, would also potentially result in the loss of your moral entitlements. There is, however, also a deeper intuition underlying this claim; an intuition that is not grounded in self-interest. If a person were to be discovered to be a member of a genetically deviant group, and, in virtue of this, not a member of the species *homo sapiens*, there is still a clear sense in which they are the same person they always were. What has been revised is one of the biological categories to which they belong, but this revision has not changed their identity as the particular person they are. Suppose it happened to you, for example. You spend all of your life regarding yourself as an ordinary member of the species *homo sapiens*. Then one morning you wake up to find that, in your sleep, scientists have been running genetic tests on you. They have dis-covered that you are in fact a genetic anomaly: although you possess all the typical phenotypic properties of a human being, genetically you are not human at all. And since species membership is a genetic concept, this means that you arc, in fact, not a member of the human race. However you might have conceived of yourself in the past, you are not a member of the species *homo sapiens*. There is a clear sense, I think, in which, despite the revision of one of the biological kinds into which you can be placed, you are still the same person you always were. After all, from your perspective nothing much has changed. You still remember things that happened to you in the past, you still have the same interests, thoughts, feelings, emotions, character traits, behavioural dispositions, and so on. In fact, if the scientists had not informed you of their discovery, you would, in all likelihood, have spent the rest of your life thinking of yourself as a human being. Intuitively, then, you are still the same person you always were. And, crucially, whatever aspects or features of you that go into making you deserving of consideration and respect, these aspects or features have not suddenly vanished with the mere discovery that assessment of your relation to a particular biological kind has been revised. As subjectively earth-shattering as it would no doubt be, the discovery is not sufficiently conceptually earth-shattering to change either your identity as the particular person you are, or the moral entitlements you possess.

The conclusion we must draw from this is that species membership is not a morally relevant property. The fact that two individuals might be members of different species is not, by itself, sufficient justification for treating them differently. In particular, a difference in species membership is no justification for treating one of the individuals with consideration and respect while withholding such treatment from the other.

The above example is, to say the least, rather far-fetched (as, of course, is the whole independence day scenario). But the outlandish character of the example is not a significant drawback. What we are examining by way of such examples is the *concept* of moral considerability. That is, we are examining how we *think* about moral entitlements. And one way of facilitating this process is by considering various counterfactual examples, and often, the more outlandish the example, the more helpful it can be in this regard. We could also use the same process with regard to more mundane and well understood concepts. We might, for example, examine the concept of a *bachelor* (to take a tried and tested philosophical example) by imagining various features that bachelors might have. Then, when we find that we cannot, without contradicting ourselves, talk about married bachelors, this tells us something important about the concept of a bachelor: the concept of a bachelor logically excludes the concept of being married. The reason, of course, that we do not do this with mundane and well understood concepts is precisely because they are mundane and well understood. There is no point in clarifying these sorts of concepts; we already understand them perfectly well. However, part of what we are trying to do in the case of moral inquiry is clarify the nature of the moral concepts we employ. And in this case, the concept we are trying to clarify is that of moral considerability; of what it means to be morally entitled to consideration and respect. In this light, what the above thought experiments seem to tell us is that the concept of moral considerability is not closely tied to the concept of species membership. In certain circumstances at least, we would be quite happy to allow that the umbrella of moral considerability extends beyond the boundary of our species. Species membership cannot be regarded as the criterion of moral considerability because it is at least possible that there could be morally considerable individuals who are not members of the species *homo sapiens*. We can hope that the namuhs will follow us in this assessment, and accept the analogical extension to their own case.

B. Phenotypic Properties

A possible namuh response to the problem of genetically distinct, but phenotypically identical, groups is to revise their criterion of moral considerability, now giving it a basis not in genetic properties but in *phenotypic* ones. On this suggestion, it is the physical appearance associated with being namuh that is decisive in determining who possesses moral entitlements in general, and the entitlement to consideration and respect in particular. Thus, it is the phenotypic properties associated with being namuh that constitute the criterion of moral considerability. Therefore, it is the different phenotypic properties possessed by namuhs and humans that provides the crucial morally relevant difference between members of the two species. And this is why all namuhs must be treated with equal consideration and respect while all humans can be sent off to the factory farm.

While this suggestion might be put forward by certain sections of the namuh population, it must be said that the more reflective namuhs would not be really happy with it. What troubles them is the possibility that there could be born a namuh who is so hideously deformed (from the namuh point of view) that he shares very few of the typical phenotypic properties of normal healthy namuhs. Nonetheless, despite his physical disfigurement, his mental powers were the same as those of a normal, healthy, namuh. This namuh is quite happy with this his life, enjoys the company of other namuhs (and as all namuhs admit, is a most agreeable host), and likes to engage in abstruse scientific and philosophical speculation. Surely, the more reflective namuhs think, it would be wrong to regard this unfortunate namuh as lacking any moral entitlements, hence as not being entitled to equal consideration and respect. To regard the namuh in this way, simply on the basis of his physical deformities, would be a particularly nasty form of chauvinism. And namuhs do not like to think of themselves as chauvinists. But, if the deformed namuh is morally considerable, despite his failure to possess a large proportion of the phenotypic properties of the average namuh, then phenotypic properties cannot provide the criterion of moral considerability. Phenotypic properties, that is, cannot be crucial in determining who, or what, possesses moral entitlements.

C. Intelligence

The more philosophically sophisticated namuhs will be unruffled by the failure to identity either a genetic or phenotypic criterion of moral considerability. They never expected there to be such a criterion. It is more realistic, they claim, to suppose that the morally relevant difference between namuhs and humans lies not in physical differences but in psychological ones. In particular, the vast gulf in intelligence between namuhs and humans is the morally relevant difference which justifies them treating all namuhs with equal consideration and respect, and sending all humans off for slaughter. Namuhs are, while humans are not, morally considerable because the latter fall below the necessary threshold of intelligence.

There is, however, a serious problem with this line of argument also. If this is the namuh case against us, then we can employ what is known as the *argument from marginal cases* against them. That is, we should point out that, while it may be true that *most* namuhs are more intelligent than *most* humans, there is a class of namuhs for which this is not so. Firstly, some namuhs, for example, are born with severe brain damage resulting in severe retardation of their intellectual powers. Secondly, the intelligence of levels of namuh infants is not noticeably different from those of adult humans. Finally, many ageing namuhs, through a variety of causes, suffer from a progressive deterioration in brain structure and function, and the intelligence of these is certainly no greater, and in many advanced cases, less than that of adult humans. Therefore, if the namuhs want to claim that humans, because of their inferior intelligence, lack moral entitlements, including the entitlement to respectful treatment, then it seems that, if they are to be consistent, they must also claim that these classes of namuhs lack such entitlements. Happily for us, most namuhs are not willing to endorse this latter claim, and they accept, therefore, that they must reject intelligence as the criterion of moral entitlement. Since there is no difference in intelligence between these classes of namuhs and adult humans, intelligence cannot be a morally relevant difference between the two. Therefore, if the namuhs want to regard the unfortunate class of namuhs as morally considerable, while denying this status to adult humans, they cannot be relying on a criterion of intelligence in making this judgement. As far as any criterion based on intelligence is concerned, if the former are morally considerable then the latter must be also.

This argument from marginal cases, in fact, gives us an extremely powerful negotiating instrument. The reason is that the argument is completely neutral with respect to the property advanced as the criterion of moral entitlement. If, for example, the namuhs claimed that the morally relevant difference between them and us was their ability to appreciate *cisum*, an auditory art form of which humans had no comprehension, then all we would have to do in order to apply the argument from marginal cases is show that there are at least some namuhs who are unable to appreciate cisum, or whose ability to appreciate cisum is no greater than that of humans. If we can do this, then the namuhs face a choice: either they deny any moral entitlements to the relevant class of namuhs, or they abandon the capacity to appreciate cisum as the criterion of moral entitlement. Thus, the argument from marginal cases is completely neutral with respect to any proposed criterion of moral entitlement, and can, therefore, be applied independently of any particular criterion. The argument has the following general form of a dilemma:

(1) X is proposed, by group G, as the criterion of moral entitlement.

(2) There are certain members of G which do not possess X.

(3) Therefore, either (a) those members of G possess no moral entitlements, or (b) X must be abandoned as the criterion of moral entitlement.

The argument is applicable no matter what X is, and no matter what the group G that is proposing X as the criterion of moral entitlement. Much of the power of the argument lies in its generality.

We humans, of course, will be hoping that the namuhs adopt option 3(b). And, happily for us, I think many of the namuhs would be willing to take this option. However, this may not be true for all of them. Some namuhs, in fact, may be willing to adopt option 3(a). According to proponents of this option, the fact that some namuh fail to measure up to the levels of intelligence required for possession of moral entitlements does not entail that the intelligence criterion should be abandoned. All it means is: so much the worse for those namuh. These unfortunate namuh are not, in fact, genuine possessors of moral entitlements. They are not, in reality, morally entitled to anything. To make his position more palatable, the defender of this view might employ a distinction between being a *direct* and being an *indirect* bearer of moral entitlements. The namuh who measure up to whatever level of intelligence is demanded by the criterion are direct bearers of moral entitlements. The namuh who fail to measure up lack such entitlements, at least directly. However, it is also true that the namuh who are direct bearers of rights may, in various ways, be attached to those who are not. In various ways, and to various degrees, they sympathise with their brothers, sisters, sons and daughters, mothers and fathers who fail to meet the requirements of the criterion. Moreover, in various ways, and to various degrees, they would be upset should harm befall these unfortunate namuh. Furthermore, as it has often been noted, the namuh who is cruel, callous, or indifferent in his dealings with those less fortunate namuh who are not direct bearers of rights tends also to be more cruel, callous, or indifferent in his dealings with those namuh who are the bearers of direct rights. If we sanction harm being done to the less fortunate namuh, we immediately put ourselves on a slippery slope, the inevitable conclusion of which is that harm will be done to those more fortunate namuh who are direct possessors of moral entitlements. Therefore, the namuh defender of option 3(a) could argue that although those namuh who fail to meet the requirements of the criterion thereby fail to be direct bearers of moral entitlements, they do, nonetheless, possess such entitlements in a derivative sense. Since harm done to them can result in harm being done to those namuh who are bearers of direct rights, harm should not be done to those namuh who lack moral entitlements. This is not because they are entitled to not being unnecessarily harmed, but because of the connections they have to namuh who are entitled to not being unnecessarily harmed. Thus, the namuh who fail to measure up to the level of intelligence demanded by the criterion, it could be argued, possess entitlements in a derivative sense. They are indirect possessors of entitlements.

Even with this qualification in place, however, option 3(a), and the intelligence criterion upon which it is based, faces formidable difficulties. In particular, it is difficult to see how intelligence can be the crucial feature determining which entities are, and which entities are not, possessors of moral entitlements, direct or otherwise. Part of the worry here is that there are fundamental difficulties in identifying any non-arbitrary level of intelligence as constituting the criterion of moral entitlement. Suppose, for example, the namuh were to be attacked by yet another species who are significantly more intelligent than them. Whereas the average namuh IQ is, let us suppose, about 900, the average IQ of this invading species is more than double this. Consequently this new species regards the namuh in much the same way as they regard us, and as we regard other higher mammals. The new species, we will suppose, are also *intelligencists*: they regard a certain level of intelligence as constituting the criterion of moral considerability, and they identify this level as significantly higher than that of the most intelligent namuh – 1500 on the human scale, let us suppose. But what justification could there be for identifying this as the crucial threshold level? Why 1500? Why not, say, 700? Or 100? Or 10? What does any one of these numbers have to recommend it over any of the others?

This problem, it should be recognized, is not an epistemological one. That is, it is not simply a problem about the limits of our knowledge. It is not as if there is a certain numerical level of intelligence which provides the morally relevant threshold but that we just can't work out what it is. The problem is that any number we pick, any level of intelligence we identify, is equally arbitrary. There is nothing, no fact of the matter, that could recommend any one number over any other. And, since any particular level of intelligence we happen to identify, not just seems, but actually is, equally arbitrary, this shows that intelligence cannot be the crucial factor determining who possesses moral entitlements. Therefore, option 3(a) should be rejected.

4. 'THOU ART THE MAN'

The biblical passage quoted at the beginning of the chapter pertains to the behaviour of David, the king of Israel. David apparently lusted after Bathsheba who, unfortunately from David's point of view, was married to Uriah. Not to let a little thing like this thwart him, he ordered Uriah off to fight in the front line on his army thus, effectively, ensuring his death. The point of Nathan's anecdote, of course, is to get David to see his behaviour from a new perspective, one unclouded by his libidinal promptings. Thus, David comes to see his behaviour not as a clever piece of manoeuvring in the game of love, but as a cruel and vicious act against an essentially defenceless opponent.

The independence day scenario is, of course, a thinly veiled parable for our treatment of animals. (Subtlety, I'm afraid, was never my strong point.) For, with respect to our treatment of non-human animals, we are the namuh, the animals are us! And, in the argument we might have used against the namuh, we have the essential argument for animal liberation, where, for the present, we can understand this simply as the attempt to show that non-human animals possess substantially more moral entitlements than we humans typically accord them. The argument has the following general form:

P1. Human beings possess a substantial set of moral entitlements including, fundamentally, the entitlement to equal consideration and respect.

P2. There are no morally relevant differences between humans and non-human animals.

C. Therefore, non-human animals also possess a substantial set of moral entitlements including, fundamentally, the entitlement to equal consideration and respect.

Defenders of the idea of animal liberation often point out the conceptual connections between this idea and the claims of certain oppressed groups, arguing that just as the treatment of one group by another can be, and often is, racist or sexist in character, so too the treatment of non-humans by humans is typically *speciesist* in nature.

Remarkably, defenders of animal liberation are sometimes attacked for this claim, as if it somehow demeaned the fight against racism or sexism to have non-human animals mentioned in the same breath. However, the comparison is perfectly legitimate. This can be seen simply from the fact that the argument described above is simply one instance of a more general argument form:

P1. Individual members of group X possess a substantial set of moral entitlements including, fundamentally, the entitlement to equal consideration and respect.

P2. There are no morally relevant differences between individual members of group X and individual members of group Y.

C. Therefore, individual members of group Y also possess a substantial set of moral entitlements including, fundamentally, the entitlement to equal consideration and respect.

It is because the fundamental argument for animal liberation is an instance of this more general form that we could make use of essentially the same argument against the namuh in a bid to achieve human liberation. And it is because the argument for animal liberation is an instance of this more general form that the comparison with arguments against racism and sexism is both legitimate and logically compelling. If there is a difference between the cases against racism and sexism, on the one hand, and the case against speciesism on the other, it is not in virtue of the logical form of the arguments these cases instantiate. The logical form is, in each case, identical.

There may, of course, be other reasons for thinking that the case against speciesism is disanalogous to the cases against racism and sexism. If one could show, for example, that there were morally relevant differences between humans and non-humans, while there were not between male humans and female humans, or between white humans and non-white humans, then one would have justification for one's claim that the cases are disanalogous. In any event, the crucial premise in the above argument for animal liberation is P2: the claim that there are no morally relevant differences between human and non-human animals which could justify the claim that the former are morally entitled to be treated with consideration and respect while the latter are not.

With respect to P2, much of the arguments of animal liberationists have been essentially, and necessarily, defensive in character. That is, they consist in demolishing suggestions of in what the morally relevant

difference might consist. The most common suggestions of anti-liber-
ationists, in this regard, mirror those of our imagined namuh
interlocutors. These suggestions, as we have seen, can be objected to
on the grounds that they are either morally arbitrary (genotype,
phenotype, intelligence) or fall victim to the argument from marginal
cases (intelligence, and most other qualities possessed by typical
humans). And, it remains true that opponents of animal liberation
have failed to put forward any satisfactory suggestion for in what the
morally relevant difference between humans and non-humans might
consist. Therefore, I think, the burden of argument is clearly with
those who want to maintain that there is a morally relevant difference
between human and non-human species.

In this book, despite the indisputable success for the animal liberationist of the negative tactic, I want to explore a more positive
approach. This approach consists in examining the other crucial, but
obviously neglected, concept involved in the animal liberation argument. This is the idea of *treating individuals with equal consideration
and respect*. If we want to know what is involved in treating non-
humans with consideration and respect equal to that accorded
humans, we shall first have to know what is involved in treating
humans with equal consideration and respect. Moreover, I shall argue
that once we understand what is involved in treating humans with
equal consideration and respect, and once we understand the basis of
the requirement to do so, we shall automatically see that (at least
some sorts of) non-humans must be treated with consideration and
respect equal to that we accord ourselves. That is, proper understanding of the concept of equal consideration itself reveals that there
are no morally relevant differences between human and non-human
animals. This is the central argument of this book.

5. WHO SPEAKS FOR WOLF?

Since the chapter opened with a parable, it seems appropriate to close
with one. I make no claims for the historical accuracy of this story,
indeed, it strikes me as extremely implausible. But, historical veracity,
of course, is not its point. The parable runs as follows.[2] For their
council meetings, Native Americans of the Cheyenne nation were
reported to have had a person whose function was to represent not the
interests of any particular tribe, but those of the non-human inhabitants of the plains; the four legged creatures, the winged creatures, the

crawling creatures. This person would be invited to speak by the question: who speaks for wolf? This book is, in effect, a piece of philosophical advocacy, an attempt to speak for wolf. But with such an attempt, sentiment is, at least in philosophical contexts, inappropriate. And this somewhat misty-eyed invocation of the wisdom and decency of aboriginal Americans is the last thing even approaching sentimentality that will be found in this book. Any piece of philosophical advocacy must stand or fall on nothing other than the validity and soundness of its arguments. And if the arguments of this book are correct, our treatment of many non-human creatures – four-legged, winged, and crawling – is of a piece with, and morally no more defensible than, the namuhs' imagined treatment of us. And, in the absence of morally relevant differences, to speak for humans is, logically, to speak for wolf.

3 Liberalism and the Expanding Circle

1. THE EXPANDING CIRCLE

Philosophical defences of the idea of animal liberation often invoke the imagery of the *expanding circle*. The circle comprises perceived moral entitlements, that is the moral entitlements we perceive ourselves and others to possess. This circle is said to be expanding in the sense that these entitlements, which we once, perhaps, perceived as being restricted to members of our own family or tribe, have gradually broadened, to include, in the first instance, all members of our nation, then all members of our race, all members of our gender, and, finally, all members of our species. Animal liberationists typically claim that re-evaluation of our understanding of the moral entitlements possessed by at least some non-human animals is the next logical step in this expansion. What underwrites this claim is not simply the fact, or alleged fact, of this expansion but, rather, the basis of it. Once we come to realize that a certain group of individuals possess a certain set of moral entitlements, we also come to understand that, in the absence of any morally relevant differences between members of this group, each member will have the same entitlements. However, this claim naturally lends itself to extension in the following sort of way. Suppose there is a certain group of individuals, S_1, who are generally perceived by us to have a certain set of moral entitlements. Then, in the absence of any morally relevant differences between the members of S_1, we must also agree that each member possesses the same moral entitlements. However, suppose S_1 is subsumed by a larger group of individuals, S_2. Then, if it can be shown that there are no morally relevant differences between, on the one hand, the members of S_1 and, on the other, those members of S_2 who are not members of S_1, then we are also committed to granting the same moral entitlements to the latter as we do to the former.

Most animal liberationist thinking can be seen to proceed on the basis of this sort of framework of assumptions, and the present book is no exception. In fact, the central argument of this book is that once we understand the content, or meaning, of the claim that all human

31

beings should be accorded equal consideration and respect, then we will also understand that this principle of equal consideration must be extended beyond the circle of human beings. Involving, as it does, the imagery of the expanding circle, this idea is common to most animal liberationist argument. And my disagreements with other authors, to be dealt with in future chapters, stems not from any disagreement about this general framework, but, rather, from a disagreement about what they consider to be the basis of the claim that all human beings should be treated with equal consideration and respect. I shall argue that they misunderstand the reason why non-human animals should be treated with consideration and respect equal to that accorded humans because they misunderstand why human beings should all be treated with equal consideration and respect. To begin with, however, we first have to examine this principle of equal consideration.

2. THE PRINCIPLE OF EQUAL CONSIDERATION

Restricted to the category of human beings, the principle of equal consideration says:

> All human beings should be treated with equal consideration and respect.

This principle can perhaps best be understood as comprising two components, each partly constitutive of its content. The first specifies an abstract principle of justice: as a matter of strict justice, each person is to be given their due, what they are owed. Such a principle is axiomatic in any plausible moral or political inquiry. Even, for example, avowedly *perfectionist* accounts of moral entitlement, such as those of Aristotle or Nietzsche, adhere to this abstract principle. It's just that, according to perfectionist theories, what a person is owed, as a matter of justice, is dependent on their level of worth, excellence, or perfection.

The second component functions essentially to place an important restriction of this abstract principle of justice. All people are owed, as a matter of strict justice, *equal* consideration and respect, irrespective of their level of excellence. That is, according to the second component, level of excellence, however excellence is defined, is not a morally relevant difference that could justify treating a person with more, or less, respect than another. And today, unlike the time of Aristotle, or even Nietzsche, with our conception of justice shaped as it is by the democratic ideal, it is difficult to imagine finding any satisfactory justification for claiming that level of excellence, however defined, can constitute a morally relevant difference between one person and another.

The first thing to note about the principle of equal consideration is that it does not, in any straightforward way, entail equal (in the sense of identical) treatment. As we saw in the previous chapter, if there is a disease which, like sickle cell anaemia, because of slight genetic differences within a population, only affects one clearly defined segment of that population, it would not be a departure from the principle of equal consideration to withhold access to suitable screening and prevention procedures from the non-affected segment. Similarly, it is no obvious departure from the principle of equal consideration to withhold the right to vote from humans who are unfortunately sufficiently mentally defective that they can in no way understand or meaningfully exercise this right. The principle of equal consideration is, in fact, not only compatible with differential treatment of human beings, it may, in certain cases, require such treatment.

The principle of equal consideration requires not equal (in the sense of identical treatment) but *equitable* treatment of all human beings. All human beings should, as a matter of strict justice, receive their due, what they are owed. And it is not always, and perhaps not even typically, true that what they are owed is identical treatment. And while there must, presumably, be some connection between equity and equality, the connection is by no means straightforward or easy to discern.

Whatever else may be involved in the idea of equal consideration, it is obviously intimately connected with the equal consideration of *interests*. More precisely, it is bound up with the equal consideration of *relevantly similar interests*. The notion of a relevantly similar interest can, perhaps, be made clearer by way of the following example, borrowed from Singer.[1] If I give a horse a slap across its rump with my hand, it presumably feels little pain, whereas if I slap a baby in the same way, it will presumably feel significantly more pain. However, there must be some kind of blow, perhaps a blow with a heavy stick, that would cause the horse as much pain as the baby feels when slapped by my hand. The horse, then, has a relevantly similar interest in avoiding being hit with the stick as the baby has in avoiding being hit with my hand. Both us and non-human animals, Singer argues, therefore have a relevantly similar interest in avoiding similar amounts of pain. And this is not to say, of course, that we share all relevantly similar interests with non-humans. Clearly we can have interests that they lack, and vice versa. Interestingly, all philosophers writing on animal ethics regard life, the interest in staying alive, as a relevantly *different* interest for humans and non-humans. That is, it is commonly thought that a normal human loses more in dying than does a non-human animal. Thus, a normal human's interest in life is not relevantly similar to that of a non-human animal. And if this is true, then treating humans and non-humans with equal consideration is compatible with according greater moral significance to the life of a normal human.

Some way can be made in the interpretation of the concept of equal consideration, then, by viewing it as requiring equal consideration of all relevantly similar interests. However, this, by itself, is not enough. The claim that the concept of equal consideration can be interpreted as the claim that all relevantly similar interests should be accorded equal moral weight is not so much mistaken as incomplete. It leaves most of the hard philosophical work undone. This is for two reasons.

Firstly, while acknowledging that all interests are important, we also often regard some as more important than others and, to this end, provide a *lexical* ordering of interests; an ordering which specifies which interests can be traded off against others, and which can not. Providing this sort of ordering is one of the central projects of political philosophy. Thus, in discussions of political equality, we frequently find discussions of what quantity a political system should attempt to distribute equally. Some political theories emphasize equality of opportunity, others emphasize equality of income or wealth, and yet others emphasize equality of welfare. Thus while political theories of a broadly socialist orientation might claim that equality of income is a precondition of treating people with equal consideration, libertarian theories will tend to claim that equal rights over one's labour and property are necessary prerequisites of such treatment. In fact, not only does the concept of equal consideration vary from one theory to another, these distinct interpretations of the concept are often incompatible with each other. Equality of opportunity, for example, is incompatible with equality of income, since people differ with respect to their abilities; and equality of income is incompatible with equality of welfare, since people differ with respect to their needs.

The relevance of these considerations to understanding the principle of equal consideration is as follows. We cannot arrive at a complete understanding of the principle of equal consideration simply by way of the idea of the equal consideration of relevantly similar interests because, it is generally thought, some interests are more important than, and should be protected at the expense of, others. Proper understanding of the principle of equal consideration, then, requires defence of a particular lexical ordering of interests. And this, as the proliferation of debates in contemporary political philosophy indicates, is no easy matter.

Secondly, and even more importantly, even if we could arrive at a defensible lexical ordering of interests, the principle of equal consideration of relevantly similar interests is still seriously incomplete. Even if a defensible lexical ordering of interests could be established, we would still need to work out what is involved in giving equal moral weight to relevantly similar, and equally important, interests. This debate is, in fact, one of the central concerns of moral theory. Utilitarians, as we shall see, have a very different understanding of what is involved in giving equal moral weight to interests than do more deontological approaches of the sort exemplified by, for example, John Rawls. For the utilitarian, according equal moral weight to interests involves, in some way, aggregating them. With deontological approaches, on the other hand, strict limits on such aggregation are imposed by the need to respect the rights of the individuals involved. If we, as we surely must, regard the content of the principle of equal consideration as, in part, constituted by the idea of equal consideration of relevantly similar interests, then we find that what counts as equal consideration varies from one moral theory to another.

The moral of the preceding considerations is, essentially, this. There can be no theory-neutral conception of the principle of equal consideration. The specific content of this principle will vary along two dimensions, according to the specific moral and political theories one is prepared to endorse. In the political dimension, the content of the principle will depend on the specific lexical ordering of interests entailed by one's guiding political theory. In the moral dimension, on the other hand, the content of the principle will depend on the specific interpretation of what it means to accord the same moral weight to interests that is entailed by one's guiding moral theory. The concept of equal consideration, therefore, is an irredeemably theory-laden concept; there can be no invariant, theory-neutral, concept of equal consideration.

As mentioned earlier, the central argument of this book is that once we understand what is involved in treating human beings with equal consideration, we will also understand that and why such treatment should be extended beyond the human circle to include at least some types of non-human animals. There can, however, be no theory-neutral concept of what is involved in treating human beings with equal consideration and respect. If we want to identify what is involved in according all human beings equal consideration and respect, we have to fix both the political and moral factors that are partly constitutive of this concept. Consider, first, the relevant political factors. Which political theory, with its embodied conception of equality, should we adopt?

The answer to this question is: *liberalism*. This is for two reasons. Firstly, it is widely accepted that the movement towards recognizing the moral claims of non-human animals is an essentially liberal movement. As outlined at the beginning of this chapter, the movement is often presented, and, I think, rightly so, as the next logical step in a broadly liberal process of enfranchisement of the individual. Part of the aim of this book, then, is to provide a systematic examination of the connection between liberalism and the concept of animal rights.

Secondly, and more importantly, as outlined in the opening chapter, there are two importantly distinct conceptions of method in applied moral philosophy. We might call these the *ambitious* and the *modest* conceptions. The ambitious conception is closely tied to foundationalist approaches to moral theory. On this view, the correct role of moral theory is to identify moral principles that are, if not absolute, then at least objectively true; and the correct role of applied moral philosophy is to apply these principles to concrete cases and issues. The modest conception, on the other hand, coheres much more comfortably with non-foundationalist views of moral theory, and takes a somewhat more relaxed view of the relation between moral theory and its applications. While there is nothing in the modest conception which rules out either the existence or the possibility of discovery of objectively true moral principles, the modest conception does not rely on these. The modest conception focuses not on what is objectively true in ethics, but on what people generally *believe* to be objectively true, as evidenced by their behaviour including their professed moral commitments. The modest conception then tries to draw out the logical implications of these beliefs. That is, the modest conception sees the correct method of applied moral philosophy as having something like this form: if you believe X (which you profess to do, and act as if you do) then you also (logically) have to believe Y. The modest conception does not concern itself with whether the moral beliefs in question are true. What is crucial for the modest conception is not whether these beliefs are true, but that they are generally believed to be true.

In the context of this book, there are two reasons for adopting the modest conception, one strategic, the other stemming logically from the book's central arguments. The strategic reason is that, for any piece of moral argument there is a well-known problem with relying too heavily on the claim that one is in possession of objectively and demonstrably true moral principles. The problem is not so much that there are no such things as objectively true moral principles, but, rather, that even if there were such things, they would be ineffectual in moral argument unless they were widely recognized as such. If an objectively true moral principle existed but was not widely recognized as such, then it would be useless for the purposes of moral argument. That is, that a principle be widely accepted is a necessary and sufficient condition for its utility in moral argument. And the only way any realistic form of moral advocacy can be effected is by focusing on widely accepted moral beliefs. The second reason is that the very nature of the moral position defended in this book requires at least some commitment to the modest conception of ethical argument. For reasons that will become clear later in this chapter, the central philosophical argument of this book derives its efficacy from focusing on moral beliefs or intuitions that are pervasive and deeply entrenched. And if one is looking for beliefs that are pervasive and deeply entrenched in this sense, then one of the places to look is at the dominant political ideology, and at the principles and conception of equal consideration embodied therein. The dominant political ideology of today is liberalism. Liberalism, of course, here denotes not any particular political party but, rather, a set of presuppositions or sentiments that are, broadly speaking, universalist and neutral in character and which span the ideological divide between various particular democratic parties and thus provide the necessary framework for political debate and argument.

The situation is, therefore, as follows. The concept of equal consideration is a theory-relative concept: its content varies with the various moral and political theories through which it is interpreted. In order to determine a specific content for this concept, then, we have to fix both the moral and political factors that are partly constitutive of it. Chapters 4, 5, and 6 will be concerned with fixing the moral dimension of the concept. With regard to the political dimension, I have chosen to focus on what is clearly the dominant political ideology of the present time: liberalism. This is for both strategic and, as we shall see, theoretical reasons. Accordingly, part of the argument of this book runs as follows. Liberalism, the dominant political ideology of today, embodies a certain conception of what it is to treat persons with equal consideration and respect. And, once we understand this conception, and the basis of it, we will realize that the according of equal consideration and respect must, for the sake of consistency, be extended beyond the human circle to incorporate at least some types of non-human animals. The very *content* of the concept of equal consideration and respect embodied in the liberal political tradition logically requires that the principle of equal consideration be applied beyond the human sphere. At least, that is what this book will argue. The remainder of this chapter is concerned with the preliminary work of examining the idea of liberalism, the particular conception of equal consideration embedded in it, and the basis of that conception.

3. LIBERALISM: THE RIGHT AND THE GOOD

The liberal political tradition exhibits many well-known and widely accepted features. It is *meliorist* in the sense that it asserts that all existing social institutions are corrigible and capable of improvement. The tradition is also *universalist*, affirming the moral unity of all human beings and according specific ethnic, historical, civic, and cultural associations only a secondary or derivative importance. These features liberalism shares with other political traditions, notably Marxism. What is really definitive and distinctive about liberalism lies in two further elements, and, even more importantly, in the interaction between them.

The first of these is *individualism*. The liberal conception of human beings is fundamentally individualist in character in that it asserts the moral primacy of the individual against the claims of the social collective. The moral claims of collectives are always ultimately a function of the claims of individuals. Therefore, moral reasoning must start with the moral claims of individuals, and moral justification must ultimately be traceable back to the claims of individuals. This feature distinguishes liberalism quite clearly from socialism, communitarianism, and other forms of perfectionism. What is common to various strands of perfectionism is the idea that some social structures embody values that are beneficial in that they allow humans to fulfil or perfect their essential nature. The task of political theory, then, is to identify which social structures embody these values, and the task of the political activist is to attempt to bring these social structures into being, or to maintain them if already existing. It is characteristic of liberal political thought, however, that it has abandoned the project of pursuing the idea of a political community in this sense. This is not, as is commonly thought, the result of moral scepticism: the claim that there is nothing to guide us in determining the ultimate nature of right and wrong. Some liberals have been moral sceptics in this sense, but scepticism is not intrinsic to liberalism. Far more important in the liberal's abandoning of the pursuit of political community is the concept of individualism. One of the fundamental tenets of liberalism is the idea that, whatever the ultimate nature of good and bad, right and wrong, and whatever the ultimate status of our knowledge of these things, an individual's life typically goes better when it is led from, so to speak, the *inside*. That is, a person's life typically goes better when, as far as possible, he or she is allowed to develop their own conceptions of the good, or the good life, and live, again as far as possible, in accordance with the conception they have developed. Given that this is so, and given that distinct people will often have very different conceptions of the good, the function of political thought, according to the liberal conception, is to find ways to accommodate these distinct, and often incompatible, conceptions of the good within society. That is, liberalism begins with the assumption of *moral pluralism*. Different individuals will often have different, and sometimes incompatible, conceptions of the good life. This does not entail, nor is the result of, moral scepticism. Neither does it entail moral nihilism: the view that ultimately there is no such thing as right or wrong. Most importantly, and this is where confusion is most likely, this position does not even entail moral relativism: the view that there are distinct and incompatible standards of right and wrong. Moral pluralism is the view that people have different conceptions or beliefs about what is right and wrong. This, by itself, is a purely descriptive claim; a claim about the way the world happens to be. And, as such, it is scarcely contestable. It is a plain fact about the world that people do have, often very widely, differing conceptions about what is good and bad. Moral pluralism, as a descriptive claim, does not entail that all, or even any, of these people are correct in their beliefs. Therefore, moral pluralism is distinct from moral relativism, since the latter claim does entail this.

All that moral pluralism claims is that, whatever the ultimate status of the concepts of right and wrong, different people have different conceptions of the content of these concepts. Liberals then add to this descriptive claim the further one that, typically, though not always, and certainly not necessarily, a person's life goes better when he or she is allowed to live it in accordance with whatever concepts of right and wrong they have in fact adopted. The abandonment of the perfectionist ideal of political community, then, stems from liberalism's commitment to individualism, not, or not necessarily, from any commitment to moral scepticism, nihilism, or relativism.

The second constitutive feature of liberalism is its *egalitarianism*. In the liberal tradition, not only does moral primacy attach to individuals, but, further, all individuals are to count equally. Every person is to be accorded equal respect and consideration. Each individual has equal moral status. This statement of egalitarianism is, of course, extremely vague. And different versions of liberalism interpret the requirement of equal moral status in different ways. Someone whose liberalism derives from utilitarianism, for example, might interpret the condition of moral equality in terms of the idea that each person's interests or preferences are to be given equal weight in moral deliberations. An interest I, had by a person P, is to be given as much weight in determining policy or actions as is given to that interest had by any other person distinct from P. More typically, however, the liberal emphasis on moral equality generates a preoccupation with the concept of moral rights. As Dworkin puts it, in the liberal tradition, moral rights can be viewed as sort of *trumps*; devices which protect the individual from the unfair demands of the collective. Someone whose liberalism is formulated in terms of this sort of device will typically cash out the concept of moral equality in terms of the idea that all people possess equal rights.

Many non-liberal political systems, of course, are based on the notion of the moral equality of individuals. As was mentioned earlier, Dworkin has argued, quite powerfully, that the ideal of the moral equality of all persons is a presupposition of any plausible political theory. Moreover, one need think only of a Nietzschean form of perfectionism, to realize that not all forms of individualism need necessarily be liberal in character. What is truly distinctive of liberalism is not its individualism or its egalitarianism taken separately, but, rather, the combination of these two elements. It is this combination which leads to what is arguably the defining trait of liberalism, the *priority of the right over the good*.[2] The idea that the right has priority over the good may well be the defining feature of liberalism, but it is also, almost certainly, one of the most misunderstood. It will be worthwhile, therefore, taking some time to explain exactly what this idea is, and what it is not.

Liberalism, in the sense explained above, has abandoned the idea of pursuing political community, at least in the perfectionist sense of pursuing a community in which certain definite values are identified, emphasized, and encouraged by means of political structures. Moral pluralism, in the sense that different people have different conceptions of the good, has to be accepted as a base fact from which moral and political reasoning are built. Liberal political theory must, therefore, be developed around moral pluralism. Thus, the liberal accepts as a given that the conceptions of the good adopted by different people can be distinct, incompatible, and even incommensurable. It is at this point, however, that the egalitarian component of liberalism takes effect. Assigning equal moral status to individuals who have differing conceptions of the good means, among other things, respecting each person's conception of the good in the sense of allowing each person to live, in so far as this is possible, according to the conception of the good they have, in fact, adopted. In the claim that the right is prior to the good, the *good* refers to each person's conception of the good, and the *right* refers to the claim that these differing conceptions of the good, possessed by different individuals, be allowed, in so far as this is possible, to peacefully co-exist. A political system is right to the extent that it allows, in so far as this is possible, the peaceful co-existence of different conceptions of the good.

Some people – usually non-liberals – have interpreted the claim that the right is prior to the good as the idea that liberals have no conception of the good. But this is not really true. For the liberal, the right is, in effect, a second-order good. Liberals think that it is a good thing that distinct conceptions of the good should be allowed to co-exist in so far as this is possible. Therefore, it is not true to say that liberals have no conception of the good. They clearly do. However, this good – that liberals refer to as the right – is of a different logical order from the conceptions of the good between which it attempts to mediate. If we call these conceptions of the good first-order conceptions, then what liberals call the right is simply a second-order conception of the good: a conception that is satisfied by the holding of certain sorts of relations between first-order conceptions. The distinction between first- and second-order entities in this sense is well known. What is also well known is that distinct levels carry with them interestingly different logical properties. To affirm something of a second-order entity simply because what is affirmed is true of all the first-order items which it subsumes is to commit what is known as the *fallacy of composition*. To use an example made famous by Bertrand Russell, it would be fallacious to infer from the claim that every member of the human race has a mother to the claim that the human race as a whole has a mother. Liberalism is, in essence, constituted by a second-order conception of the good: it is a good thing that first-order conceptions of the good should be allowed to co-exist, in so far as this is possible. But to claim that liberalism is, therefore, simply putting forward its own conception of the good on a par with the first-order conceptions of the good between which it attempts to mediate is to seriously confuse first- and second-order conceptions of the good.

Liberalism does embody its own conception of the good, therefore. However, relative to the conceptions of the good between which it attempts to mediate, liberalism puts forward a meta-conception. And liberals often refer to this meta-conception of the good as the *right*. To say that the right is prior to the good, then, is to say that, for the purposes of constituting the basic political structures of society, what is important is not so much the particular conceptions of the good adopted by members of society, but the fact that these conceptions of the good be allowed to peacefully co-exist in so far as this is possible.

4. LIBERALISM AND NATURAL RIGHTS

Liberalism, then, is the political doctrine constituted by the interplay between the concepts of individualism and egalitarianism that culminates in the claim of the priority of the right over the good. In virtue of its egalitarian component, liberalism embodies a certain conception of what it means to treat people with equal consideration and respect. Understanding this conception, however, involves understanding the proposed justification for acceptance of liberal principles; for, as will become clear, the specific conception of equal consideration embodied in liberal ideology depends on the perceived justification of that ideology. Historically, there have been three distinct types of justification, and the remainder of the chapter will be concerned with examining these. The first of these is the doctrine of *natural rights*, given its classical liberal formulation by John Locke.

The doctrine of natural rights, in broad outline, is the claim that humans possess certain moral entitlements, and thus may make valid moral claims against each other, because they possess natural rights which mandate that they are deserving of certain types of treatment, and of certain types of freedom. According to the doctrine, humans possess these rights not in virtue of being members of any specific moral or legal community but, rather, simply in virtue of their *nature* as the type of creatures they are. These rights are natural, then, in that they derive from the nature of human beings. They are, therefore, what we might call *pre-conventional*, prior to any moral practice, legal institution, or contractual arrangement.

The claim that human beings have natural rights which they possess in virtue of their nature has itself been supported by appeal to three distinct types of argument. The doctrine of natural rights and these three underlying arguments are clearly evident in the work of Locke.

According to Locke, all men are equally the subject of natural rights that are both logically and chronologically prior to society, hence prior to conventional morality. He has three distinct strands of argument for this claim, and he tends to shuffle constantly between them. The arguments derive from *reason, nature,* and *religion.*

Locke is generally clear that natural rights derive from natural law. And he is also clear that there can be no law without a law-giver (a point that, in a secular form, would become central to Bentham's jurisprudence). And the only plausible candidate for law-giver, the creator of natural law, is, of course, God. Thus, natural rights derive from natural law, and natural law derives from God. Natural law is 'the decree of the divine will discernible by the light of nature and indicating what is and what is not in conformity with rational nature'.[3] By natural law, here, Locke is not referring to what we today call *laws of nature*; that is, descriptive principles according to which the universe actually operates. Natural law, in Locke's sense, is *moral law*: 'the eternal, immutable standard of right'. [4] Thus, natural law is *divine* law. God, then, is the source of natural law, hence of natural rights. But what of the binding force of this law? That is, what is the source of our obligation to obey this law? Why, morally speaking, should we adhere to it? At some points, for example, Locke's argument focuses on the inherent *rationality* of natural law; sometimes he even seems to identify it with reason itself:

> The *State of Nature* has a Law of Nature to govern it, which obliges everyone: And Reason, which is that Law, teaches all Mankind, who will but consult it, that being equal and independent, no one ought to harm another in his Life, Health, Liberty, or Possessions.[5]

Passages such as this suggest that natural law, or the Law of Nature as Locke puts it, is synonymous with reason. If so, it might be thought that the source of our obligation to obey natural law derives from its intrinsic rationality; obeying natural law is the rational thing to do, and this is why we should obey it.

At other points, however, Locke bases assertions for the existence of natural rights on claims about how humans actually behave. In his discussion of resistance to prerogative power in the *Second Treatise*, for example, Locke argues that the decisive test of when the executive has overstepped its rightful limits is when 'the Majority *feel it*, and are weary of it, and find a necessity to have it amended'.[6] The reason for this is, according to Locke, that 'God *and nature* never allowing a man so to abandon himself, as to neglect his own preservation' must leave him with this final authority.[7] Thus, in some passages, Locke seems to suggest that the source of our obligation to obey natural law consists in the fact that its principles accord or coalesce so completely with human nature.

However, what underlies these appeals to reason and nature is a deeper claim about the relation between man and God. The natural rights of human beings depend on the natural law created by God. And while this law may be inherently rational (so that failure to obey it would be irrational), and while it may coalesce with the requirements of human nature (so that failure to obey it would be unnatural), neither of these features is the source of our obligation to obey it. Rather, the source of our obligation is the relation in which we stand to God, the creator of the law. It is our relation to God that grounds a duty for us to obey His law.

There are three possible reasons why the fact that God created natural law gives us a duty to obey it. The first focuses on the power of God, in particular, on His ability to enforce His law. The second focuses on the nature of divine wisdom. And the third focuses on the right a creator has over his creation. We shall consider each in turn.

According to the first suggestion, we have a duty to obey natural law because (a) God created it, and (b) He has the power to enforce it. God's law is obligatory for us only (or largely) because of His power to impose sanctions on us. This is to adopt a *sanction theory* of obligation, and some passages seem to suggest that this was indeed Locke's view:

What duty is, cannot be understood without a law; nor a law be known without a lawmaker, or without reward and punishment.[8]

Moral good and evil, then, is only the conformity or disagreement of our voluntary actions to some law, whereby good and evil is drawn on us, from the will and power of the lawmaker; which good and evil ... is that we call reward and punishment.[9]

There are, however, serious problems with the sanction theory. One central problem is that it confuses *obligation* with *compulsion*. In effect, Locke himself points this out, comparing the situations of a captive 'constrained to the service of a pirate' and a subject freely 'giving obedience to a ruler'. In the former case, while one may be compelled to perform certain actions, one can hardly say that one is (morally) obligated to perform those actions. The sanction theory unacceptably blurs these two concepts. In addition, the sanction theory has political consequences that would be anathema to Locke. In the *Second Treatise*, for example, Locke attempts to make the case that the consent of the governed, not the power of the governor, is the ground of our obligation to obey civil law. Therefore, he can hardly espouse a theory of obligation which has the consequence that any powerful maker of civil law can morally obligate us to obey simply by having the power to punish us if we do not. Locke, then, cannot consistently adopt a sanction theory of obligation, and he cannot, therefore, believe that the ground of our obligation to obey natural law consists in the fact that God has the power to punish us if we fail to do so.

According to the second suggestion, the basis of our duty to obey natural law lies in the divine wisdom of God. Once again, however, this view seems to have political implications that Locke would find unacceptable. One of the central tenets of Locke's political theory is that the obligation to obey civil law derives from the consent of the governed. And this is clearly incompatible with the claim that any very wise (and good) person has natural authority over and can make morally binding rules for the rest of us simply because of his wisdom and goodness. But this latter claim seems to be just what is entailed by the claim that our obligation to obey natural law derives from the divine wisdom of its maker.

Therefore, it seems we are inevitably driven to the third suggestion. Our obligation to obey natural law derives from the claims that (a) God has created us, and, as such (b) has a natural right over His creation. We should obey natural law because it is God's law, and, as His creation, we have a natural duty to obey Him. It might be thought that this suggestion would also have untoward earthly consequences. We do not believe, for example, that parents have unrestricted rights over their children simply because they have created them. Locke's reply to this is that there is an important difference between the relation in which parents stand to their children and that in which God stands to His creation. Parents create children in only a derivative sense; they can create children only because God has first created everything. Therefore, parents do not have unrestricted rights over their children precisely because it is God who is their ultimate creator, not the parents themselves.

Even if this line of argument can be made to work, however, there are still serious problems for the suggestion that our duty to obey natural law stems from God's right over his creation. According to Locke, all persons are bound by natural law to preserve themselves and others, and forbidden to harm another in his life, health, liberty, or possessions. And this is, ultimately, because, being God's workmanship, we are also His property. And, as everyone knows, one should not harm or destroy another's property. The problem with this claim emerges, however, when we ask why we should not harm another's property. And, by his own principles, Locke seems forced to admit this can be only because it is one of the principles of natural law. That is, if we try to explain our obligation to obey God's law in terms of the right a creator has over his creation, we have to explain where this right comes from. But, according to natural law theory, moral obligations derive from natural law. And if this is so, the right a creator has over his creation would be a principle of natural law. But, then, we would be using natural law to explain the obligatory character of natural law. And, if this is so, then Locke appears trapped in a tight circle: he is using natural law to explain why we should obey natural law.

In fact, parallel problems emerge for *any* attempt to explain why we should obey natural law. The general strategy of natural rights theorists has been to try and explain our obligation to obey God's law by showing it to be simply a particular case of some familiar and universally accepted kind of obligation. Thus, we might try to argue that we are obligated to obey God's law because of His power, or His wisdom, or His goodness, or out of respect for the fact that He created us. The problem is that all these sorts of obligation are themselves principles of the very natural law whose obligatory character we are trying to explain. By adopting this strategy, we would be using natural law to explain and justify why we should adopt natural law. And this is to argue in a circle.

This brief discussion of natural law doctrine as developed by Locke is perhaps sufficient to indicate the formidable difficulties involved in constructing a theory of natural rights today. The fundamental difficulties stem from the attempt to explicate natural law in a modern conceptual framework that is decidedly alien, and distinctly hostile, to the concepts necessary to sustain the natural law *weltanschauung*. This problem manifests itself in Locke's account in at least two ways.

Firstly, in Locke's account, as we have seen, natural law is created and sustained by divine will, from which it derives its moral status. Whatever his considered view on the details of the dependency relation, it is clear that, for Locke, the principles of natural law are good because, and only because, they derive from God. However, the belief in God now has nowhere near the widespread support it had in Locke's day. Locke's God has difficulty finding a home in the framework of concepts constituted by the Enlightenment in general and modern science in particular. And this, by itself, is sufficient to render the concept of natural law problematic for the purposes of moral argument. As was noted earlier, moral argument can be successful only when it appeals to concepts and principles that are widely accepted; indeed, the more widely accepted, the better chance the argument has of being successful. The reliance of a moral argument on natural law will effectively alienate a substantial segment of the moral population, probably a majority of this population.

Essentially the same problem emerges in a second way in Locke's account. Locke, as we have seen, has serious difficulties in accounting for our obligation to obey natural law and, therefore, in accounting for what makes natural law good. It is very likely, however, that Locke would be in no way perturbed by his failure in this regard. That God, as creator, has a right over his creation, would likely strike Locke as being simply the end of the explanatory chain. The claim that we should obey God's law, therefore, stands in no need of justification. The fact that we, today, are less likely to be satisfied here is, as David Gauthier points out, simply a measure of the vast conceptual gulf between our world view and that of Locke. From our perspective, it is simply not enough to say that man should obey God because God created man; further argument is required to support the move from creation to obligation. The conceptual framework from within which Locke operates, however, is theocentric. Everything depends on God, and no further argument from creation to obligation is required.[10] Once again, we find a dissonance between the conceptual framework necessary to sustain the natural rights doctrine, and that embodied in the modern world view. In this particular case, the dissonance means that Locke, by our lights, has failed to explain the status of natural rights and hence our obligation to respect them.

It is worth noting that the same sort of problem arises for other versions of the natural rights doctrine, versions that do not explicitly derive natural law from God. Other natural rights theorists, for example, while not appealing directly to God, nonetheless require some sort of appeal to teleological principles embodied in nature. Aristotle is a case in point. He supports his moral theory with a meta-physical biology which depends, in the final analysis, on a conception of nature as a system governed by final causes and tending toward perfec-tion. There seems little room for Aristotle's concept of a final cause in the modern scientific world view. In other words, perhaps the most fundamental problem with sustaining (or resurrecting) *any* version of the doctrine of natural rights is that it requires, for its ultimate coher-ence, metaphysical assumptions that, by today's intellectual lights, seem outrageous. The conceptual framework needed to sustain a coherent version of the doctrine of natural rights has long been superceded by others that are incompatible with the doctrine.

Modern natural rights theorists, being well aware of these prob-lems, have tended to focus not on the underlying divine or teleological basis of the doctrine, but on the nature of human beings as such. In effect, they abandon two of the three justificatory strands evident in the Lockean vision, and focus, instead, on the third: natural rights derive from the nature of human beings alone. It is noticeable that this is, perhaps, the strand least favoured by Locke. Nevertheless, modern proponents of natural rights doctrine argue that a coherent doctrine can be extracted from this strand alone. Thus, according to contemporary theorists of natural rights, such rights embody the conditions necessary for the flourishing of human beings as the distinctive creatures we are. We can discern the content of these rights by, first, identifying the distinguishing characteristics of the human species and, then, the circumstances in which these character-istics might best be developed.

There are, however, also formidable difficulties with this approach to developing the natural rights doctrine. Firstly, the selection of any feature, or collection of features, taken to be distinctive of human beings, already presupposes a significant degree of evaluation.[11] Proponents of natural rights doctrine typically select features such as rationality, or creativity, or other such ennobling properties. If, however, one genuinely approached the task without preconceptions, one could equally easily end up selecting features such as the capacity to make weapons of mass destruction, or, perhaps, the desire to have sexual intercourse without regard to season, or despoiling the environment and upsetting the balance of nature, or killing things for fun, or attempting genocide, etc. Selection of any one feature is, it seems, arbitrary. The fact that defenders of natural rights doctrine have, typically, tended to select suspiciously flattering features indicates that they have already invested a significant amount of moral evaluation in the selection of features. But, natural rights doctrine is supposed to provide the basis of moral evaluation. Once again, it seems, the natural rights theorist is arguing in a circle.

Secondly, even if we could justify selection of a particular characteristic, or group of characteristics, it still does not follow that it would be a good thing to promote these characteristics. Many distinctively human characteristics are, as Bernard Williams points out, morally ambiguous. Imagination and sensitivity may be expressed in sophisticated forms of cruelty; courage may be harnessed in the promotion of mass murder.[12]

Finally, it is almost certainly true that many of the virtues in which the distinctive human powers are expressed are often incompatible and uncombinable.[13] One excellence crowds out another. A choice of one form of life may often require a deliberate suppression of a part of one's nature, as when one decides to become an athlete instead of an artist, a writer instead of a parent. Therefore, there seems to be no reason to suppose *a priori* that there is any such thing as *the* best form of life for a human being. Perhaps, instead, there is a heterogeneous set of distinct and incompatible forms of life, each one, as the particular form of life it is, equally good as any of the others. There is no reason to suppose, that is, there is any such thing as *the* good for human beings. There may be a host of distinct and incompatible *goods*, that what is good for humans is constituted by an irreducible plurality of ends; ends that often intractably conflict with one another. Indeed, some such assumption is basic to liberal thinking. And if natural rights doctrine cannot accommodate this thought, it is difficult to see how it could provide the basis for liberalism in general and the liberal conception of equal consideration in particular.

5. LIBERALISM AND UTILITARIANISM

The second historically important attempt to justify liberal principles appeals to the ethical theory known as *utilitarianism*. The work of

John Stuart Mill provides probably the best example of this type of justification of liberalism.[14] The term 'utilitarianism', in fact, denotes not a single view but a confederation of views. Nonetheless, these distinct views have certain common themes running through them, and this is what makes their subsumption under a single term appropriate. The distinct versions of utilitarianism are best organized and understood around the following two themes.

The first theme concerns the definition of the good, or, as utilitarians often refer to it, of *utility*. Utilitarianism provides one example of what Rawls calls a *teleological* theory. What is characteristic of such theories is that they begin, logically speaking, by defining what is good, or what the expression 'good' means, and they go on to explain other ethical concepts, such as justice, in terms of this definition. Different versions of utilitarianism, however, involve different characterizations of the good, or utility. Hedonistic utilitarianism, for example, identifies human good with happiness. Preference utilitarianism, on the other hand, identifies it with satisfaction of preferences, whether such satisfaction brings with it happiness or not. Nevertheless, despite these differences in the understanding of utility, some or other definition of this concept is the logical and conceptual starting point for any utilitarian theory.

The second central feature of utilitarianism is the requirement that we *maximize* utility, however this is understood. If utility is identified with preference-satisfaction, for example, then utilitarianism requires that we maximize the amount of satisfied preferences in the world. Once again, different versions of utilitarianism differ with regard to their understanding of in what maximizing utility consists. *Act* utilitarians, for example, understand utilitarianism as the requirement to perform whatever *action* promotes the maximization of utility. *Rule* utilitarians, on the other hand, understand utilitarianism as the requirement to follow whatever *rule* general observance of which promotes the maximization of utility, even if this means, in any particular case, performing an action that decreases utility. *Direct* utilitarians, understand the theory to entail that moral agents should decide how to act by consciously making utilitarian calculations, by attempting to assess how different actions would affect the maximization of utility. *Indirect* utilitarians, on the other hand, view the idea of maximizing utility as entering only indirectly into the agent's decision-making. That is, while they accept that morally right actions are those that maximize utility, indirect utilitarians claim that people are more likely to maximize utility by following non-utilitarian rules or habits than by directly following explicit utilitarian reasoning. There are other distinctions, resulting in yet further versions of utilitarianism.

Nevertheless, what unites these diverse forms, and makes them all forms of a single theory, is the following principle. It is morally right to maximize utility – whatever this utility consists in, and however this utility is best promoted. The crucial element in this principle is the commitment to maximization of utility. For utilitarians of whatever stripe, what is crucial is that utility be maximized, that is, that the general utility be promoted. Who is the beneficiary of this utility maximization does not matter morally speaking. It is the promotion of maximum utility that is crucial; who is benefited and who harmed by this promotion is not directly relevant.

It is this element of utilitarianism which is commonly thought to drive a wedge between liberalism and utilitarianism, hence to create a serious problem in using the latter to justify the former. Far from being able to use utilitarianism to ground liberal principles, it seems that the former's commitment to maximizing utility may actually make it incompatible with the latter. The reason is, as has been pointed out countless times, is that maximizing utility can often be incompatible with an essential element of liberal thought: the commitment to equality. It may be, for example, that the maximization of utility can best be achieved by sacrificing the interests of certain individuals. In fact, it does not really matter whether it is *actually* true that the maximization of utility can, in certain circumstances, best be promoted by such means. It might actually always be false that sacrifice of innocent individuals can best maximize utility. What is crucial, however, is that *if* it should turn out to be the case that sacrificing the interests of certain innocent individuals is conducive to the maximization of utility *then* utilitarianism would be committed to the claim that such sacrifice was the morally required course of action. And what this shows, it is argued, is that utilitarianism cannot accord individuals equal consideration, at least not in any genuine or full-blooded sense. That is, utilitarianism cannot, consistently with adherence to the requirement that utility be maximized, also adhere to the principle of equality. The former, ultimately, is not compatible with the latter. At best, any claim to equality or equal consideration enjoyed by an individual under a utilitarian regime must, necessarily, be a wholly contingent claim. Whether the claim is acceptable or not will depend on whether recognizing it helps maximize utility; and if it does not do so, then the claim should, on utilitarian grounds, be rejected. Thus, utilitarianism seems to be incompatible with according individuals any genuine status of equality. And, therefore, it does not seem possible, at least *prima facie*, to use utilitarianism to provide a logical foundation for liberal principles.

Perhaps the best known attempt to reconcile the principles of liberalism with those of utilitarianism is provided by J. S. Mill in his *On Liberty*.[15] Mill's attempted reconciliation makes use of a version of the distinction between direct and indirect utilitarianism, and proceeds by way of two claims:

Firstly, the fundamental requirement of utilitarianism, i.e. the maximization of utility, should be understood as an *axiological* principle and not a principle of conduct. That is, the requirement that utility be maximized should be understood as a principle which applies not at the level of rules of conduct that may be adopted by individuals, but, rather, at the level of entire social systems. In other words, the requirement that utility be maximized is best understood as the requirement to put in place and sustain a social system that maximizes utility. It should not be understood as the requirement that individuals, in their moral deliberations, should perform utilitarian calculations *vis-à-vis* anticipated utility. The requirement that utility be maximized is one which can correctly be used to evaluate only social systems, not rules of conduct adopted by individuals within such systems. Therefore, according to Mill, we are at liberty to adopt non-utilitarian maxims to guide our conduct in our everyday life. Non-utilitarian maxims can, therefore, be given a utilitarian justification: the maxims will be justified on utilitarian grounds if they lead or help sustain a social system that maximizes utility.

Secondly, according to Mill, individuality must be understood as a necessary condition of human utility. A social system must, therefore, promote individuality if it is to successfully maximize utility. And, given that the requirement that utility be maximized applies only to social systems as a whole, and not to the rules of conduct adopted by individuals, the general promotion of individuality will satisfy this requirement even if individual attempts at promoting individuality do not succeed in maximizing utility. Therefore, according to Mill, one of the conditions of maximizing utility, understood as an axiological principle, is the general promotion of individuality. However, Mill argues, individuality requires freedom, and, therefore, promotion of individuality requires promotion of freedom. Indeed, maximization of utility would seem to involve the maximization of individuality, and this, in turn, would seem to involve the maximization of freedom. And, maximizing freedom, it seems, requires maximizing the number of people who are free. And this, it seems, requires freedom for all; that is, equal freedom.

This move is, in many ways, ingenious. However, it does not successfully avoid the original problem, since this immediately arises again in a slightly different form. The basic problem is that one cannot assume that maximization of individuality involves maximization of the number of free individuals. It could be, for example, that development of one person's individuality is incompatible with development of that of another. And if this is so, promotion of the general welfare – understood here as promotion of individuality – might actually require the sacrifice of the opportunity of some individuals to develop their individuality. That is, the maximization of utility might require that the development of the individuality of certain persons be sacrificed so that as many people as possible can develop their individuality. This, in effect, is the same problem as the one which arose with the original understanding of utilitarianism. The problem there was that the utility of certain individuals might, on utilitarian grounds, legitimately be sacrificed so that utility, in general, might be maximized. The present problem is that the development of the individuality of certain persons might, on utilitarian grounds, legitimately be sacrificed so that individuality might be developed by as many people as possible.

Once again, it seems that utilitarianism cannot be committed both to the requirement that utility, or individuality, be maximized and to the principle of equal consideration. Utilitarians can embrace the principle of equal consideration only in so far as it maximizes utility, and if the principle of equal consideration should ever clash with the requirement that utility be maximized, it is the former which the utilitarian must sacrifice. Utilitarianism, therefore, does not necessarily treat people with equal consideration; it does so only if such treatment maximizes utility. And this, at least *prima facie*, is not to genuinely accord that person equal consideration at all.

It is very unlikely, of course, that a utilitarian would accept the above diagnosis of her clash with liberalism. In particular, most utilitarians would be very reluctant to accept the inference from (1) the claim that, in certain circumstances, the utility (individuality) of certain individuals should, on utilitarian grounds, be sacrificed, to (2) the claim that utilitarianism, therefore, does not accord those individuals equal status or consideration. The utilitarian is likely to reply that considering the interests of all individuals concerned is precisely what it means to treat those individuals with equal consideration. And this remains true even when consideration of all affected interests entails, on utilitarian grounds, the sacrifice of certain individuals. Nevertheless, there is a clear divergence between the utilitarian conception of what it means to treat an individual with equal consideration and our intuitive understanding of this notion. And this raises the question of whether utilitarianism is genuinely capable of accounting for the conception of justice embodied in liberal ideology. It is not possible to deal with this question here. In a later chapter, however, one specifically focusing upon utilitarian attempts to underwrite the concept of animal liberation, I shall argue that it can not.

6. LIBERALISM AND CONTRACTARIANISM

The third historically important attempt to provide a logical grounding for liberal principles derives from the ethical tradition known as *contractarianism*. Very roughly, according to contractarian approaches to ethics, the requirements of morality are determined by the agreements that humans make, or would make, to regulate their social interaction. There are, however, two importantly different types of contractarian theory, based on very different assumptions, and yielding very different moral principles.[16] Identifying the extent to which liberalism can be supported by contractarianism requires first distinguishing these two distinct types.

Both types of contractarian theory recognize that people, or at least most people, are, by nature, equal. However, they have very different conceptions of in what this natural equality consists. The first form of contractarianism derives, in a straightforward way, from the work of Hobbes, and, like him, emphasizes a natural equality of power possessed by most human beings. We can call this form *Hobbesian contractarianism*.[17]

According to Hobbesian contractarians, there is nothing objectively right or wrong either about the goals one chooses or the means by which one pursues these goals. In particular, there is nothing inherently wrong with harming others in order to achieve one's goals. However, while there is nothing inherently wrong with harming others, doing so may often be imprudent. Typically, I would be better off refraining from harming you if, in turn, you and every other person refrains from harming me. Thus, a convention that forbids deliberately harming people is mutually advantageous; we do not have to waste time, effort, money, etc. defending our own person and property, and it enables us to enter into stable, and mutually beneficial, co-operation. While deliberately harming another is not inherently or objectively wrong, it is nonetheless imprudent, and, therefore, wise to treat it as if it were wrong.

Thus, according to Hobbesian contractarianism, the basis of morality can be understood as a hypothetical contract consisting of mutually advantageous rules of conduct. The content of such conventions will be fixed by bargaining: each person will want the resulting agreement to serve the dual purpose of protecting their own interests as much as possible while restricting their freedom as little as possible. While this bargaining never really took place, we can view this hypothetical bargaining over mutually advantageous conventions as the means by which a community establishes its *social contract*. The principles established by this imaginary bargaining process are to be obeyed not because it is inherently wrong to transgress them, but, ultimately, because it is irrational to do so. To this extent, and to this extent only, the hypothetical social contract can be thought of as yielding a moral code.

However, while there is a sense in which mutually advantageous conventions supply a type of moral code, this code will differ crucially from more traditional conceptions. The reason is that, according to Hobbesian contractarianism, whether it is advantageous to adopt a particular rule of conduct depends on one's bargaining power. And the strong and talented have greater power than the weak and talentless. The talentless might produce little of value, for example, and whatever value is produced by the weak can be simply appropriated by the strong without fear of retaliation. Thus, there seems little to be gained from co-operation with the talentless, and nothing to fear, by way of retaliation, from the weak. Therefore, the strong have little reason, and certainly no prudential reason, to accept rules of conduct which help these groups of people. Thus, Hobbesian contractarianism seems to entail that it is legitimate to allow some people to be killed, and others enslaved or in other ways exploited. For the Hobbesian contractarian, therefore, infants, the congenitally handicapped, and many other types of human being seem to fall outside the scope of morality. Moral constraints can arise only between individuals who are roughly equal in power. When this condition is not satisfied, as in the case of individuals who are unusually weak for some reason, such individuals fall outside the scope of morality. The strong, therefore, have no obligations towards them.

The most common criticisms of Hobbesian contractarianism tend to focus on this conflict with our intuitive understanding of morality. Our ordinary intuitive conception tells us that any mutually beneficial activity must, in order to be legitimate, first respect the rights of others including, crucially, the rights of those too weak to defend their interests. And, therefore, according to our ordinary intuitive conception of morality, mutual advantage cannot be the *foundation* of morality, for there are considerations that are morally prior to the pursuit of mutual advantage. This, however, can scarcely be regarded as a *refutation* of Hobbesian contractarianism. One cannot refute Hobbesian contractarianism by appealing to our ordinary intuitive conception of morality because the whole point of the Hobbesian view is that our ordinary intuitive conception is seriously mistaken. On the Hobbesian view, there is no objective moral right and wrong, and, hence, there are no objective moral rights, and we have no objective moral duties to others. Thus to claim that Hobbesian contractarianism ignores the right of the vulnerable to our protection is not to give an argument against the theory, for the existence of such moral rights is precisely what is at issue.

However, while this straightforward objection to the Hobbesian approach clearly begs the question, it is enough for our purposes to point out that Hobbesian contractarianism cannot, by any stretch of the imagination, provide a logical foundation for liberal principles. Hobbesian contractarianism is patently incompatible with the egalitarianism that is constitutive of liberal theory as such. Hobbesian contractarians can make no sense of the idea that all people have equal moral status. In fact, the Hobbesian approach would explicitly deny this. The moral status any individual has, on the Hobbesian view, is a function of their power. There is no room in the Hobbesian approach, then, for the claim that all people have equal moral status. If there is to be a contractarian justification for liberalism, then, it will have to be other than Hobbesian in character.

The second version of contractarianism is of a very different character to the Hobbesian version. Hobbesian contractarianism uses the idea of a (hypothetical) social contract to ground morality, in the sense of providing a justification for a moral code and an explanation of why we should adopt the rules of conduct embodied in this code. The second version of contractarianism, however, uses the idea of a contract in a fundamentally different way. The contract idea, here, is used not as a method of grounding or justifying any particular moral code, but, rather, as a heuristic device in terms of which we can identify and express the principles embodied, often in a half hidden and implicit manner, in the moral code that we have, for whatever reason, in fact adopted. The contract device can be used in this way to express and reflect the idea of the equal moral status of persons, rather than as an account of how persons come to have moral standing. And the device can be used in this way to eliminate, rather than reflect, differences in the bargaining power of the contractors. This second version of the contract theory has its roots in the work of Kant, and we can therefore refer to it as *Kantian contractarianism*.[18]

The most famous exponent of Kantian contractarianism is John Rawls. Rawls takes as his starting point the idea of the moral equality of individuals: in some fundamental, but, as yet, only partially understood way, each and every person matters equally and is, therefore, entitled to equal consideration and respect. The device of the social contract, in Rawls's hands, becomes a means of identifying and expressing exactly what is involved in this basic idea.

Contracts are not always necessarily between individuals with equal bargaining power, and, thus, they have a natural tendency to override the needs of the weak. According to Rawls, however, this fact stems not from the nature of the contract as such, but from the conditions under which the contract is determined. A contract *can* give equal consideration to each of the contractors whatever their inherent power or abilities, but only if it is negotiated from a position of equality. This position of equality Rawls calls the *original position*. The contractors in the original position find themselves in a position of equality because of a peculiar feature of their epistemological situation: the contractors in the original position find themselves behind a *veil of ignorance*. What this means is that each contractor has no knowledge of his natural talents and characteristics – his or her intelligence, physical appearance, athletic aptitudes, etc. Nor do they know their position in society. In fact, behind the veil of ignorance, each contractor does not even know his or her conception of the good, the things they value, the things they despise, etc. Each contractor is still assumed to be trying to do the best they can for themselves; to formulate and advocate rules of conduct that will secure them the maximum advantage. But, since they are behind the veil of ignorance, this essentially has the consequence that each contractor will try to secure maximum advantage for all persons potentially affected by the contract. From behind the veil of ignorance, attempting to secure maximum advantage for oneself entails trying to secure maximum advantage for all. In order to decide from behind a veil of ignorance which principles will promote my good, I must put myself in the shoes of every person in the society and see what promotes his or her good, since I may end up being any one of these people. Therefore, agreements made in the original position give equal consideration to each person.

The fundamental idea underlying Kantian contractarianism is that all persons are moral equals. It then uses the contract idea to replace the manifest physical inequality of individuals with their substantive or moral equality. Kantian contractarianism, then, provides an expression of the idea that people have equal moral status, whatever their physical or intellectual capacities, whatever their socio-economic status, and whatever their conception of the good. And it uses the contract device to identify what is involved in treating people as moral equals. It is important to realize, however, that Kantian contractarianism does not provide, nor when it is properly understood does it purport to provide, a *defence* of the idea of the moral equality of individuals nor of the principle of equal consideration that follows from it.

Consider, for example, Rawls's derivation of what he calls the *difference principle*. According to this principle, all resources should be distributed equally unless the inequality is to the benefit of the least well-off. Rawls's derivation of this principle is based on the claim that contractors in the original position would, or rationally should, agree to this principle. And they would agree to this because they are, according to Rawls, unwilling to risk being one of the losers in an inegalitarian society, even if that risk is small compared to the likelihood of being one of the winners. Thus, in order to derive the difference principle, Rawls is obliged to make an assumption about the psychological dispositions of the contractors: he assumes they are not risk-takers. But, as Rawls admits, other assumptions about the dispositions of contractors are possible, in which case other principles would be chosen. If contractors are disposed to gamble, for example, they might choose utilitarian principles which maximize the utility each contractor is likely to have in society, but which create the risk that they may end up being one of the people who is sacrificed for the greater good of others. In fact, there are many possible variations in the description of the original position, so that 'for each traditional conception of justice there exists an interpretation of the initial situation in which its principles are the preferred solution'.[19] Given that this is so, then, the only way we can identify which interpretation of the original position is preferable is to determine which interpretation yields principles that match our intuitive convictions of justice. If the principles chosen on one interpretation of the original position do not match our intuitive convictions, or considered opinions as Rawls puts it, then we move to another interpretation which yields principles more in line with these convictions. But, if each theory of justice relies on its own interpretation of the original contracting situation, then we have to decide *beforehand* which theory of justice we accept in order to know which description of the original position is suitable. Therefore, the contract device in its Kantian incarnation, cannot be used to *ground* or justify any particular conception of justice.

This is the major problem with trying to use any version of Kantian contractarianism to provide a logical foundation or justification for liberalism. Which principles of justice are derivable from the contracting situation depends essentially on which description we give of that situation. And which description we give of this situation will depend essentially on our prior acceptance of certain principles of justice. It would, therefore, beg the question to try to use Kantian contractarianism to provide a justification for liberalism or, for that matter, any moral or political position.

There is, however, another way of viewing the function of the contract device in the context of Kantian contractarianism. This is to see it as a device not for grounding, or providing a logical justification for, liberal principles, but, rather, as one for *elucidating* those principles. While the idea of contracting from an original position cannot justify basic liberal principles, it can, nonetheless, elucidate them in several ways. Firstly, since contractual agreements must be explicitly and publicly formulated, the contract device can render these principles more determinate. Secondly, since the veil of ignorance is a vivid way of expressing the moral requirement of putting ourselves in other people's shoes, the contract device can be used to render the principles more vivid. Viewed in this way, the contract idea is a heuristic device used not for grounding or justifying moral principles but for identifying and expressing more clearly principles that have been antecedently accepted for other reasons. In these and other ways, the contract device can be used to illuminate – to identify and express more clearly – the basic principles of liberalism and, in particular, the principle of equal consideration. It is to this purpose that the contract idea will be put in this book.

7. LIBERALISM AND ANIMAL RIGHTS

This chapter has been concerned with what I have called the principle of equal consideration, and with its central place in liberal thought.

Three historically important justifications of liberal principles were then examined with a view to understanding how they underwrite the principle of equal consideration.

The first thing to note is that the natural rights approach, the utilitarian approach, and the contractarian approach towards explaining the content of liberal principles are not, in any straightforward sense, incompatible with each other. This is because they are, in effect, concerned with distinct questions.

Natural rights doctrine is best understood as being concerned with the question: in virtue of what is a person entitled to equal consideration and respect. And, in broad outline, the answer that this doctrine gives us is that a person is entitled to equal consideration and respect in virtue of possessing a certain nature. Thus, in Locke's development of the natural rights view, it is because God has created a law – natural law – which requires that all creatures with a certain nature be treated a certain way, and because human beings possess this type of nature, that all human beings possess natural rights. And it is possession of these sorts of natural rights which grounds or justifies the claim that all human beings are entitled to equal consideration and respect. Seen in this light, then, natural rights doctrine, by itself, is not directly concerned with the question of in what treating a person with equal consideration consists. It is concerned with the conditions that an individual must satisfy in order to fall under the scope of the principle of equal consideration.

Utilitarianism, on the other hand, is not directly concerned with the question of what conditions are necessary for an individual to fall under the scope of the principle of equal consideration, although it almost certainly does have important implications for this question. Rather, it is concerned with explaining what it means to treat someone with equal consideration. Broadly speaking, the answer utilitarianism gives us is that we treat all persons with equal consideration when we take into account the *interests* of all of them. The notion of interest, here, is construed broadly to encompass states as diverse as happiness and preference-satisfaction. And, utilitarianism claims that to treat all persons equally is to treat the interests of all persons as counting equally in the moral calculus.

The central concern of contractarianism, at least in its Kantian incarnation, is still different. Kantian contractarianism must, necessarily, begin with a certain conception of justice as given, and then tries to identify the, often partly concealed and implicit, principles that make up this conception. Unlike natural rights doctrine, there is no attempt to say what conditions must be satisfied by an individual in order for it to fall under the scope of the principle of equal consideration. And, unlike utilitarianism, there is no attempt to advocate or justify a particular interpretation of the principle of equal consideration. The purpose of Kantian contractarianism is elucidation, not justification. Kantian contractarianism must begin with a concrete exemplar of the principle of equal consideration as that principle is embodied in a particular moral or political theory, and then attempts to elucidate the precise content of this principle as thus embodied.

Utilitarianism and what is, in effect, a version of natural rights doctrine have both figured prominently in recent attempts to develop a consistent animal liberationist position. Later chapters will examine these attempts. The contractarian position, even in its Kantian form, has, however, been neglected. Indeed, received wisdom has it that a contractarian understanding of morality is incompatible with the animal liberationist position. I shall argue that this is a serious mistake. Indeed, I shall try to show that, far from being anathema to the idea of animal liberation, contractarianism, in its Kantian form, provides the best defence of the idea of animal liberation in general and the concept of animal rights in particular. Given the above comments on the status of Kantian contractarianism, the defence of the notion of animal liberation is a defence that proceeds by way of elucidation. The contract device, as employed in Kantian contractarianism, can be used to elucidate the particular conception of the principle of equal consideration as it is embodied in modern, essentially liberal, thought. And, I shall argue, once we have adequately elucidated the content of this conception, we will see that non-human animals must be included under the scope of the principle. That is, I shall argue, the most adequate understanding of the concept of equal consideration embodied in modern thought, commits us to the attribution, to at least certain sorts of non-human animals, of a substantial set of moral rights.

4 Utilitarianism and Animals: Peter Singer's Case for Animal Liberation

Peter Singer can, with justification, be regarded as the founding father of the contemporary animal liberation movement. The increased public awareness of what exactly transpires in our treatment of non-humans – in factory farming, medical research, product testing, and so on – is, to a significant extent, due to the wide circulation of his work. Consequently, anyone who cares about the welfare of non-human animals must acknowledge an enormous debt to Singer. However, it is important to distinguish the beneficial impact Singer's work has had on public awareness from the philosophical arguments he uses to defend the moral claims of non-humans. The two are logically independent of each other. And this chapter is concerned purely with the philosophical arguments.

In the opening chapter of *Animal Liberation*, Singer presents a powerful argument for the claim that justice requires equal consideration of the interests of non-human as well as human animals.[1] And Singer also places the idea of equal consideration at the centre of the conceptual stage. The notion of moral equality, and the requirement of equal consideration that stems from it, Singer argues, is not a *description* of how the world is. Whether we like it or not, we humans come in different shapes and sizes, with different intellectual abilities, different moral capacities, different capacities to experience pleasure and pain, and so on. Thus, if the demand for equal consideration were based on the actual equality of human beings, it would be a manifestly unrealistic demand. In fact, however, the concept of equal consideration derives not from any actual equality between humans beings. Its function is not to describe human beings, but *prescribe* how we should treat them. Then, given this understanding of the nature of the requirement of equal consideration, Singer goes on to argue that we are also committed to applying the requirement in our treatment of non-humans.

As I have hopefully made clear in the preceding chapters, I believe that this is precisely the right strategy. That is, the case for the moral claims of non-humans turns decisively around the concept of equal consideration. The central flaw in Singer's case, I shall argue, stems not from its *adoption* of this strategy, but from its *implementation*. Singer, I shall argue, operates with an inadequate understanding of the concept of equal consideration. The reason for this, as is made clear in some of his other writings, is that Singer is a *utilitarian*, and interprets the concept of equal consideration in terms of the central principles of utilitarian moral theory.[2] The principal aim of this chapter is to examine utilitarianism, in its various forms, with particular reference to the idea of equal consideration which it supports. I shall argue that the concept of equal consideration underwritten by utilitarian moral theory is crucially deficient and that this, effectively, undermines Singer's case for animal liberation.

1. UTILITARIANISM I: DEFINITION OF UTILITY

Utilitarianism, in all its forms, is essentially made up of two separate components:

1. A definition of human welfare, or *utility*.
2. A requirement to maximize utility.

This section deals with utilitarian ideas of human welfare. The next section deals with why utilitarians think we should maximize it.

There are two clearly distinct conceptions of human welfare evident in utilitarian writings. The first identifies such welfare with *pleasure*, or, more generally, with *happiness*. The second identifies it with the satisfaction of preferences. The former is known as *hedonistic utilitarianism*; the latter as *preference utilitarianism*.

Hedonistic Utilitarianism

Hedonistic utilitarianism has, historically, been perhaps the most influential in the utilitarian tradition. In its more restricted versions, this view claims that human welfare principally consists in the sensation or experience of pleasure. Pleasure is the primary human good because it is the one good which is an end in itself, to which all other goods are merely means. Bentham, one of the founders of utilitarianism, notoriously said that 'pushpin is as good as poetry' if it gives the same intensity and duration of pleasure. Poetry is better than pushpin only if it gives people more pleasure.

The problems with hedonistic utilitarianism are well known. Jack Smart, for example, asks us to imagine a pleasure machine, a device which injects drugs into us, thus creating in us the most pleasurable mental states imaginable.[3] It seems that if pleasure were our greatest good, then logically we should all want to be hooked up to this machine for ever, living a life of nothing but intense pleasure. The problem is, however, that, in the eyes of most philosophers at least, volunteers for this procedure would be few and far between. In the eyes of many critics of utilitarianism, such a life would not be a life most worth living; on the contrary it would be a rather sad waste of a life. And if this is true, pleasure cannot be our ultimate value.[4]

For these sorts of reasons, many hedonistic utilitarians reject the identification of welfare with pleasure. Pleasure, it is argued, is simply far too restricted in content to be the principal human good. For many of us at least, it is argued, the things worth doing and having in life are not all reducible to one mental state like pleasure. Not all valuable experiences need be pleasurable. On the contrary, many different kinds of experiences are valuable, and the best sort of life is one which promotes the entire range of valuable mental states. And utilitarianism, therefore, should be concerned with all valuable experiences, whatever form they take. If we denote the set of all such experiences with the term 'happiness', then we can reformulate hedonistic utilitarianism as the claim that human welfare principally consists in happiness.

This extended notion of human welfare, however, does not allow the utilitarian to avoid Smart's objection. To see this, all we need do is imagine the machine suitably extended in its capacities to produce any desired mental state – not just intrinsically pleasurable ones.[5] Thus, the machine might be able to produce the experience of love, the sense of accomplishment from achieving a difficult task, etc. Even with this extension of its capacities, many critics of hedonistic utilitarianism contend that we would still be hard pressed to find any volunteers willing to be hooked up for life. What we want in life, they claim, is something more than simply the acquisition of any kind of mental state. We do not just want the sense of satisfaction engendered by accomplishing a difficult task, we want to accomplish the task itself. We do not simply want the experience of writing a respected philosophical tract, or a Booker prize winning novel, we want to actually write these things. What this seems to show, these critics contend, is that while we do find certain sorts of experiences valuable, we also find other things, over and above experiences, to be valuable. Moreover, the value of these sorts of things is of a sort that is not replaceable by the value of the experiences that might accompany them. This is why not many of us, it is claimed, would volunteer to be hooked up for life to the suitably extended experience machine.

Preference Utilitarianism

According to the most straightforward version of preference utilitarianism, human welfare consists in the satisfaction of human preferences, whatever these might happen to be. A person might want the experience of accomplishing a difficult task, or writing a Booker prize winning novel; and these are preferences that could be satisfied in Smart's machine. However, a person might also actually want to accomplish the task or write the novel; and this is a preference that cannot be satisfied in the machine. According to the most basic form of preference utilitarianism, then, the principal welfare of a human being consists in the satisfaction of his or her preferences, whatever those preferences might be.

The problem with this view, as stated, is that, intuitively, our preferences do not always contribute to our welfare. I might have a preference to drink vast quantities of alcohol every night, but this would probably not contribute to my general welfare. Our welfare and our preferences do not necessarily coincide. This, by itself, does not show that there is anything more to our welfare than our preferences. After all, the reason why my current preference for large amounts of alcohol is not in my long-term welfare is that it conflicts with other preferences of mine – to stay healthy, live a reasonably long life, hold on to my job, and retain a viable bank balance, for example. But what this does show is that our preferences can, often without us realizing it, conflict. And, given this is so, not *all* of our preferences can coincide with our welfare.

A more sophisticated version of preference utilitarianism attempts to accommodate the problem of mistaken preferences by defining welfare as the satisfaction of *informed* or *rational* preferences. Human welfare, on this view, consists in the satisfaction of informed human preferences; that is, satisfaction of those preferences which are based on full information and correct judgements, while rejecting those that are mistaken or irrational. This position does seem far more plausible. However, it also seems extremely vague. It places very few constraints on what counts as utility. Pleasure at least had the merit of being reasonably easy to identify, and its presence easy to discern in others. We also have a reasonably good idea of how to promote pleasure. Once, however, we view utility in terms of informed or rational preferences, these features disappear. There are many different kinds of informed preferences, and no obvious way of aggregating them. How do we know whether to promote poetry or pushpin if there is no single overarching value like pleasure by which to measure them? And, more generally, how do we know what preferences people would have if they were informed and rational?

There are, of course, genuine difficulties here. However, it would be unfair to use them to criticize utilitarianism, since the same difficulties emerge in connection with almost any moral theory. Ultimately, every moral theory has to confront the difficult issue of the nature of human welfare. The problems here, therefore, are not peculiar to utilitarianism. Indeed, nothing prevents the utilitarian from adopting whatever account of welfare her critics favour. If there is a damaging objection to utilitarianism, therefore, it will have to be found in the second part of the theory – that is, in the instruction to maximize utility, whichever definition of utility we finally adopt.

2. UTILITARIANISM II: MAXIMIZING UTILITY

The second component of utilitarianism is the instruction to maximize human welfare or utility, however this latter notion is defined. According to utilitarianism, the morally right action, in any given situation, is the one that maximizes utility – for example, produces the greatest amount of happiness, or satisfies as many informed preferences as possible. In any such maximization, some people's preferences will necessarily go unsatisfied; the satisfaction of the preferences of some people is incompatible with the satisfaction of those of others. Therefore, if a person's preferences conflict with what maximizes utility overall, then that person's preferences will, in this situation, be overridden. However, since the number of preferences satisfied necessarily outnumber the number of preferences frustrated, there is no reason, utilitarians claim, why the preferences of the losers should take precedence over the more numerous, or more intense, preferences of the winners. Notice also, that to override a person's preferences in a given situation is not, according to the utilitarian, the same as to ignore those preferences. The preferences have been considered and added into the preference calculus which determines the best course of action; i.e. the course of action which results in the satisfaction of the greatest number of preferences. It is just that, once the results of the calculation have been determined, some preferences will have to be sacrificed in order to bring about the greatest number of satisfied preferences. The overriding of some preferences, then, is perfectly compatible with the equal consideration of all preferences.

There are two distinct arguments for maximizing utility that can be identified in utilitarian writings. These arguments are quite distinct, indeed even incompatible, and they generate two very different interpretations of utilitarianism. The difference turns on the conceptual role of the concept of justice in each interpretation.

Teleological Utilitarianism: Individuals as Receptacles

John Rawls defines a teleological moral theory as one which (i) provides an independent definition of the good for humans, and (ii) defines justice in terms of the maximization of the good.[6] This, according to Rawls, is precisely what utilitarianism does; and for this reason, we can refer to this interpretation of utilitarianism as the *teleological* interpretation.

According to the teleological interpretation, our primary moral duty is to maximize utility, however this is defined. That is, our primary duty is not to treat people as equals, but to bring about valuable situations or states of affairs; and the more utility possessed by a state of affairs, the more valuable that state of affairs is. On this view, people don't have value intrinsically, but they are, or can be, the *bearers* of what has value. These intrinsically valuable things will be states such as happiness, or preference-satisfaction, depending on one's view of what utility is. And the prime moral directive of utilitarianism is to maximize the number or amount of these intrinsically valuable things. How we maximize these things, and, in particular, in whom we maximize them, is of no direct moral concern. Thus, on this view, people can be viewed as *receptacles* of what has value, and not things which are themselves intrinsically valuable. In this connection, Regan introduces a rather striking and helpful analogy: we can compare people to cups that are capable of containing either sweet-tasting liquid (utility) or bitter-tasting liquid (disutility).[7] The primary goal of moral action is to produce as much sweet-tasting liquid, and as little bitter-tasting liquid, as possible. It doesn't matter, at least not

directly, into which cups we pour the sweet-tasting liquid, as long as
we introduce as much sweet-tasting liquid into the world as possible.
Thus, if, for example, it should prove necessary to fill some cups
entirely with bitter-tasting liquid so as to produce the maximum
amount of sweet-tasting liquid elsewhere, then this is what we should
do. In fact, if the maximization of the quantity of sweet-tasting liquid
required filling some cups entirely with bitter-tasting liquid, then this
is what *justice* requires we do. Similarly, if maximization of utility
requires sacrificing the welfare of certain individuals, then justice
requires that we sacrifice these individuals. This is so because justice,
according to the teleological interpretation of utilitarianism, consists
in the maximization of utility. Individuals who are sacrificed in this
way, then, cannot, according to the teleological interpretation,
complain that they are being treated unjustly.

The teleological interpretation is actually found in very few utilitarian writings – G. E. Moore being its only notable advocate.[8]
Indeed, the teleological interpretation seems to be one primarily
found in the writings of critics of utilitarianism. As mentioned above,
Rawls, for example, sees utilitarianism as fundamentally a teleological theory in this sense.[9] And this is the basis of his charge that
utilitarianism essentially collapses the distinction between different
people. Tom Regan, another vociferous critic of utilitarianism, also
sees it as primarily a theory of the teleological sort.[10] This provides
the basis of his claim that utilitarianism treats people as merely receptacles of what has value, and not as inherently valuable in themselves.
The teleological interpretation, then, seems largely to be an interpretation foisted on utilitarianism by its critics.

There are, in fact, good reasons why utilitarians should not adopt
the teleological interpretation. One of the things a moral theory
attempts to do is not only to spell out a set of duties that a moral agent
can reasonably be thought to possess, but also to identify those individuals towards whom the agent has these duties. The teleological
interpretation of utilitarianism is committed to the claim that we have
a duty to maximize valuable states of affairs, but leaves it wholly
mysterious as to whom we have this duty. On the teleological interpretation of utilitarianism, there seems to be no identifiable
individual or group of individuals who can plausibly be regarded as
the beneficiary of such a duty. It is implausible to claim that we have
this duty to the maximally valuable state of affairs itself, for it is not
clear how states of affairs can have moral claims. The most natural
response is to claim that we have the duty to whichever individuals

would benefit from the maximization of utility. But then it seems our primary moral duty is to individuals, and that we have only a derivative duty to produce maximally valuable states of affairs. And in this case, the teleological interpretation of utilitarianism collapses into another, quite distinct, version of that theory. It is to this second interpretation that we now turn.

Egalitarian Utilitarianism: Individuals as Counting Equally

The teleological interpretation of utilitarianism begins by defining human welfare – happiness, preference-satisfaction, etc. – and then defines justice as the maximization of this welfare. The concept of justice is derivative upon the concept of welfare. What we can call the *egalitarian* interpretation of utilitarianism, on the other hand, treats the concept of justice as basic, and the requirement to maximize utiltity is then derived from this. Thus, in the writings of many utilitarians, we find the following sort of argument. Each person should be regarded as a moral equal, and we must, therefore, treat everyone with equal consideration and respect. To this end, the preferences of each person should be regarded as having equal weight, irrespective of the content of their preferences, and regardless of the specific talents, capacities, endowments, and physical and economic circumstances of the person. Giving these preferences equal weight is what is required to treat people as equals, to treat them with equal consideration and respect.

In other words, on the egalitarian interpretation, we can regard the content of utilitarianism as being factored into three components. The first is a formal principle of justice:

U1. Each person should be treated with equal consideration and respect.

This principle, as we have seen, is generally regarded as constitutive of, or essential to, the moral point of view as such, and is in no way peculiar to utilitarianism. What is peculiar to utilitarianism, however, is its interpretation of this formal principle. This interpretation consists of two principles. The first is:

U2. The interests of each and every person should be given equal weight in moral deliberations.

The notion of an interest, here, functions simply as a place-holder for the slightly more concrete concepts of pleasure, happiness, preference-satisfaction, and the like. U2 is an interpretation of U1. We are to treat each person with equal consideration by allowing their interests (e.g. their preferences) to count equally. The final principle is an interpretation of U2.

U3. The maximum possible number of interests should be satisfied.

U3 is an interpretation of U2. According to U3, the best way to make each person's interests count equally is to ensure maximal satisfaction of interests.

The crucial difference between the teleological and the egalitarian interpretation of utilitarianism can be understood as follows. The teleological interpretation makes maximization of utility *constitutive* of justice. The egalitarian interpretation, on the other hand, begins with a prior conception of justice (all people should be treated with equal consideration and respect) and interprets this conception as the requirement that utility should be maximized. What is crucial to the egalitarian conception is that the requirement to maximize utility is derived entirely from the prior requirement to treat people with equal consideration. This sort of justification for maximizing utility can clearly be found in the writings of utilitarians such as Mill, Hare, Griffin, and Harsanyi.[11]

The egalitarian interpretation is also clearly the interpretation adopted by Singer. In the opening chapter of *Animal Liberation*, as in other writings, Singer claims that his arguments for the moral claims of non-humans derive from what he refers to as 'the basic moral principle of equality'. This principle, he points out, is not based on any alleged factual equality between different people. Whether we like it or not, people come in different shapes and sizes, they come with different moral capacities, different intellectual abilities, different abilities to communicate effectively, and so on. In short, if the truth of the principle of equality depended on there being any factual equality between human beings, the principle would be certainly false. However, Singer argues, the principle does not function to *describe* any factual equality between humans. Its function is *prescription* not *description*. The principle prescribes how people should be treated, not describes how they are. Singer's utilitarianism, then, derives from his viewing the equal consideration of all interests as the best means of satisfying the basic moral principle of equality.

Since it is the egalitarian interpretation which is clearly adhered to by most defenders of utilitarianism, and since, as outlined above, there are significant problems with the teleological interpretation, in the sections to follow I shall focus on the egalitarian interpretation. Given this interpretation, the central problem with utilitarianism can, I think, be stated as follows: *principles U2 and U3 provide a poor interpretation of the formal principle of justice U1*. The section to follow will develop arguments that attempt to show exactly why this is so. These arguments, however, can easily be adapted to apply to the teleological interpretation of utilitarianism. That is, although arguments will be presented as showing that utilitarianism provides a poor *interpretation* of the formal principle of justice, they can also be taken to show that utilitarian deliberations cannot, plausibly, be regarded as *constitutive* of the formal principle of justice.

3. PROBLEMS WITH UTILITARIANISM

The principal motivation for utilitarianism, then, at least in the eyes of many of its advocates, is egalitarian; it is essentially motivated by a concern for treating all people with equal consideration. Indeed, as Hare says, if we believe that each person's welfare consists in the satisfaction of their informed preferences, then, in order to treat each person with equal consideration, what else can we do except give equal weight to their preferences, everyone counting for one, no one for more than one.[12] Hare, that is, sees utilitarianism as providing the only possible way of giving equal consideration to everyone. Thus, underpinning the egalitarian conception of utilitarianism is the inference from treating people with equal consideration to giving equal weight to each person's interests or preferences. The former, on the egalitarian conception of utilitarianism, requires the latter.

This inference, I shall argue, is fallacious. To interpret the principle of equal consideration in terms of the principle of equal consideration, via maximization of interests, is to badly misunderstand the principle of equal consideration. More precisely, U2 and U3 amount to what we can call an *aggregation requirement*. We are to treat people with equal consideration by giving equal moral weight to all their interests. And we give equal moral weight to all their interests by satisfying the maximum possible number of them. And this means we have to aggregate interests and adopt whatever course of action is required to bring about the maximum number of satisfied interests. I shall argue that to understand the concept of equal consideration in terms of this sort of aggregation requirement is to badly misunderstand the concept. Utilitarianism, then, has misinterpreted the ideal of equal consideration. And, as a result, it allows some people to be treated as less than equals, as a means to other people's ends.

Other-directed Preferences

One central component of our intuitive conception of equal consideration is surely this: the moral entitlements an individual can be legitimately thought to possess do not depend on, and are in no way altered by, the attitudes that other individuals bear towards them. If I, for example, dislike Smith, and want him to be deprived of certain goods, resources or opportunities to which he claims entitlement, then my attitudes do not entail that Smith should be deprived of these things. If Smith is genuinely entitled to these goods, resources or opportunities, then my hostility towards him can do nothing to change this. Indeed, if everyone in the world harbours inimical feelings towards Smith, then this in no way alters his moral entitlements. We do, of course, sometimes restrict an individual's access to certain goods, resources or opportunities, and often when we do so we also actively dislike the individual in question. Our treatment of certain convicts provides an obvious example. However, our active dislike of someone who has committed a particularly heinous crime is, in this sort of case, simply an *accompaniment* to the restrictions imposed on them, not a *justification*. The justification for restricting their goods, resources, opportunities, and the like lies in the crime they have committed, not in the hostility this crime arouses in us.

It is fairly clear, then, that the claim that the moral entitlements possessed by an individual do not depend on the attitudes that other people bear towards him or her is absolutely constitutive of our intuitive understanding of the principle of equal consideration. One of the problems with utilitarianism is that it is simply unable to accommodate this fact.

To see this, consider the following scenario. Suppose the vast majority of the populace of a society become increasingly desensitized to violence, perhaps due to the proliferation of violent films or whatever it is which is supposed to desensitize one to violence. And they decide that the usual offerings of contact sports – boxing, rugby, gridiron, hockey, etc. – simply don't hold the same fascination for them any more. What is needed is something far more violent. Therefore, in the quest for better weekend entertainment, network television decides to reinstitute the old Roman tradition of gladiatorial combat to the death. The viewing population who, you remember, has become severely desensitized to violence, is very excited about the idea. So too, therefore, are the advertisers. And so too, therefore, are the networks. The only problem is: finding the gladiators. The problem is solved when a young ambitious network executive hits upon the idea of using convicts on death row (or, in countries where there is no death penalty, those sentenced to life without the possibility of remission). The convicts are not given a choice, they are simply forced to fight.

In this scenario, we seem to have a situation where the preferences of a large number of people – the bloodthirsty populace of our imagined society – are set against the preferences of what is, in comparison, a vanishingly small number of people – the unwilling gladiators. If the imagined society were the United States, for example, the population would number about 250 million, compared to, say, a few hundred convicts a year. In China, the disparity would be even greater. Even allowing for the fact that the preferences of the convicts are greater or more intense than those of the viewing population, it still seems that the preferences of this vast majority would outweigh those of the convicts. Therefore, it seems that utilitarianism would, in this sort of situation, be committed to the reintroduction of gladiatorial combat to the death as the morally right thing to do. But, intuitively at least, something here seems to be seriously unjust.

Of course, there could be complications in instituting such a programme, complications that the utilitarian might cite as tipping the preference calculus back against the gladiatorial system. Thus, for example, the gladiators might have friends or relatives who would be greatly saddened by their public slaughter. This sort of consideration is often referred to as a *side effect*. However, we can eliminate these sorts of complications by slight articulation of the scenario. Suppose, for example, the names of the convicts were drawn by public lottery a week or so before their fight. Viewers then had a week to register a complaint, and the prisoner would go to the arena only if no one of the general populace objected. Presumably, gladiatorial candidates would be harder to find in these circumstances, but, in principle, there might well be enough friendless and familyless death row convicts to meet the network's requirements. The utilitarian, it seems, would be committed to claiming that, in this case, reintroduction of the gladiatorial system is not only morally legitimate but actually morally required.

The above scenario is admittedly somewhat far-fetched.

Nevertheless, the same sort of points can be made in relation to cases much closer to home. Some people, for example, are racists. And one form such racism might take is wanting a certain minority, or minorities, to have fewer goods, resources and opportunities than one wants available to members of one's preferred racial group. One might, for example, want to exclude blacks from certain jobs, or certain educational opportunities, because one thinks they are not worthy of them. And if the minority in question were of sufficiently small size, and if the racist members of society were sufficiently large in number relative to the minority group, and if the relevant beliefs of the racists were held with sufficient fervour, then taking proper account of the preferences of the racists might, on utilitarian grounds, justify repressing the minority group in the way preferred by the racists. Once again, whatever else we have here, we do not have a case of equal consideration. On the contrary, adopting the utilitarian calculus would entail that what treatment should be accorded the minority group is a function of what *other* people – in this case a group of racists – happen to think about them.

Furthermore, the situation would not be significantly changed if we replace the group of racists with a group of, say, benevolent despots who are much more favourably disposed to the minority group to the extent, for example, of even granting them preferred status with regard to employment and educational opportunities. The point remains the same. In this case, the treatment we accord the minority group is again a function of what *other* people happen to think about them; it's just that here the others happen to be a group who are more favourably disposed towards the minority group. The principle of equal consideration is incompatible with the idea that what a person, or a group of people, are rightfully owed is a matter of what other people happen to think about them. And this is true no matter what the specific content of those other people's attitudes; that is, no matter whether those attitudes are favourable or unfavourable.

There is a crucial distinction implicated in both of the above examples, a distinction that any plausible account of the principle of equal consideration needs to take into account: that between *self-directed* and *other-directed* preferences.[13] Self-directed preferences are preferences about the goods, resources, and opportunities etc. one wants available to oneself. Other-directed preferences concern the goods, resources, and opportunities one wants available to others. Other-directed preferences can often be prejudiced. As in one of the above cases, someone may want blacks to have fewer resources because he thinks them less worthy of respect. Because of this there is a clear and serious tension between the primary motivation for utilitarianism and its inclusion of other-directed preferences in the preference calculus. As we have seen, the primary motivation for utilitarianism is the egalitarian principle of equal consideration. Each person has moral standing, each person matters as much as any other. And utilitarians interpret this idea in terms of the aggregation of interests – each person's interests should count as much as, but no more than, every other person's interests. But if this is the primary motivation for utilitarianism, then utilitarianism cannot, on pain of inconsistency, count other-directed preferences. For if such preferences are counted, then what I am rightfully owed depends on how others think of me. If they think I am unworthy of equal concern, then I will do less well in the utilitarian calculus. But utilitarians cannot accept that result, because utilitarianism is premised on the view that everyone ought to be treated as equals.

What is in fact going on here is a clash between two principles which utilitarians have conflated. On the one hand there is the principle of *equal consideration*: the principle that every person should be treated with equal consideration. On the other hand is the principle of the *aggregation of interests*: we are to aggregate the interests of all people and adopt whatever course of action maximally satisfies the aggregation. Utilitarians, as we have seen, interpret the former in terms of the latter. However, as the above examples make clear, the principles are not only non-equivalent, they are, in fact, incompatible. If we adopt the principle of the aggregation of interests, as do utilitarians, then, because individuals can have other-directed preferences as well as self-directed ones, this entails that what people are rightfully owed depends on what others happen to think of them. That is, the principle of the aggregation of interests entails that the moral status of each person depends, in part, on the content of the attitudes that every other person bears towards them. And this is incompatible with the principle of equal consideration, which says that every person should be treated with equal consideration, irrespective of the attitudes of others towards them. Thus, the principle of the aggregation of interests, far from being the correct interpretation of the principle of equal consideration, is, in fact, incompatible with this latter principle.

If we believe that everyone is to be treated as equals, then we cannot allow that it is acceptable for some people to suffer because others do not want them treated as equals. Therefore, if utilitarianism is to remain true to its perceived motivation – the principle of equal consideration – then other-directed preferences must be excluded from the utilitarian calculus. The consequences of this will be examined later in the chapter, where I shall argue that this commits the utilitarian to a prior, and non-utilitarian, standard of justice.

Self-directed Preferences

It is not possible to avoid the above objection simply by excluding other-directed preferences *en bloc* from utilitarian aggregative calculations. For the category of self-directed attitudes also carries within it a problematic set of preferences. The relevant category here is that of *selfish* preferences. Selfish preferences involve the elevation of one's own position – in terms of access to goods, resources, opportunities, etc. – relative to others. Now clearly, selfish preferences can often be productive of utility. However, I shall argue that the utilitarian is not able to include selfish preferences in the calculus.

Kymlicka gives the following useful example.[14] Suppose all my neighbours have flower gardens, but decide they would like my lawn left open as a public space for children to play on, dogs to walk on, etc. I, however, want a flower garden. The desires of others to use my lawn as a public space may well outweigh, in terms of overall utility, my desire to have a garden. In such circumstances the utilitarian must think it right to sacrifice my desire for the more numerous desires of others. This, however, seems implausible.

The utilitarian would claim that, in this case, my sacrifice is required in order that everyone be treated with equal consideration. If I keep my garden then my neighbours are not being treated with equal consideration since their preferences, when aggregated, outweigh mine. Thus, if I keep my garden, their preferences are, in effect, being treated as less important than mine; more importance is being placed on my preferences than on anyone else's. Utilitarians are committed to the idea that the preference of my neighbours *vis-à-vis* the use of my lawn is a legitimate preference that grounds a moral claim. And this reveals the gulf between the utilitarian and the intuitive understanding of equal consideration. It is extremely implausible to suppose that the principle of equal consideration gives my neighbours any claim over my share of resources. If they already have their own lawn, then surely I am not treating them unjustly in saying that my preferences concerning my lawn outweigh theirs, outweigh even the aggregation of all their preferences. If this were not so, then surely it is I who would not be treated with equal consideration. I still respect them as equals since I make no claim on their resources. But they do not respect me as an equal when they expect me to give up my share of resources to satisfy their desire to have more than their fair share.

What is going on here is once again a clash of two principles conflated by utilitarianism. On the one hand, there is the principle of equal consideration: the claim that each individual should be treated with equal consideration. On the other hand, there is the principle of the aggregation of interests: the claim that the interests or preferences of each individual should be aggregated and the resulting aggregation be maximally satisfied. However, as the above example makes clear, these principles are, in fact, non-equivalent and potentially conflicting. In the above example, if we adopt the principle of aggregation of interests, and accord the preferences of each individual equal weight, then we are led to the conclusion that my lawn should be used as a public area. But if we adopt the principle of equal consideration, and treat each of the individuals involved with equal consideration, then we seem to be led to the conclusion that my lawn should not be used as a public area. The principle of the aggregation of interests provides a poor interpretation of the principle of equal consideration.

Now, it may be objected that the above way of setting up the problem begs the question against utilitarianism. Utilitarians, after all, will deny that there is such a thing as a fair share, and hence such a thing as a selfish preference, independently of utilitarian calculations. For utilitarians, a fair distribution just is one that maximizes utility, and so no preference can be identified as selfish prior to utility calculations. So, it begs the question against the utilitarianism to assume that we can identify such things as selfish preferences prior to utilitarian calculations.

The problem with this objection, however, is that it relies heavily on what was earlier identified as a teleological interpretation of utilitarianism: the claim that the primary directive of utilitarianism is to maximize utility. However, it was argued that this interpretation is not the one adopted by most utilitarians. On the contrary, most utilitarians understand their theory as providing the best way to interpret a formal principle of justice, a principle motivated independently of considerations of utility maximization. And, if this is so, utilitarianism will involve a commitment to our intuitive understanding of the formal principle of justice. Therefore, the above objection does not substantially affect the present issue. The present issue is simply whether utilitarianism provides an adequate interpretation of the principle of equal consideration. And, as the above case hopefully makes it clear, it does not do so; at least it does not provide an adequate interpretation of our intuitive understanding of what this principle entails. If selfish preferences are included, then there will be cases where the principle of aggregation of interests leads to violations of the principle of equal consideration. Therefore, the former cannot be regarded as providing an adequate interpretation of the latter.

Therefore, as with the case of other-directed preferences, if utilitarianism is to remain true to its motivation, namely, the principle of equal consideration, it must systematically exclude from the preference calculus both external and selfish preferences. The consequences of such exclusion will be examined in the next section.

4. UTILITARIANISM AND JUSTICE

It might be thought that the objections based on other-directed and selfish preferences outlined in the previous section could be accommodated by utilitarianism with only minor modifications. Surely, it might be thought, the utilitarian can simply modify her position to the claim that the morally correct course of action is the one which produces the greatest number of satisfied self-directed but nonselfish preferences. However, I shall argue, the exclusion of these sorts of preferences cannot be justified by the utilitarian without recourse to non-utilitarian principles of justice. Provision of any principled justification for excluding other-directed and selfish preferences requires a prior non-utilitarian account of justice. And thus, exclusion of other-directed and selfish preferences in any principled way requires, in effect, rejection of utilitarianism as a foundational moral theory.

The motivation for utilitarianism, it has been argued, is the principle of equal consideration. Utilitarians, however, interpret this principle in terms of the principle of the aggregation of interests. That is, to treat each individual with equal consideration requires giving equal weight to each of their interests or preferences. However, if we include other-directed and selfish preferences among those to which we are to give equal weight, then the principle of the aggregation of interests is actually incompatible with the principle of equal consideration, at least as this is intuitively understood. By interpreting the principle of equal consideration in this way, therefore, utilitarianism, in effect, undermines its own motivation.

Nevertheless, it is also true that the interpretation of the principle of equal consideration in terms of the principle of the aggregation of interests is definitive of utilitarianism. For utilitarianism, in addition to being committed to the former, is also committed to the idea of a calculus, and therefore to things which can be weighed, aggregated, and measured against one another. It makes little sense to talk of entering individuals into the calculus in this sense. So, utilitarianism needs things such as interests, or informed preferences, as suitable material for the calculus.

Therefore, not only is utilitarianism committed to the principle of equal consideration, it is also, it seems, committed to interpreting this principle in terms of the principle of aggregation of interests. Without this principle, it seems, we would lose much (or all) of what is distinctive about utilitarianism. The problem is, however, that, without the exclusion of other-directed and selfish preferences, the principle of the aggregation of interests is actually incompatible with the principle of equal consideration, at least as this is intuitively understood. Therefore, on pain of violating our intuitive understanding of the concept of equal consideration, the utilitarian is committed to excluding other-directed and selfish preferences from the principle of aggregation of interests. Not all interests are, in fact, to be given the same weight. Some are to be given no weight at all.

However, this creates a serious problem for the utilitarian. According to utilitarianism, which actions count as right, and which count as wrong, can emerge only *subsequent* to the calculus of interests or preferences. The possibility of moral evaluation, then, can emerge only as a result of the calculus. It therefore makes no sense, on utilitarian grounds, to exclude certain preferences on the grounds that they are illegitimate preferences *prior* to the calculus. For what counts as a legitimate or illegitimate preference can only be determined by the calculus itself. Therefore, the exclusion of other-directed and selfish preferences, an exclusion which utilitarianism requires to safeguard our intuitive conception of equal consideration, cannot be justified on utilitarian grounds. It is an exclusion required by utilitarianism, but one that cannot in any way be motivated or justified by it.

This means that any exclusion of other-directed and selfish preferences will have to be justified by a prior standard of legitimacy. And since utilitarianism is committed to this exclusion, utilitarianism is, therefore, also committed to a prior standard of legitimacy. But, then, utilitarianism cannot be thought of as providing the sole standard of morality. It must already incorporate, in a tacit manner, prior standards of moral legitimacy. In other words, in order for utilitarianism to work, there would have to be prior, non-utilitarian, standards of morality. Utilitarianism, therefore, cannot provide the sole standard of morality.

What is required, in fact, as a non-utilitarian standard of morality, is an adequate *theory of justice*. That this is so is clearly recognized by John Rawls, and he regards this as the fundamental difference between his account of justice and that of the utilitarians. For Rawls, it is a defining feature of our sense of justice that 'interests requiring the violation of justice have no value', and so the presence of illegitimate preferences 'cannot distort our claims upon one another'.[15] An adequate theory of justice, for Rawls, limits the admissible conceptions of the good, so that those conceptions the pursuit of which violates the principles of justice are ruled out absolutely: the claims to pursue inadmissible conceptions have no weight at all. Because unfair preferences never enter into the preference calculus, people's claims are made secure from the unreasonable demands of others. Utilitarianism fails to exclude illegitimate preferences because utilitarianism is committed to interpreting the concept of equal consideration in terms of the aggregation of pre-existing preferences, whatever those preferences happen to be. And standards of equality can emerge only subsequent to the calculus. That is, what counts as equal consideration is, for the utilitarian, constituted by the results of the calculus itself. The problem, however, is that the notion of equality should enter into the very decision whether to take into account a particular preference; whether to enter it in the calculus in the first place. Thus, we need a prior standard of justice in order to even begin to engage in deliberation of consequences. Part of what it means to show equal consideration for others is taking into account what rightfully belongs to them. Hence other-directed and selfish preferences must be excluded from the start, for they already reflect a failure to show equal consideration. Utilitarianism, however, can make no sense of this claim. Therefore, utilitarianism provides an inadequate interpretation of the principle of equal consideration.

5. RULE UTILITARIANISM

The conclusion of the arguments developed in the previous two sections is this: utilitarianism cannot do justice to our intuitive conception of equal consideration because it entails that the treatment someone is owed, as a matter of justice, depends, in part, on the attitudes other people bear towards him (other-directed preferences) and on the (illegitimate) attitudes he bears towards himself (selfish preferences). This clashes with our intuitive conception of equal consideration which claims that an individual's moral entitlements, and, in particular, the entitlements they can claim as a matter of justice, do not depend on these factors. Some utilitarians, however, would deny that there is this incompatibility between the concept of equal consideration and that of the equal consideration of interests. They admit that utilitarian reasoning can *appear* to have implications that are incompatible with the principle of equal consideration. But they claim that these implications can be avoided if we switch to a more sophisticated form of utilitarianism. According to this, it is not individual acts that are subject to the test of utility but, rather, the *rules* they embody. According to this view, since society is impossible without individuals adhering to rules, we should assess the consequences not simply of acting in a particular way on a particular occasion but of making it a rule that we act in this way. Thus, we should perform whatever act is required by the best rule; and the best rule is one consistent adherence to which will maximize utility. Thus, we are to adhere to utility maximizing rules, even when doing so results in our failing to perform utility maximizing acts. This view is known as rule utilitarianism. There are well-known problems with rule utilitarianism. Some have argued that rule utilitarianism ultimately collapses into act utilitarianism. To see this, suppose there is an action A_1 which would, in a particular situation S, maximize utility. However, there is also a rule R consistent adherence to which also maximizes utility in the long run, and R, let us suppose, requires us to perform, in situation S, the distinct act A_2. However, if this were the case, then it seems possible to replace R with another rule R^* which states: 'perform act A_2 unless in situation S; but when in situation S, perform A_1'. This is a rule which seems to be more productive of utility than R since it inherits all the usual utility maximizing power of R and at the same time avoids the problem that R does not maximize utility in situation S. Thus, consistent adherence to R^* would generate more utility than consistent adherence to R. Therefore, it seems that the rule utilitarian is committed to adoption of R^* rather than R. However, this procedure can be repeated for all those situations S_2, S_3 ...S_n in which adherence to R results in less than maximal production of utility. And this will result in the further rules, R^{**}, R^{***}, etc. And if this is so, there is a clear danger that our specification of the rules becomes so specific as to make rule utilitarianism indistinguishable from act utilitarianism.

Even if this problem can be surmounted, however, it is still very doubtful that rule utilitarianism can provide an adequate interpretation of our intuitive conception of equal consideration. The reason is that even rule utilitarianism makes the treatment a person is owed, as a matter of justice, contingent on the attitudes of other people. To see this, consider, for example, the rule utilitarian position with regard to selfish preferences such as racist ones. According to rule utilitarianism, the wrong done in discriminating against a minority group consists in the increased fear caused to others by having a rule allowing discrimination. But this claim is surely no closer to our intuitive conception of equality than is the corresponding claim of act utilitarians. The rule utilitarian claim entails that the treatment someone is owed, as a matter of justice, depends, at least in part, on the presence or absence of certain psychological attitudes in others. If discriminating against a minority group happens to result in increased fear in individuals outside that group, then it is morally wrong. If, on the other hand, such a rule did not result in this sort of increased fear, perhaps because the members of the majority group were too dimwitted to see the connection, then the rule should be regarded as morally legitimate. So, the rule utilitarian is also committed to the view that the treatment someone is owed, as a matter of justice, depends on the contingent presence or absence of certain psychological states in others. Rule utilitarianism, then, is no closer than act utilitarianism to our intuitive conception of equal consideration.

6. UTILITARIANISM AND ANIMALS

The strength of utilitarianism, as a moral theory, is that it frequently, so to speak, gets the right answer. Its weakness is that it does so for the wrong reasons. That this is sometimes difficult to see is due to the fact that the sorts of situations necessary to highlight the problematic implications of utilitarianism are often, necessarily, outlandish. The example of the institution of gladiatorial combat provides an obvious example. In more realistic cases, racism for example, it is often difficult to see the implications of utilitarianism. It is difficult to imagine, for example, the desires of racists to restrict the opportunities of minorities possibly outweighing the preferences of those minorities not to be so restricted. The latter sorts of preferences would, by their very nature, presumably be far more intense than the former. Thus, in order to make the example at all plausible, we would have to imagine a vast disparity in size between the two groups. And, once again, we veer towards the outlandish. Nevertheless, it remains true that, since utilitarianism, in both its act and rule forms, is committed to the claim that the treatment an individual is due as a matter of justice depends on the contingent psychological states of both that individual and others, utilitarianism, in both its forms, is incompatible with our intuitive understanding of the idea of equal consideration. Intuitively, to treat individuals with equal consideration requires treating them without regard to such contingent psychological features. Utilitarianism, then, often gets the intuitively right answer with respect to particular moral issues. It does so, however, for the wrong sorts of reasons; because, for example, of contingent features of the world such as the disparity in size between exploiting and exploited groups not being too great. Nowhere is this combination of right answer arrived at for the wrong reason more evident than in the utilitarian account of our moral commitments to non-humans. Let us consider Singer's utilitarian argument for vegetarianism.

The utilitarian case for vegetarianism is simple. If we are preference-utilitarians, for example, we will have to weigh up the preferences satisfied and frustrated by a policy of continuing to eat meat against the preferences satisfied and frustrated by a policy of abandoning meat-eating. And since the preferences of those non-human animals involved in the animal husbandry process will have to be included, it may seem that utilitarianism licenses a straightforward and clear-cut result. Singer writes:

> Since, as I have said, none of these practices (of raising animals intensively) cater for anything more than our pleasures of taste, our practice of rearing and killing other animals in order to eat them is a clear instance of the sacrifice of the most important interests of other beings in order to satisfy trivial interests of our own ... we must stop this practice, and each of us has a moral obligation to cease supporting this practice.[16]

As Singer sees it, the issue is simply one of weighing our relatively trivial preferences for gustatory satisfaction against the preferences of cattle, pigs, chickens etc. for a decent life free from undue suffering. And, seen in these terms, it is clear that utilitarianism would license the policy of abandoning meat-eating.

Tom Regan, however, feels that matters are not quite as clear-cut as this.[17] After all, there are more human preferences involved than those of the merely gustatory sort. The animal industry is big business. It is uncertain exactly how many people are involved in it, both directly and indirectly, but certainly the number must run into the tens, and probably hundreds, of thousands. Firstly, there are those who actually raise and sell the animals. Then, there are the feed producers and retailers; cage manufacturers and designers; producers of growth stimulants and other chemicals; those who butcher, package and ship the produce. Then there are extension personnel and veterinarians whose lives revolve around the success or failure of the animal industry. Moreover, also to consider are all the members of the families who are the dependants of these employees or employers. These interests these people have in raising animals intensively go well beyond pleasures of taste and are far from trivial. These people have a stake in the animal industry as rudimentary and important as having a job, feeding a family, and so on. When you add in these interests to the utilitarian calculations, things are perhaps not as clear-cut as Singer would have us believe.

Things become even more cloudy when we add in to the calculations the *side effects* which Singer, as a utilitarian, is obliged to take into account. Singer must take into account the preferences of *everyone* affected by the consequences of altering the animal industry, not just those who happen to be directly involved in it. The short- and long-term global economic consequences of a sudden or gradual transition to vegetarianism, must be investigated by any utilitarian. For example, it has been shown that the rate of inflation in countries such as the US follows, quite closely, the price of beef. What would be the economic implications of a widespread abandoning of meat-eating? As the price of beef rose, as it almost certainly would in these circumstances, would there be a consequent rise in inflation, and, as a result, perhaps an increase in unemployment even for people not connected with the animal industry? These sorts of questions would have to be seriously addressed by the utilitarian. It is simply not enough to see the issue as a weighing up of the vital interests of animals over the trivial gustatory interests of human beings.

I think Regan's case is probably empirically implausible in this regard. That is, when you in fact weigh up the preferences of the humans directly and indirectly involved in the animal husbandry industry against the preferences of the vastly greater number of animals used in this industry, my suspicion is that the latter will significantly outweigh the former. Therefore, utilitarianism does entail that the practice of animal husbandry is unjust. And, as I shall argue in a later chapter, this conclusion is correct; the practice is seriously unjust. This is a case, then, where I think utilitarianism yields the right answer. The problem is that it does so for the wrong reasons.

To see this, imagine a few contingent changes in the circumstances underlying the practice of animal husbandry. By imaginatively varying the circumstances, we can presumably imagine a case where the interests of humans outweigh those of animals. Indeed, given the aggregative nature of utilitarianism it seems that there must necessarily be such a situation. All we have to do to arrive at such a situation is gradually reduce the number of animals involved in the industry, or gradually increase the interests humans have in the results of the process, or both, and, due to its aggregative nature utilitarianism entails that we must eventually reach a situation where the interests of humans outweigh those of animals.

To see this, consider the following scenario. Suppose animal protein had a different effect on humans than the one it in fact has. Suppose animal protein has no nutritional role in human growth or maintenance, but, instead, acts as a drug which induced in humans intense states of euphoria without the side effects associated with most euphoriants. Suppose also that humans could take very little animal protein at any given time, but that the effects lasted for weeks. Thus, far fewer animals were involved in the husbandry industry: numbering, say, only a few thousand worldwide at any given time. In this sort of situation, utilitarianism, it seems, would be committed to the idea that this level of animal husbandry is morally good. (If you don't think it would, just tinker around with the circumstances until you find a situation where you think it would.) Now, the central question, here, is not whether this would, in fact, actually be a morally good situation, although the theory to be developed in Chapter 6 entails that it is not. Rather, the central question, here, is what the fact that utilitarianism is committed to claiming that it is a good situation entails about the utilitarian concept of equal consideration. And, it is pretty clear, the utilitarian is committed to the following position: the treatment a human or animal is due is a function of the effects such treatment has on everyone effected by it. The animals who are involved in our imagined case are not being treated with equal consideration. The treatment they receive is a function not of any feature they possess in themselves, but of the effects of their treatment on others. They are being treated simply as means. And to endorse this claim is to reject the principle of equal consideration.

Utilitarianism can support no robust concept of equal consideration. Ultimately, utilitarianism is committed to the idea that the treatment an individual deserves is a function of the interests everyone – and not just the individual – has in such treatment. Thus, if a robust concept of equal consideration is to be found, it will have to be in other, non-utilitarian, moral theories. In the next chapter, we look at such a theory.

5 Tom Regan: Animal Rights as Natural Rights

In his seminal work *The Case for Animal Rights*, justifiably regarded as a classic of the animal liberation movement, Tom Regan presents a forceful and compelling account of why non-human animals should be regarded as making direct moral claims upon us. The reason, according to Regan, is that non-humans possess moral rights; and he presents an elegant and systematic theoretical underpinning for this claim. I think it is fair to regard Regan's case as proceeding from within the framework of natural rights approaches to morality. This is for three reasons. Firstly, Regan argues that many kinds of non-human animals possess moral rights in virtue of their *nature*; in virtue of the fact that they are, as he puts it, *subjects-of-a-life*. Secondly, his argument appeals quite centrally to the concept of *inherent value*, viewed as an objective moral property which attaches to certain things, and which does so irrespective of whether those things happen to be valued or not. Thus, Regan views at least some non-human animals as possessors of moral rights which are objective in the sense that they do not depend on whether they are recognized as rights. Third, these rights are logically prior to any contractual arrangement, since they stem from the nature of the individuals and not from the agreements such individuals might enter into. In this sense at least, Regan is an inheritor of the conceptual framework embodied in natural rights doctrine.

One of the central claims of this book is also that at least some sorts of non-human animals possess moral rights. However, the argument for this claim, to be developed in Chapter 6, differs substantially from that of Regan. In fact, I find myself unable to accept Regan's theory, not, or not primarily, because of the content of the rights it adduces and defends, but because of their metaphysical basis. The first part of this chapter presents an overview of Regan's theory, with particular reference to its metaphysical basis: the concepts of a subject-of-a-life and inherent value. The final sections offer a critique of Regan's position, again with particular reference to its reliance on these concepts. This sets up discussion of Chapter 6, where an alternative account of moral rights is developed.

1. SUBJECTS-OF-A-LIFE

The conceptual edifice upon which Regan's rights-based view is built is composed of two concepts: *subject-of-a-life* and *inherent value*. This section deals with the notion of a subject-of-a-life, the following with inherent value. According to Regan, an individual is a subject-of-a-life if it possesses the following sorts of features:

> Individuals are subjects-of-a-life if they have beliefs and desires; perception, memory, and a sense of the future, including their own future; an emotional life together with feelings of pleasure and pain; preference and welfare-interests; the ability to initiate action in pursuit of their desires and goals; a psychophysical identity over time; and an individual welfare in the sense that their experiential life fares well or ill for them, logically independently of their utility for others and logically independently of their being the object of anyone else's interests.[1]

These conditions are collectively referred to as the *subject-of-a-life criterion*. Many creatures, according to Regan, satisfy these conditions. The conditions are, for Regan, certainly satisfied by almost all humans, including young children and the mentally enfeebled. Living human beings in persistent vegetative states might not satisfy this criterion, however, and humans in irreversible coma almost certainly would not. The criterion is also satisfied by all normal members of mammalian species (the exceptions would, presumably, be analogous to the human exceptions listed above). It is also likely to be satisfied by many species of birds, and quite possibly by reptiles, amphibians and fish, although Regan does not wish to take a stand on these latter types of case. And, thus, his eventual case for animal rights will, strictly speaking, be restricted to mammals. Regan will, in effect, present a case for mammalian rights. The question of whether birds, reptiles, amphibians and fish satisfy the subject-of-a-life criterion is, ultimately, an empirical one; but, if it should turn out that they do, then Regan's case can easily be extended to include them. It is primarily to avoid any controversial, or at least questionable, empirical assumptions that Regan restricts his arguments to mammals.

What is crucial to the role that the subject-of-a-life criterion will play in Regan's argument is that it cuts across the distinction between moral agents and moral patients. Both can be subjects-of-a-life. This, Regan argues, is a (morally) relevant similarity between moral agents and patients, a similarity that he will exploit in the arguments to follow.

It should be noted that there are two different ways in which the subject-of-a-life criterion might be understood. According to what I shall call the *strong* interpretation, an individual must satisfy all of the conditions listed above in order to qualify as a subject-of-a-life. That is, the conditions collectively constitute a set of necessary and sufficient conditions for something being a subject-of-a-life. In order to be a subject-of-a-life, you must possess *all* the features listed in Regan's description. According to the *weak* interpretation, the constraints imposed by the features on Regan's list are somewhat softer. On this view, in order to be a subject-of-a-life you must satisfy *most* of the above conditions, but not necessarily all. And which conditions must be satisfied can vary from case to case. Thus, on the weak interpretation, one creature might qualify as a subject-of-a-life because it satisfies the conditions of perception, belief, desire, memory, emotional life, psychophysical identity over time etc., but does not have a sense of the future. Another might have a sense of the future (for example, it can anticipate), but no clear psychophysical identity over time. On this weaker view, then, creatures satisfying the subject-of-a-life criterion need bear only what Wittgenstein has called a relation of *family resemblance* to each other. They need not share precisely the same features. Or, to employ somewhat more up-to-date jargon (borrowed from artificial intelligence), the conditions listed under the subject-of-a-life criterion function as *soft constraints* – conditions which are significant but not necessarily of overriding importance.

Regan is not explicit on whether he advances the subject-of-a-life criterion in the strong or weak sense. However, the context provided by his later arguments suggests pretty strongly that he intends the strong interpretation of the criterion. This, as we shall see later in the chapter, might well be a mistake. It leaves Regan's argument open to essentially irrelevant objections.

2. INHERENT VALUE

According to Regan, all creatures which are subjects-of-a-life have *inherent value*. Being a subject-of-a-life is a *sufficient* condition for having inherent value, not a *necessary* one. That is, if you are a subject-of-a-life then you have inherent value, but if you are not a subject-of-a-life, it does not necessarily mean that you don't have inherent value. It is possible, therefore, that humans and animals who don't meet the subject-of-a-life criterion nonetheless do have inherent value.

There are four features central to the concept of inherent value. Firstly, the inherent value possessed by an individual is independent of their being the object of anyone else's interests. Possession of inherent value does not depend on whether, or how much, one is liked, respected or in any other way valued by others. As Regan puts it, the lonely, forsaken, unwanted, and unloved have no less (and no more) inherent value than those in more fortuitous social circumstances.

Secondly, the inherent value of an individual does not vary according to the extent to which they have utility *vis-à-vis* the interests of others. The unscrupulous used-car salesman, or even a lawyer, has just as much inherent value as the most beneficent philanthropist.

Third, the inherent value of an individual is not something they can earn or cultivate by dint of their efforts; and it is not something they can lose by what they do or fail to do. A criminal, no matter what his crime, is no less inherently valuable than a saint.

Fourth, and, for Regan's purposes, perhaps most importantly, the inherent value of an individual is conceptually distinct from, and not reducible to, whatever value attaches to the experiences had by that individual (Regan refers to this as *intrinsic* value). It is not possible to determine the inherent value of an individual by totalling up the intrinsic values of their experiences. Inherent value is simply *incommensurable* with intrinsic value: the two simply cannot be compared; they cannot be assessed by the same scale of measurement. Thus, those who have a generally happy life do not have more inherent value than those who do not, even though they presumably undergo more experiences with intrinsic value. Nor do those with more 'sophisticated' or 'cultivated' preferences have more inherent value than those whose pleasures tend towards the vulgar or earthy. The inherent value of an individual is something which is distinct from, not reducible to, and actually incommensurate with the values of those experiences which that individual undergoes during the course of its life.

The notion of inherent value thus allows Regan to draw a clear distinction between his view and utilitarianism. Utilitarianism, for Regan, treats individuals as *receptacles* of value.[2] For utilitarians, the primary locus of value lies in the experiences which a person undergoes (usually pleasures or preference-satisfactions). An individual human or animal, on this view, is a like a cup which, in itself, has no value but, circumstances permitting, can become the container of valuable things – namely pleasures or preference-satisfactions, depending on the type of utilitarianism in question. For Regan, on the other hand, an individual is like a cup which has value in itself, that is, inherent value. This cup can contain things that are valuable – for example, certain sorts of experiences – but the value of the cup is distinct from, not reducible to, and cannot even be compared with, the value of these things that it contains. Individuals who satisfy the subject-of-a-life criterion have, according to Regan, this kind of inherent value.

Thus, according to Regan, the *inherent* value of an individual subject-of-a-life is incommensurate with the *intrinsic* value of that subject's experiences or other mental states. Therefore, Regan argues, the former can never be overridden or outweighed by the latter. It is not legitimate, then, in a sense to be made clear, to justify a situation which involves riding roughshod over someone's inherent value merely by appealing to the more favourable aggregation of intrinsic value that this situation involves or produces. This is not to say, however, that the intrinsic value of experiences is irrelevant to moral decision-making. As we shall see, there are, even on Regan's account, situations in which such value clearly is relevant. It does mean, however, that inherent value is a sort of moral *trump* with respect to the intrinsic value of experiences. One cannot legitimately override the inherent value of an individual by appeal to the value of the experiences, either in that individual or in others, which this would bring about.

3. INHERENT VALUE AS A THEORETICAL POSTULATE

It seems, at least at first glance, that Regan's argument is a straight-forward version of the so called *naturalistic fallacy*; very roughly, the fallacy (if indeed it is a fallacy) of inferring values from facts. That is, it seems as if Regan has simply presented us with an argument of the following form:

Premise. Creature X is a subject-of-a-life

Conclusion. Creature X has inherent value

To view Regan's argument in this way, however, would be to seriously misrepresent it. The argument for inherent value is not a version of the naturalistic fallacy, but, rather, has the form of an *inference to the best explanation*.

An inference to the best explanation has the following form. We start off with a phenomenon, or set of phenomena, which need explaining. We then hypothesize the existence of a certain entity (or, in some cases, law or principle) which is capable of explaining that phenomenon. Finally, it is argued that the hypothesized entity is the most plausible explanation of the phenomenon because all competing explanations are manifestly, or at least arguably, false. This is essentially the type of argument Regan is giving for inherent value.

The phenomenon which needs explaining in this case is what Regan calls our *considered beliefs* about moral issues. In particular, one of our considered beliefs about morality, indeed perhaps the most fundamental, is that we have a duty to treat people justly. Treating people with justice is not an optional or *supererogatory* moral principle, it is essential to the nature of morality as such. Moreover, our considered moral beliefs also incorporate a fairly definite conception of what is involved in treating someone with justice. Thus, Regan points out that our considered moral beliefs rule out a perfectionist view of justice, according to which what individuals are due, as a matter of justice, depends on the degree to which they possess a certain cluster of virtues or excellences. These might include intellectual and artistic talents, and/or a certain sort of character. According to perfectionist views of justice, individuals who possess these virtues in abundance are due more, as a matter of justice, than those who do not. This sort of view is, as Regan points out, morally pernicious, providing a justification for seriously objectionable forms of social and political discrimination – slavery, caste systems, etc. And these forms of discrimination, our considered moral beliefs inform us, should be rejected. Thus, perfectionist views of justice do not cohere with our considered moral beliefs.

Utilitarian accounts of justice also do not seem to cohere very well with our considered beliefs about justice. As we have seen, standard objections to utilitarianism point out that it seems, in principle, to legitimize many forms of what we would regard as serious injustice, as long as the overall aggregate of pleasure or preference satisfaction is increased. Thus, we would be justified in treating an individual with what we would intuitively regard as injustice, as long as doing so secured a greater amount of happiness or preference-satisfaction in the world. In other words, innocent individuals could, in principle, be sacrificed for the greater good of the community. And, at least intuitively, our considered moral beliefs tell us that such a situation is a paradigm case of injustice.

Regan believes that in order to account for our considered beliefs about justice, we must postulate that certain sorts of individuals – individuals who are subjects-of-a-life – possess inherent value in the sense explained above. If we suppose that subjects-of-a-life do possess inherent value, then we can explain our considered beliefs about the importance of justice and about what just treatment amounts to. So, the postulation of inherent value, at least on Regan's view, is an explanation of our considered moral beliefs – or as Rawls would put it, our *reflective intuitions* – concerning justice. And given the manifest, or at least arguable, failure of other theories to account for these beliefs or intuitions, we have good reason for supposing that the postulation of inherent value is the *best* explanation of these beliefs. Thus, inherent value is a theoretical postulate, justified, on Regan's view, as an inference to the best explanation. It is no different in kind, he would claim, to the postulation of, for example, atomic particles to explain characteristic patterns in a cloud chamber; or the postulation of an additional planet to explain perturbations in the orbit of Neptune.

4. THE RESPECT PRINCIPLE

Once we allow that all subjects-of-a-life have inherent value, we can derive several important moral principles concerning how they should be treated. The first of these Regan calls the *respect principle*:

> We are to treat those individuals who have inherent value in ways that respect their inherent value.

That is, all individuals who are subjects-of-lives must, as a matter of justice, be treated in ways that respect this fact. The respect principle sets forth an egalitarian, anti-perfectionist interpretation of the formal principle of justice. Treating an individual that possesses inherent value in ways, and only in ways, that respect this value is not supererogatory, not an optional moral extra. It is required by justice; any contrary treatment is unjust.

We fail to treat individuals who have inherent value with the respect they are due whenever we treat them as if they lacked inherent value. And we treat them in this way whenever we treat them, as the utilitarian does, as if they were mere receptacles of valuable experiences such as pleasures or preference-satisfactions. We also treat them as if they lacked inherent value when we treat them as if their

value depended upon their utility relative to the interests of others.
And we also treat them as if they lacked inherent value when we harm
them simply so that we may bring about the best aggregate consequences for everyone affected by the outcome of such treatment. All
these are, in fact, just variations on the same theme: treating an individual with inherent value as if he, she or it were nothing more than a
receptacle of value. That is, it is to treat something with inherent
value as if it lacked inherent value; and this is unjust.

The respect principle, however, requires more than that we abjure
from treating an inherently valuable individual in disrespectful ways.
The principle, in fact, imposes on us a *prima facie* duty to assist those
who are the victims of disrespectful treatment (i.e. injustice) at the
hands of others. This is, in fact, a common view of justice, and not
peculiar to Regan's account. That is, it is commonly accepted that
justice, whatever its interpretation, not only imposes duties of non-
harm; it also places us under a *prima facie* obligation to aid those who
are the victims of injustice. As Regan puts it, all those who have inherent value are to be given what, as a matter of justice, they are due; and
sometimes what they are due is our assistance.

The respect principle, for Regan, may or may not be morally fundamental in that it may or may not be derivable from a more
fundamental principle. Regan leaves the question of its ultimate
logical status open. The justification for the principle, however, is
essentially the same as the justification for the postulation of inherent
value. That is, no moral theory which fails to incorporate the respect
principle can hope to systematize, justify, and, above all cohere with,
our considered beliefs about justice.[3]

5. THE HARM PRINCIPLE

Unlike the respect principle, the *harm principle* is not a candidate for
basic moral principle: it can, in fact, be derived from the respect principle. The harm principle states that:

We have a direct *prima facie* duty not to harm individuals.

According to the respect principle, any individual who has inherent
value is owed, as a matter of strict justice, treatment that is respectful
of this value. And this amounts to the claim that any individual who is
a subject-of-a-life is owed, again as a matter of justice, treatment
which respects this fact. Now, any individual who is a subject-of-a-life

has an *experiential welfare*; that is, their life can, from their perspective, fare well or ill for them. Their life, that is, can go experientially better or worse for them, logically independently of their utility for others and of their being the object of another's interests. Therefore, the concepts of benefit and harm apply to these sorts of beings in virtue of the fact that they are subjects-of-a-life. That is, being the subject-of-a-life bestows on an individual the distinctive sort of value which consists in having an experiential welfare. Therefore, at least *prima facie*, we fail to treat individuals in ways that respect their value when we treat them in ways that detract from their welfare. And we detract from the welfare of this type of an individual when we harm them. Therefore, Regan claims, we have a *prima facie* direct duty not to harm those individuals who have an experiential welfare. And this is precisely what the harm principle claims. Thus, the harm principle is derivable from the respect principle.

According to Regan, therefore, we have a *prima facie* duty not to harm those individuals who are subjects-of-a-life. The qualification *prima facie* signifies that the duty can, in certain circumstances, be overridden. That is, the harm principle does *not* entail that, no matter what the circumstances, it is always wrong to harm an individual who is subject-of-a-life. As we shall see, there are, according to Regan, circumstances when harming an individual with inherent value, even an innocent individual, is morally legitimate. This issue will be explored in later sections.

6. MORAL RIGHTS

Justice requires, then, that we should treat those individuals who possess inherent value – that is, who are subjects-of-a-life – in accordance with the respect principle and the harm principle. This provides the basis for Regan's claim that individuals with inherent value also possess moral rights. Regan's demonstration of this latter claim proceeds by way of an analysis of the concept of a right.

Regan adopts the widely accepted view of moral rights as *valid claims*.[4] The relevant sort of valid claims, here, have two aspects, (i) a valid claim-to, and (ii) a valid claim-against.

A claim-to, in this context, is a claim to a certain commodity, freedom, or type of treatment by others. And to be a valid claim-to, the claim must be backed, or validated, by an appeal to a correct moral principle or principles. Thus, the claimant can demonstrate that she is owed the commodity, freedom, or treatment in question by appeal to the relevant moral principles.

In order to be a valid claim-against, a claim must be made against assignable individuals who do in fact owe what the claimant asserts. And, again, whether the individuals in question do owe the commodity or treatment must again be decided by appeal to correct moral principles.

When both a claim-to and a claim-against has been validated by appeal to correct moral principles we can speak of a *valid claim all things considered*. And this, according to the present analysis, is what constitutes a moral right. To have a moral right to a certain commodity or treatment is to have a valid claim all things considered to that commodity or treatment, and a valid claim all things considered against whatever individuals are to provide the commodity or treatment.

Regan has, of course, already argued that the respect principle and the harm principle are valid moral principles. Therefore, a claim, made against assignable individuals, to a certain commodity or treatment will be a valid claim all things considered if it is backed or validated by an appeal to either the respect or the harm principle. Therefore, any individual with inherent value has a moral right to treatment that respects this value. The right to such treatment is a valid claim-against assignable individuals (i.e. all moral agents) and a valid claim-to a certain type of treatment, the validity of each claim being backed by the respect principle, a valid moral principle. Similarly, any individual with inherent value has a *prima facie* right not to be harmed. Such a right is again a valid claim-to and a valid claim-against, the validity of each being backed by the harm principle, a correct moral principle. Therefore, any individual who has inherent value (i.e. a subject-of-a-life) has a moral right to treatment that respects this value and a *prima facie* moral right not to be harmed.

Two points should be noted. Firstly, the right not to be harmed is a *prima facie* moral right only. That is, it can be overridden in certain circumstances (to be clarified shortly). The *prima facie* status of the right, here, is due to the *prima facie* status of the harm principle from which it derives.

Secondly, according to Regan, one consequence of this analysis is that one can have moral rights only against moral agents; not against moral patients or inanimate objects. The reason for this stems from the nature of claims-against. A claim-against can be a valid one only if the individual against whom the claim is made is capable of meeting the requirements of the claim. That is, the individual must be capable of providing the treatment or commodity that, according to the claim, is due. Thus, for example, we can have no moral rights against nature. We would have such rights only if nature was capable of providing us with the commodity or treatment we claimed was due. But nature is obviously incapable of acting in such a way. More precisely, we could have valid claims-against nature only if nature has direct duties to us to do or forbear doing certain acts that are our due. But nature, in this sense, is capable neither of doing nor forbearing from doing things. To say that nature *ought* to do certain things, or forbear from doing certain things, is to presuppose that nature *can* choose in the relevant sort of way. But nature obviously cannot choose what it does. Therefore, we have no rights against nature because we have no valid claims-against nature.[5]

This also allows us to dispense very neatly with a frequently raised objection to the concept of animal rights: the claim that the concept leads to absurdity.[6] The argument runs as follows. If sheep have rights, then these are violated by wolves who prey on them. Therefore, it seems that if we have a duty of assistance to sheep to stop those who violate their rights, then it seems we have a duty to stop wolves from preying on sheep. However, if we were to do this, we would be violating the wolves' rights by harming them (e.g. by consigning them to a slow painful death through starvation). Thus, either way we end up violating some creature's rights. And, therefore, the whole concept of animal rights leads to logical absurdity.

Once, however, we understand that moral rights are valid claims, this objection can be stopped, so to speak, before it even starts. The sheep has no moral rights with respect to wolves. That is, the sheep does not have a valid claim-against the wolf to refrain from eating it. This is because the wolf is not a moral agent, hence is not capable of choosing, in any morally relevant sense, whether or not to eat the sheep. The sheep would have a valid claim-against the wolf in this regard only if the wolf had the capacity to forbear from eating the sheep. And the wolf has no such capacity. That is, to say that the sheep has a right against the wolf not to eat it is to imply that the wolf ought not to eat the sheep. And to say that the wolf ought not to eat the sheep is to imply that the wolf is capable of choosing whether or not to eat the sheep. But the wolf has no such capacity. Therefore, the sheep has no valid claim-against the wolf not to eat it. And, therefore, the sheep has no moral right against the wolf in this regard. Neither, for that matter, do humans (not that wolves ever eat humans). It makes no sense to speak simply of a moral right to X as such. To speak of a moral right is always an elliptical way of referring to the individual against whom the right is claimed; it presupposes such an individual or individuals. And we can only have rights against moral agents.

7. THE MINIRIDE PRINCIPLE

According to Regan, the moral right not to be harmed, possessed by an individual with inherent value, is a *prima facie* moral right. That is, the right can, in certain circumstances, be overridden. The task Regan now has, then, is to show in a *principled* way what these circumstances are. That is, he does not just want to claim, in an *ad hoc* fashion, that the right can be overturned in circumstances X. In order to make the exceptions theoretically satisfactory, he must show how they can be derived from the respect or harm principles themselves. If this cannot be done, then the exceptions, in effect, count as objections to Regan's theory. However, if the exceptions can be derived from Regan's theory itself, then they count not as objections to the theory but, in an importance sense, as confirmations of it. Therefore, Regan describes two principles which govern the circumstances under which the harm principle can be overridden, and tries to show how these can be derived from the respect principle.

The first of these is what Regan calls the *miniride principle* (the minimize overriding principle):

> Special considerations aside, when we must choose between overriding the rights of many who are innocent or the rights of few who are innocent, and when each affected individual will be harmed in a *prima facie* comparable way, then we ought to choose to override the rights of the few in preference to overriding the rights of the many.[7]

This principle, Regan argues, is derivable from the respect principle. The derivation runs as follows.

The respect principle entails that all individuals with inherent value have a *prima facie* right not to be harmed, and all those who have this right have it equally. Therefore, precisely because this right is equal, no one individual's right can count for more than the right of another, at least when the harm that will befall both is *prima facie* comparable. But, therefore, for any individual with inherent value, precisely because each individual's possession of the right not to be harmed is equal to the right of every other individual one should, in a situation where one is forced to choose between overriding the right not to be harmed of few and overriding the right not to be harmed of many, choose to override the right not to be harmed of the few. To choose otherwise would be to accord inordinate status to the rights of the few. That is, it would be to imbue the rights of the few with greater value or significance than the same rights of the many. And this is precisely what the respect principle says you should not do. To choose in favour of the few, that is, would involve not treating the many with the respect that they deserve as bearers of inherent value. But to choose in favour of the many does not entail that one fails to treat the few with the respect they deserve. In this way, therefore, the miniride principle is derivable from the respect principle.

The miniride principle, as the above formulation makes clear, has two qualifications. The principle is restricted to cases where the harm suffered by each inherently valuable individual is *prima facie comparable*. And the principle is restricted to situations where no *special considerations* obtain. Consider an example to illustrate each of these in turn.[8]

Fifty-one miners are trapped in a mine cave-in and are certain to die in a very short time if nothing is done. Fifty of the trapped men are located on the pit floor, and the other one is located in a shaft leading down to the floor. Suppose the only one way to reach the fifty miners in time is to place an explosive charge in the shaft through which the trapped men can then escape. However, suppose also that this method is certain to kill the lone miner. The one miner could be saved, however, if we simply dug him out, but the time this would take would certainly lead to the death of the fifty trapped men. What ought we to do? In this case, the miniride principle says that we should save the fifty men at the expense of the one.

In the above case, the harm facing each of the trapped men is comparable – all fifty-one of them stand to die if nothing is done. However, suppose the potential harm facing the two groups was not comparable. Suppose there was a way of getting the single miner out while also saving the lives of the fifty. Suppose, for example, that we did have time to dig the single man out, but that this would lead to substantial delay in rescuing the other miners. We have, however, every reason to think that the mine has stabilized and that there would be no further cave-ins, nor is there any danger of explosions etc. We know that several of the group of fifty miners have suffered painful injuries – broken legs, etc.; but that none of these injuries are life-threatening. We thus have a choice between sacrificing the life of the lone man, or allowing the group of fifty to remain for, say, forty-eight hours in a state of quite significant pain coupled with the fear of the mine collapsing at any point. Now, in this scenario, what ought we to do? Well, whatever we ought to do in this case, the miniride principle does not apply. The reason is that the harm suffered by the single miner and that suffered by the group of fifty is not, *prima facie*, comparable. The harm facing the lone miner is death; that facing the group of fifty is pain and fear. The harms are not comparable, and, therefore, the miniride principle does not apply in this case.

Consider, now, the notion of special considerations. Suppose the single trapped man had been kidnapped by the group of fifty who hoped to reap the financial rewards of his forced labour. This would be a special consideration, and, once again, the miniride principle would not apply in this case. Or perhaps the group of fifty had, for some difficult to imagine reason, each signed a legal document requesting that in the event of this sort of situation, person X should be saved before them. And suppose the lone miner was person X (this is a difficult situation to imagine, I know, but the point concerns not the plausibility of the scenario but the principle underlying it). There are, in fact, several different types of special consideration Regan is prepared to allow as morally significant, but the details do not concern us here. The point is that, as soon as special considerations obtain, the miniride principle no longer applies.

8. THE WORSE-OFF PRINCIPLE

The second principle determining when the harm principle may justifiably be overridden is what Regan calls the *worse-off principle*:

> Special considerations aside, when we must decide to override the rights of the many or the rights of the few who are innocent, and when the harm faced by the few would make them worse-off than any of the many would be if the other option were chosen, then we ought to override the rights of the many.[9]

Although the principle is formulated in terms of the rights of the many and the few, such formulation is not essential to the principle as such. If we were forced to choose between harming *one* innocent individual and harming another, the worse-off principle would still apply and legislate in favour of the individual who would be made worse-off.

The worse-off principle is also derivable from the respect principle. The derivation goes like this. Suppose we have two individuals, P_1 and P_2, both of whom have inherent value. The respect principle entails that P_1 and P_2 have an equal right not to be harmed, a right which derives from the equal inherent value possessed by each. However, despite the fact that they possess an equal right not to be harmed, this does not entail that each and every harm either may suffer is equally harmful. All things being equal, P_1's death is a greater harm than P_2's (non-fatal dose of) flu, even if both possess an equal right not to be harmed. But this means, that in order to show equal respect for the equal rights of the two, one must count their equal harms equally; one must not count their unequal harms equally. If we were to count unequal harms equally, this would imply that we were not, in fact, according due respect to the equal rights of each individual. To attempt to alleviate P_2's flu, at the expense of P_1's death would be to give P_2 more than his due. P_1 and P_2, as inherently valuable individuals, have an equal right to respect, and, consequently, an equal *prima facie* right not to be harmed. And precisely because of this, and because the harm P_1 faces is greater than the harm faced by P_2, equal respect for the two requires that we not choose to override the right of P_1 but choose, instead, to override that of P_2.

Now, according to Regan, adding numbers in this case makes no difference. Suppose we have to weigh the death of P_1 against the (non-fatal) flu suffered by P_2, P_3 ... P_{1000}. The death of P_1 would, according to Regan, still be a greater harm because it is greater than the individual harm suffered by each and every of the remaining 999. There is, after all, no aggregate individual who suffers the sum of the harms suffered by the remaining 999 individuals. There are just the 999 individuals, none of whom will be worse off than P_1 would be. It is the magnitude of the harm done to P_1 and each individual member of the remaining 999, not the sum of P_1's harm compared with the sum of the harms done to the 999 that determines whose right overrides whose. Thus, according to Regan, since the harm done to P_1 would be greater than that done to, and would make P_1 worse off than any other individual involved, respect for the equal rights of everyone involved requires overriding the rights of the many rather than those of the individual. In general, in the absence of special considerations, if the few who are innocent would be made worse off than any of the many who are innocent if we chose to override the rights of the few, the respect principle requires that we override the rights of the many.

And this is precisely what the worse-off principle states. Therefore, the worse-off principle is derivable from the respect principle.

It might be thought that, in putting forward this argument, Regan is undermining his own rights-based position. After all, the rights view is supposed to deny the moral relevance of consequences; this is the basis of its oppposition to utilitarianism. But now Regan seems to be relying on the notion of comparable harm and invokes considerations about who will be harmed most. Thus, in defending the worse-off principle, Regan's position seems to be inconsistent.

However, there is, in fact, nothing in Regan's position which commits him to the claim that consequences are irrelevant to moral decision-making. What the rights view *does* deny is that moral decisions can legitimately be made *merely* by determining which alternative will bring about the best aggregate consequences for all those affected by the decision. Consequences, in other words, are relevant; it's just that they are not the only relevant factor. The rights view, therefore, does *not* claim that consequences are morally irrelevant. *A fortiori*, it does *not* claim that we can dispense with consideration of consequences in making our moral decisions and determinations. Indeed, it would be a very strange, and extremely implausible, view if it did make these claims. The rights view, in fact, entails that the consequences of actions *are* extremely relevant considerations in moral decision-making. It would not be possible to show equal respect toward each of the individuals affected by an action if we did not weigh up how much each would be harmed by that action. Therefore, the rights view does not entail that consequences in general, and consequences for the specific welfare of individuals in particular, are morally irrelevant. In fact, when the rights view is properly understood, it entails just the opposite. It denies only that consequences are the *sole* basis upon which moral decisions should be reached.

The miniride and worse-off principles can be, roughly, summed up in the following slogan: *special considerations aside, when the harms are comparable numbers count, when the harms are not comparable numbers don't count.* Both of these principles should be clearly distinguished from a third one which Regan does *not* endorse. This is what Regan refers to as the *minimize harm principle*: act so as to minimize the total aggregate of harm of the innocent. The minimize harm principle is a purely consequentialist principle. It instructs us to act so as to avoid the worst consequences, where these are understood as the greatest sum of harm done to all the innocents affected by the outcome. And to accept this principle, therefore, is to assume that inherently valuable individuals are mere receptacles of value. They are receptacles, in this case, not of pleasures and pains but of harms and benefits. And the minimize harm principles tells us that we should minimize the total amount of harm irrespective of what inherently valuable individuals we have to sacrifice toward this end. Both the miniride and worse-off principles, therefore, should be clearly distinguished from the minimize harm principle.

9. REGAN ON VEGETARIANISM

So far then, Regan has used the notion of a subject-of-a-life to motivate and defend the concept of inherent value. He has used the concept of inherent value to justify the respect principle, and from the respect principle he derived the harm principle. These, being valid moral principles, were used to defend the idea that all inherently valuable individuals have a moral right to be treated in ways which respect this value, and a *prima facie* moral right not to be harmed. Exceptions to the right not to be harmed are governed by the miniride and worse-off principles, both of which, Regan argues, can be derived from the respect principle. In short, what Regan has provided here is a consistent, cogent, and systematic moral theory which not only attempts to justify the concept of a moral right but also to determine priority rules for the moral rights thus justified. It is an elegant theory, and this is never more evident than in its application to particular moral issues. This section tries to provide a feel for the ways in which Regan's theory has application to the world. The particular moral issue we shall look at is the raising, killing and eating of animals (specifically, mammals) for food.

Vegetarianism, according to Regan, is morally obligatory. That is, it is not simply a morally good thing to be a vegetarian; it is a morally bad thing not to be a vegetarian. The basic reason for this should be quite evident from his overall theory. In fact, Regan's basic argument for vegetarianism looks something like this.

P1. Mammals are subjects-of-a-life.
P2. Therefore, mammals have inherent value.
P3. Therefore, the respect principle, and the harm principle derivable from it, apply to mammals.
P4. Therefore, mammals have a right to be treated with respect, and a *prima facie* right not to be harmed.

P5. Raising, killing and eating of mammals harms them.

C. Therefore, we should not raise, kill, and eat mammals.

This, in any event, is the most obvious way in which Regan's theory applies to the issue of raising, killing and eating of mammals. The restriction to mammals is because of the earlier mentioned restriction on the scope of the subject-of-a-life criterion. It is fairly clear, Regan thinks, that the criterion applies to mammals; but its application to non-mammals is more controversial. And in wishing to keep the premises of his argument as non-controversial, and therefore as widely acceptable, as possible, Regan restricts his case to mammals.

However, this is not the end of the argument. The right not to be harmed is, after all, a *prima facie* right; a right that can be legitimately overridden in certain circumstances. Any support for the raising, killing and eating of mammals, therefore, will likely focus on the *prima facie* status of the right not to be harmed, and try to show that, in this case, the right can be overridden for legitimate moral reasons. And this, in effect, is where the hard work begins.

The claim that the *prima facie* right of non-human mammals not to be harmed can be overridden to allow us to use them for food is often thought to gain support from another principle; a principle which is also derivable from the respect principle. Regan refers to this as the *liberty principle*:

> Provided that all those involved are treated with respect, and assuming that no special considerations obtain, any innocent individual has the right to act to avoid being made worse-off even if doing so harms other innocents.[10]

The liberty principle is derivable from the respect principle. As an individual with inherent value, I am always to be treated with respect and thus am never to be viewed or treated as a mere receptacle or as one who has value merely relative to the interests of others. Furthermore, I also have a welfare, and I should be allowed to do whatever is necessary to advance this welfare, as long as I treat others with respect. To deny me the liberty to pursue my welfare simply because others will be worse-off if I do is to fail to treat me with the respect that I, as a possessor inherent value, am due, as a matter of justice. Thus, for example, I should be able to compete for a job with another even if my success means that he is destined for the poor house. He will be made worse-off, and undoubtedly harmed, by my success, but to deny me the liberty to pursue the job simply because of this is to give me less than my due: it is to assume that the treatment I am due, as a matter of justice, is contingent upon how others will be affected as a result. It is to fail to give my inherent value proper consideration. The qualification of 'special considerations' is meant to handle such cases as where, for example, I steal my neighbour's Mercedes on the grounds that not to do so would be to make me worse-off relative to him. The liberty principle would not permit this action, on the grounds that the ownership of the car by my neighbour is a special consideration and hence is not covered by the liberty principle.

The second proviso – namely 'provided that all those involved are treated with respect' – is more complicated, and has an extremely important consequence. Suppose I were a sadist whose greatest pleasure was the torturing of innocents. Then, if I were not able to indulge my passion in this regard, I would, at least arguably, be made worse-off. However, to engage in my interest in torture would, manifestly, not respect the inherent value of my victims. What this shows is that it is only possible to respect the inherent value of those affected by my actions if the standard of me being made worse-off is set relative to them. That is, according to the liberty principle, I can legitimately harm innocents only if this is to avoid being made worse-off *than them*. That is, *it is not being made worse-off as such which is crucial, but being made worse-off than those innocents I must harm*. That is, the liberty principle only justifies overriding the harm principle when I must act to avoid being made worse-off than those I must harm in the process. Since it is hard to see how by not torturing innocents I would thereby be made worse-off than they would be if I had tortured them, the liberty principle rules out this sort of action. This is an extremely important qualification. Without it, it is difficult to see how any defence of vegetarianism could get off the ground; since it is at least arguable that we are made worse-off by not eating meat. The crucial point is not whether we are made worse-off, but whether, by not eating meat, we are thereby made worse-off than the animals we raise and kill would be if we were to eat meat.

Therefore, in addition to the respect, the harm, the miniride, and the worse-off principles then, the rights view recognizes a fifth principle, the liberty principle, to be understood in accordance with the above qualifications. And opponents of Regan's claim that vegetarianism is morally obligatory are likely to appeal to this principle. For since both farmers and meat-eaters are authorized to act as the liberty principle allows, they may claim that they are at liberty to raise and eat animals, even though this involves harming them, because not to do so would make them worse-off relative to any of those individuals who are harmed in the process – that is, relative to any farm animal. Moreover, Regan's defence of the worse-off principle has already ruled out aggregating the harms done to farm animals in order to defend vegetarianism.[11] But what, however, could be the grounds for claiming that the harm done to farm animals is justified by the liberty principle? The following by no means constitutes an exhaustive treatment of Regan's argument for vegetarianism. I have chosen, instead, to focus on those arguments which might be thought to constitute the biggest threat to Regan's position. That is, I have chosen to focus on those arguments, used to defend the practice of animal husbandry, which might, *prima facie*, be thought to be justified by appeal to the very principles Regan himself defends. Focusing on these arguments will allow us to see more clearly the subtlety and power of Regan's position.

One argument commonly raised in favour of animal husbandry focuses on the pleasure human beings get from both eating and preparing meat dishes. Animal flesh, it is argued, tastes very nice, and to abstain from eating it is to forgo certain pleasures of the palate. Moreover, from a culinary standpoint, it is personally rewarding to prepare dishes of this nature. Therefore, should human beings choose to forgo eating meat, they would be clearly worse-off from being denied these sorts of pleasures. Therefore, it might be argued, the liberty principle itself licenses the continuing practice of animal husbandry: it is legitimate for us to continue with this practice since not to do so would make us worse-off than we would otherwise have been.

There are several fairly obvious problems with this argument. Firstly, no one has a right to eat something just because they happen to find it tasty. If I happen to find babies good to eat, it does not mean that I have the right to eat them. Nor does it mean that if I find the cooking of babies to be a rewarding culinary adventure I thereby have the right to cook them. Secondly, there are many other tasty foods besides meat, and other foods beside meat can offer similar, or greater, culinary rewards. So, it is not even clear that we are harmed by not being able to eat meat. But third, and most importantly, even supposing we were harmed (i.e. made worse-off) by not eating meat, the harms we would be called upon to endure could not reasonably be viewed as *prima facie* comparable to the harm visited upon farm animals. That is, even if we were made worse-off by not eating meat, we would be nowhere near as badly off as farm animals would be were we to eat meat. Our being made worse-off by forgoing certain pleasures of the palate or kitchen can, by no stretch of the imagination, be compared to the daily suffering, deprivation, and untimely death of farm animals. Now, the liberty principle, remember, does not claim that we are morally entitled to harm innocents in order to avoid being made worse-off. It says that we are entitled to do so *if* all those involved are treated with respect. And this amounts to the claim that we are entitled to harm innocents to avoid being made worse-off only if not doing so would make us worse-off than the innocents would be if we chose to harm them. Therefore, the liberty principle does not, at least in this case, justify our consumption of meat, since, by forgoing cooking and eating meat we would not be made anywhere near as badly off as farm animals are made by our not forgoing these activities. Moreover, as Regan points out, matters do not substantially change if the farm animals in question are raised and slaughtered 'humanely'. Death is one of the greatest harms that can be inflicted on an inherently valuable individual, and one cannot compare the harm of death with the harm of abstaining from certain adventures of the kitchen or palate. In fact, once we get clear on the principles involved here, we see that animal husbandry is ruled out by the worse-off principle. The death and suffering inflicted on animals by this practice makes them substantially worse-off than we would be made if we chose, or were prevented from eating meat.

Another common argument in favour of animal husbandry focuses on economic considerations. Some people, it is argued, have a strong economic interest in continuing to raise farm animals, and the quality of their life as well as that of their dependants is tied to the continuation of this practice. This claim might be thought to be backed by both the worse-off principle and the liberty principle. Consider, first, the worse-off principle. The farmer, it might be claimed, will be made worse-off relative to the animals he raises if we, the consumers, became vegetarians and thereby failed to support him. He would lose his livelihood, and, with this loss, the harm done to him would outweigh any harm done to any one animal, even one kept in close confinement. And remember, on the rights view, we cannot aggregate the lesser *prima facie* harms of the many as a way of justifying causing greater *prima facie* harm to the few. Therefore, we ought to eat meat because we owe it to the farmer – this is what he is due as a matter of justice. And the principle backing this claim is the worse-off principle.

However, proper understanding of the worse-off principle, Regan argues, reveals that this is, in fact, not the case.

The basic reason for this is that to enter into any business is to run the risk of failure. It is also to acknowledge, at least tacitly, both that no one has a duty to purchase one's products or services and that such purchase cannot be claimed as one's due. Voluntary participation in a competitive activity such as a business constitutes a *special consideration*. And the worse-off principle is explicitly formulated to begin 'Special considerations aside'. Therefore, the worse-off principle cannot legitimately be applied in this case. As Regan points out, a businessperson who would be made worse-off if her products or services were not purchased has no valid claim on anyone to make the necessary purchases to keep her business afloat. Business is a competitive activity, and those who voluntarily participate must understand that the worse-off principle is suspended. We do not, therefore, *owe* it to the farmer who sells meat to purchase his products.

Another argument relates the farmer's economic interests to the liberty principle. Even if we have no duty to purchase the farmer's products, it could be argued, the farmer has a legitimate moral right to engage in animal husbandry. The reason for this is that he would be worse-off if he did not raise them. We, as consumers, might only be marginally worse-off if we should forgo meat, but the farmer might face financial ruin. Therefore the liberty principle itself permits him to continue raising animals for food, since not to do so would make him worse-off than the animals he raises.

The problem with this argument, however, is that it neglects a crucial qualification on the liberty principle: *provided that all those involved are treated with respect*. But, as Regan points out, this is a requirement that the present practice of animal husbandry fails to meet. The reason is that present animal husbandry practices treat individuals with inherent value as if they were *renewable resources*. An individual with inherent value is treated as if it were a renewable resource if, before it has reached a state or condition where terminating its life can be defended on grounds of preference-respecting or paternalistic euthanasia, it is killed, its place to be filled by another similar individual whose life will be similarly terminated. Such a practice is unjust because it violates the respect principle. The practice treats an individual with inherent value as if it lacks any independent value of its own, and has value only in relation to the interest of another, i.e the farmer or consumer. A practice of this type treats inherently valuable individuals as *renewable* because it regards them as replaceable without any *prima facie* wrong having been done to those who are killed; and it regards them as *resources* because what value they are assumed to have is viewed as being solely a function of their utility relative to the interest of others. And to treat an individual with inherent value as if it were a renewable resource is, on Regan's view, even worse than treating them as receptacles. At least when treated as a receptacle, the individual's *goods* (e.g. pleasures or preference-satisfactions) and their *harms* (e.g. pains or preference-frustrations) are viewed as being directly morally relevant to the determination of what ought to be done. When individuals are viewed as renewable resources, however, their goods and their harms have no direct moral significance whatsoever. To view individuals with inherent value as renewable resources is, thus, to view them as even less than receptacles. And, therefore, any practice, institution, or undertaking that permits or requires treating individuals with inherent value as if they were renewable resources, therefore, permits or requires treatment of these individuals that violates the respect principle. As such, the practice, institution or undertaking are unjust. To treat farm animals as renewable resources, therefore, is to fail to treat them with the respect they deserve as individuals with inherent value. But this means that the liberty principle fails to apply, and the farmer cannot, therefore, use it to justify his activities. He could invoke the liberty principle to this end only if those who are harmed by what he does (i.e. the animals he raises) are treated with respect. But, they are not treated with the respect they are owed as a matter of justice, and they cannot be so treated while they are viewed as renewable resources.

As mentioned earlier, the foregoing does not in any way provide an exhaustive account of Regan's treatment of the vegetarianism issue. Nonetheless, it does show pretty clearly that the theoretical framework constructed by Regan provides a clear and consistent account of our duties to non-human mammals. When properly understood, the principles – respect, liberty, miniride, worse-off, and liberty – derived by Regan are more than capable of handling the usual objections to vegetarianism. It is also worth noting that the principles show not only that vegetarianism is morally obligatory. They also show, in an equally clear and consistent manner, why trapping, hunting and blood sports in general are morally wrong; and why the use of animals in science is wrong. In short, Regan has provided us with a moral theory that is systematic, coherent, consistent, and of adequate scope to account for our moral dealings with non-human animals. He has, that is, provided

us with an extremely powerful moral theory. Nevertheless, it is a
theory which I think, ultimately, we should not accept. The remaining
sections of this chapter will try to explain why.

10. INHERENT VALUE IS MYSTERIOUS

It is possible, I think, to attack Regan both from the point of view of
the *content* of the moral principles he adduces and from the point of
view of the logical *basis* from which they are adduced. As an example
of the former approach, consider Regan's *worse-off* principle.
According to this principle, when we must decide whether to override
the rights of the innocent few or the innocent many, and when the few
would be made worse-off should we adopt the former course than the
many would be if we adopted the latter, then we should choose to
override the rights of the many. When the harms are not comparable,
in other words, numbers don't count. This seems to have counterintuitive consequences. If, for example, we assume that losing one's
legs is a harm that is not comparable with losing one's life, that in the
latter situation one is made worse-off than in the former, and if we are
somehow forced to choose between saving the life of one person and
saving the legs of a million others, then the worse-off principle claims
that we should choose to save the life of the one. We should allow the
million to lose their legs in order to save the life of one person. And
this does seem rather counterintuitive.[12] Nevertheless, the criticism of
Regan I want to develop in the following pages focuses not on the
content of his central moral principles but, rather, on their basis. The
basis of these principles is provided by the concepts of *inherent value*
and *subject-of-a-life*.

The notion of inherent value is, upon reflection, a mysterious one.
What sort of thing is inherent value? Regan is, to say the least, not very
explicit about this. One thing, however, is clear. According to Regan,
inherent value exists logically independently of valuers; that is, of individuals who recognize value. That is, for Regan, an individual having
inherent value should be clearly distinguished from that individual
being valued by others. Being valued by others is certainly not a necessary condition, and probably not a sufficient condition, for an
individual having inherent value. It is not a necessary condition
because an individual can have inherent value even if it is not valued in
this way by others. A subject-of-a-life, such as, for example, a veal calf,
raised in isolation from members of its own kind, has inherent value

for Regan even though it is not inherently valued by the humans who raise it. For these it is only *instrumentally* valued – that is, valued for its utility relative to the projects of humans. The calf has inherent value even though it is not inherently valued. And being inherently valued may well not be a sufficient condition of having inherent value. We humans, as we all know, have a great capacity to value useless things. This claim does, in fact, raise other issues which we neither need nor want to get immersed in here. It is enough for present purposes to note that Regan wants to clearly distinguish the property of having inherent value from the property of being inherently valued, and all he needs for this claim is that the latter is not a necessary condition of the former. The two properties, therefore, are, for Regan, distinct.

Once we distinguish the property of having inherent value from that of being inherently valued, however, a puzzle merges. Is inherent value a basic feature of the world, or does it somehow *emerge* from more basic features? Sooner or later, I suppose, scientists might arrive at a complete description of the basic furniture of the universe. And the sort of things which might be referred to in this description are features such as *charm, charge, quark, spin,* and so on. These are basic in the sense that all other things which exist are made up of these sorts of thing. Now, what of inherent value? Is it basic, having the same ontological status as the above items. Or does inherent value somehow *emerge from* or, as philosophers now put it, *supervene upon,* these more basic items. On the one hand, to claim that inherent value is part of the basic furniture of the universe seems implausible; investigation of the sub-atomic world, it seems, is going to tell us very little about inherent value. But, on the other hand, if inherent value emerges from the combination of more basic items, it seems we need some account of how this is so, under what conditions it arises, and so on.

These are, of course, difficult issues, and it would be unreasonable to expect Regan's theory to answer everything relevant to the moral domain. Inherent value, according to Regan, is a theoretical posit: we may not know exactly what it is, but, if Regan is right, we have to suppose it exists in order to make sense of our reflective moral intuitions (i.e. our considered moral beliefs). This reply is reasonable, but only to a point. The fundamental problem is that Regan has done nothing to clarify the nature of inherent value, and this undercuts the validity of his claim that inherent value is a genuine theoretical posit.

As was explained earlier, the basic structure of Regan's argument for inherent value is what is known as *inference to the best explanation.*

And this, in itself, is a perfectly legitimate form of argument, even though it is not deductively valid. However, once we have posited an entity using this argument form, it is then surely incumbent upon us to try and say something about the nature of this entity. More generally, any theorist who wants to posit the existence of a certain theoretical entity, in order to explain a certain range of phenomena, is then placed under a fairly pressing methodological burden to investigate, and to try to say something about, the nature of the postulated entity. Otherwise she has not provided us with a theory at all, but only with a theoretical hole waiting for a theory to be put in its place.

Consider an analogous case. Cartesian dualists claim that the mind is a non-physical entity. One of the arguments for this claim is an inference to the best explanation. No physical system, like the brain, dualists claim, could possibly explain the capacity of people to reason, or use language, or be aware, etc. (the list can be extended, and which feature is focused upon varies from one dualist to another). Therefore, we must suppose that there is some non-physical part of us which is responsible for our being able to do these things. Now this inference, in itself, is perfectly legitimate. But, having made this inference, it is then surely incumbent on the dualist to, firstly, investigate the nature of this non-physical mind, and, secondly, show, from this investigation, how this non-physical mind allows us to do the things it was introduced to explain (i.e. to reason, use language, etc.). Dualists have, typically, not even attempted this task. And, therefore, in the absence of this sort of investigation, dualism is seen to be not a theory of the mind at all. And the inference to it was, therefore, not, ultimately, a legitimate theoretical inference either. Dualism, in other words, is not a theory of the mind, it is a theoretical hole or vacuum just waiting for a genuine theory to be put in its place.

The same point can, I think, legitimately be made with respect to Regan's postulation of inherent value. Above all, we must be careful to distinguish two things; two things constantly confused in just about every empirical and quasi-empirical endeavour. On the one hand, there is a theory which seeks to explain a certain phenomenon, on the other there is an admission that you have no idea what the explanation of that phenomenon is. And, without a serious and concerted attempt to say something about the theoretical entities one has postulated to do the explanatory work, we don't really have a theoretical posit at all. What we have is a simple, though disguised, admission that we have no idea what the explanation is. And, ultimately, I think this is all Regan's postulation of inherent value turns out to be.

11. INHERENT VALUE IS *AD HOC*

Not only is inherent value mysterious, its postulation is arguably *ad hoc*. To see this, consider the sorts of reason one has for introducing the concept of inherent value, and for postulating it in particular cases. One context in which such postulation occurs is in connection with the failure of utilitarian accounts of justice. One central problem with utilitarianism, as we have seen, is that, at least *prima facie*, it seems to license all sorts of intuitively unjust practices. That is, there is legit-imate moral reason to sacrifice individuals as long as this contributes to the greater overall good (understood in terms of pleasures, preference-satisfactions, or whatever). In order to avoid the counterintuitive consequences of utilitarianism in this regard we must, Regan claims, suppose that certain individuals have inherent value and, therefore, cannot be sacrificed in this way.

Consider, again, the institution of gladiatorial combat discussed in the previous chapter. Suppose society, increasingly inured to violence, decided that traditional sporting fare had become just too tame, and, therefore, decided to reinstate the Roman institution of gladiatorial combat to the death. The gladiators, let us suppose, were selected from people who fulfilled no useful purpose in society, and who had no friends or family. In addition, let us suppose, these people did not want to become gladiators, but were forced to by the authorities on pain of torture and death. Now, it could turn out that the very real misery of the unwilling gladiators was outweighed by the pleasure of the spectators. The extreme misery of a few hundred gladiators, for example, might be outweighed by the individually lesser, but aggregatively greater, pleasure of the several hundred million spectators. If this turned out to be the case, it could be argued, utilitarianism would have to say that instituting this practice of forced gladiatorial combat to the death was the morally right thing to do. But, the argument continues, it is, intuitively, the morally wrong thing to do; it is unjust because it overrides the rights of the victims. To avoid this sort of conclusion, Regan would argue, we must introduce the concept of inherent value. The people who are forced to become gladiators, we must suppose, being subjects-of-a-life, have inherent value. And to force them to fight to the death in this way is to fail to treat them with the respect they are owed as a matter of justice; it is to fail to respect their inherent value. Therefore, we should not, as a matter of justice, treat them in this way – irrespect-ive of whatever pleasure this might bring to the majority, and irrespective of whatever socially useful functions this practice might have.

Now I'm not suggesting that utilitarianism has no means of circumventing this scenario. There are, in fact, several ways in which, I think, a utilitarian might avoid the conclusion we are asked to draw here. What I want to focus on, however, is one particular way; a way which seems, to me at least, irredeemably *ad hoc*.

Suppose the utilitarian tried to avoid the conclusion of the above scenario by adopting the following strategy. Firstly, the notion of incommensurable benefits and harms is introduced. The basic idea is that certain sorts of benefits and harms simply cannot be compared with certain other sorts of benefits and harms. The two do not occupy the same scale of measurement. Now, if, for example, a certain type of pleasure P_1 is incommensurable with a certain other type of pleasure P_2, then the two cannot be compared. And it simply makes no sense to ask, for example, how many people have to enjoy pleasure P_2 in order to add up to one person's enjoyment of P_1. The two pleasures simply cannot be compared in this way. A similar point holds for the attempt to compare incommensurable pleasures and pains. Thus, if a pleasure P_1 is incommensurable with a pain N_1, then it makes no sense to ask, for example, how many people have to enjoy pleasure P_1 in order to make up for one person suffering N_1. Again, a comparison of this sort would only make sense if P_1 and N_1 were commensurable. But, let us suppose, they are not. Given this distinction, the utilitarian would then be able to respond to the case of the unwilling gladiators in the following way. The misery suffered by each individual gladiator through being forced to participate in this practice is incommensurable with the pleasure of the spectators. They do not exist on the same scale of measurement. Therefore, it is nonsense to ask how much pleasure has to be enjoyed by how many spectators in order to make up for the misery of the gladiator. No amount of pleasure enjoyed by the spectators could possibly make up for, or balance out, the misery of the gladiator because these particular examples of benefits and harms are incommensurable; they cannot be compared in the relevant way.

The same approach might then be employed more generally by the utilitarian. That is, whenever we are presented with a case which seems to show that utilitarianism clashes with our considered convictions about justice, we can simply introduce the distinction between commensurable and incommensurable benefits and harms, and assert that, in this case, we are, in fact, dealing with incommensurable benefits and harms; and, therefore, the threat to our considered convictions is only an apparent one.

Now there is a clear sense in which this is an *ad hoc* manoeuvre. On the face of it at least, it is a blatant attempt to save utilitarianism from falsification. Crucially, the method of introducing the distinction is theoretically unprincipled. We bring in the distinction when, and only when, the theory seems to face a serious counterexample. That is, the criteria for when the distinction is to be employed – its criteria of application, if you like – are nothing more than the theory being under threat. And if the distinction is to be both legitimate and legitimately employed, surely some criteria other than the potential falsification of the theory is required. Therefore, the manoeuvre seems to be clearly *ad hoc*.

However, and this is the crucial point, the above manoeuvre of the utilitarian seems to be no more *ad hoc* than the corresponding strategy of Regan. The criterion of application for Regan's notion of inherent value is essentially identical with that of the utilitarian. Regan introduces inherent value when, *and only when*, it is needed to make his theory consistent with his considered moral beliefs. That is the sole criterion for applying the concept in any particular case. Therefore, if the utilitarian's employment of the concept of incommensurable value is *ad hoc* – and it certainly seems to be – there is no reason why Regan's employment of the concept of inherent value is not equally *ad hoc*. It is true that Regan postulates the existence of an entity – inherent value – while our imagined utilitarian posits the existence of a relation – a relation between certain types of harm and benefit. But, whether or not a posit is *ad hoc* turns only on the criteria according to which the posit is made. The status of the posit itself, and, in particular whether one posits an entity or relation, is irrelevant to this issue.

Therefore, with regard to inherent value, in addition to the postulated entity being essentially mysterious, the postulation itself seems to be seriously *ad hoc*.

12. INHERENT VALUE IS UNNECESSARY

Postulation of inherent value is also unnecessary. There are two, importantly different, ways of understanding and defending the notion of a moral right.

The first of these is adopted by Regan. We introduce the concept of inherent value; argue that certain individuals satisfy the conditions for possessing this value; and then argue that, on the basis of this, that those individuals possess certain moral rights – the right to treatment in accordance with this value, and various other rights derivable from this one. According to this strategy, then, the possession of moral rights is grounded in inherent value, where this is understood as an objective feature of the world.

The second way of understanding the notion of a moral right is based not on the concept of inherent value, but on the concept of *being inherently valued*. That is, the role played by the concept of inherent value in Regan's understanding of a moral right is, in this case, taken over by the concept of being inherently valued. We can define the notion of something being inherently valued as follows:

A thing X is inherently valued by individual I if and only if (a) X is valued by I, and (b) X is not instrumentally valued by I, and (c) X is not subjectively valued by I.

The notion of something being instrumentally valued is explained as follows. You value something instrumentally if you value it only because of the benefit it affords you. We value money, to use a standard example, only because of what it can do for us, not for what it is in itself. Similarly, medicine is only instrumentally valued by us. Perhaps most of the things we value, we do so only instrumentally. More generally, something is instrumentally valued if it is valued only for its usefulness, its capacity to help us get something else that we want.

Something is subjectively valuable if it is valued only by people who happen to desire it. Lying in the sun, living on spongecake and margaritas, are valued only by people, like myself, and Jimmy Buffett, who happen to enjoy them. As the name implies, something can be subjectively valued by one person and detested by another.

In addition to being instrumentally valued and subjectively valued, however, we have to allow that at least some things are inherently valued. Most of us, in our behaviour, treat some objects as if they are inherently valuable. Thus, they are inherently valued by us. Certain paintings, for example, are inherently valued by some people. That is, many people feel that certain works of art should be respected and protected because of their inherent quality (as they see it) and not simply because people happen to enjoy looking at them (although this is also a legitimate reason). For many people, the theft and possible destruction of Edward Munch's *The Scream* was a disaster, and its return a relief, even if they themselves did not particularly like the painting. The work was inherently valued by those people.

It seems fairly clear, then, that at least some things are inherently valued by people. It is important to realize that the fact that certain things are inherently valued does not entail that they are inherently valuable. People who find things inherently valuable could simply be deluded. There could be no such thing as inherent value, it could be a metaphysical illusion, but still be the case that people treated certain objects *as if* they were inherently valuable. That some things are inherently valued, then, entails that people treat them as if they were inherently valuable. It does not entail that they actually are inherently valuable. And to claim that some things are inherently valued by some people, or all people for that matter, does not commit one to the claim that those things are inherently valuable. The claim that some things are inherently valued, then, commits one to a lot less than the claim that those things are inherently valuable.

The reason why Regan's postulation of inherent value is unnecessary is because precisely the same role played by that concept in deriving a rights-based moral philosophy can also be played, instead, by the concept of being inherently valued. That is, beginning with the concept of certain things being inherently valued we can erect substantially the same edifice of rights and obligations that Regan builds on the bedrock of inherent value. Thus, for example, whereas Regan, starting from inherent value, derives the duty to treat things with such value in ways which respect this value, we, starting from the concept of being inherently valued, can derive the duty of treating things which are inherently valued in ways which respect the fact that they are inherently valued. And, whereas Regan, starting from inherent value, derives the *prima facie* duty not to harm individuals with this value, we, starting from an individual's being inherently valued, can derive the *prima facie* duty not to harm individuals who are valued in this way. In fact, a recognizable form of Regan's rights-based theory can be constructed on the basis not of inherent value, but on the less ontologically dubious fact that certain things are inherently valued. This is, fundamentally, the project of the next chapter.

But surely this project is doomed to fail? Surely the project of deriving a rights-based view from the fact that certain things are inherently valued is certain to founder on the fact that different things are inherently valued by different people? And surely it will founder on the fact that many people, most people in fact, do not inherently value non-human animals? Is this not more than evident in their treatment of them? And this, of course, is all true. And while this is not the place to anticipate the arguments of the next chapter, I can say this. In the project of deriving a rights-based view from the concept of being inherently valued, we have more to work with than just the claim that certain things are inherently valued by certain people and that certain things are not. That is, we have more to go on than just the brute facts about what people, as a matter of fact, inherently value (i.e. profess to find inherently valuable). That is, our focus is not restricted to individuals and their behaviour, but also encompasses the principles that these individuals have adopted in order to regulate their social interactions. Thus, what we also have to go on is the fact that people, whatever society they may belong to, belong to a social structure that will be built on fundamental principles; principles which regulate what things people should find, and treat as if they were, inherently valuable. And these fundamental principles, whether we realize it or not, entail that we should find other things inherently valuable also. Thus, we are committed by the fundamental principles upon which our society is based, to treat certain things as if they were inherently valuable. And this is true independently of whether we do so in fact treat them in this way. We are committed, then, on pain of inconsistency, to treat certain things as if they were inherently valuable – whether we know it or not, and whether we do in fact so treat them or not. And, I shall argue, we, as members of a society built broadly on the principles of liberal democracy, are committed to treating non-human animals as if they were inherently valuable; whether we know it or not, and whether we do so or not.

If this is correct, then a rights-based view capable of underwriting the claim that human animals have substantial direct moral duties to non-human animals does not need to be based on any assumption of inherent value. And this is a good thing. As Rawls has pointed out, the fewer controversial assumptions a moral theory is based on, the wider its force and appeal is likely to be. The assumption that certain things have a mysterious property of inherent value is a controversial metaphysical assumption if ever there was one. Therefore, all things being equal, it is better to avoid basing one's moral theory on it if at all possible. The arguments of the next chapter will try to demonstrate that it is possible.

13. SUBJECT-OF-A-LIFE: DEFENSIBLE BUT QUESTIONABLE

As Rawls among others has pointed out, when engaging in moral argument it is wise to base one's case on assumptions that are as uncontroversial as possible. The more humdrum one's assumptions are, the more likely they are to receive the sort of widespread acceptance necessary for the success of one's moral stance. This being so, Regan's heavy reliance on the concept of a subject-of-a-life is, at the very least, tactically unwise. According to Regan, an individual is a subject-of-a-life if it has beliefs, desires, perceptions, memory, and a sense of the future including its own future; an emotional life together with feelings of pleasure and pain; preference and welfare interests, the ability to initiate action in pursuit of its goals, a psychophysical identity over time, and so on. To rests one's position on the claim that some non-human animals are subjects-of-a-life is, I think, a bad idea, but not because the claim is indefensible. On the contrary, if we except the condition of a psychophysical identity over time (controversial even for humans) and a sense of the future (extremely difficult to establish), the claim that non-human animals are subjects-of-a-life is eminently defensible and very likely true. The claim does, however, require that a substantial amount of work be given in its defence. Often complex arguments have to be mustered, and these themselves will often rely on assumptions that are controversial. Because, of this, the claim is not only questionable; it is frequently questioned. Relying so heavily on the concept of a subject-of-a-life constitutes, I shall try to show, an unnecessary exposure of one's flank. The arguments of the next chapter will try to show that one can defend the claim that at least some non-human animals possess moral rights without appealing to anywhere near as controversial an assumption about the status of their mental lives.

In short, the most serious problems with Regan's case for animal rights issue, I think, not from the content of the rights he derives, but from the metaphysical assumptions underlying the derivation. To rely on the concept of inherent value is to rely on a concept that is *mysterious*, *ad hoc* and, ultimately, *unnecessary*. And to rely on the concept of a subject-of-a-life is, at the very least, tactically unwise. The next chapter will develop a case for animal rights that does not rely on these sorts of dubious metaphysical assumptions.

6 Contractarianism and Animal Rights

1. CONTRACTARIANISM AND RIGHTS

In this chapter, I shall argue that the best case for the moral claims of non-human animals can be made using the apparatus of contractarian theory as developed by John Rawls and others. In particular, it will be argued that contractarian theory can be used to defend the claim that many types of non-human animals are the bearers of moral *rights*. However, the concept of a right employed here is pretty minimalist in character, and bears little relation to the concept seen to be employed by Regan in the previous chapter. More precisely, this chapter will employ almost what we might call a quasi-*Benthamesque* notion of rights: rights are simply entailments of moral theories. Thus, if one adopts a moral theory that contains as one of its central principles 'Thou shalt not kill!', then, on the present understanding of a moral right, this entails that all those individuals who fall under the scope of the principle have at least a *prima facie* right not to be killed. Rights, that is, will be understood here as simply moral entitlements. And whether or not one possesses a moral right is essentially a theory-relative matter: an individual, I, possesses a moral right R, relative to theory T, if among the entailments of T is the proposition that I is entitled to the treatment, or to the freedom, prescribed by R. Thus, if theory T contains the principle 'Thou shalt not kill!', and if you fall under the scope of this principle, then you are, according to T, entitled, at least *prima facie*, not to be killed (by anyone else who falls under the scope of this principle). And, on the present understanding of the concept of a moral right, this means that, relative to T, you have a right not to be killed by any other individual who falls under the scope of the principle. It is in this fairly unencumbered sense that, I shall argue, many sorts of non-human animals possess moral rights. Rights are not the sorts of thing that can be possessed in the way in which one might possess broad shoulders, or a Rolex watch. And, *a fortiori*, one does not possess moral rights in virtue of also possessing a mysterious quality of inherent value. One possesses moral rights only relative to moral theories and principles, and to the extent that one falls under the scope of these. The notion of the contract, then, will be employed in the Kantian manner described in Chapter 3; that is, it will be used as a means of clarifying and identifying the entailments of certain moral principles that are sufficiently fundamental to be regarded as constitutive of our moral point of view.

2. DIRECT AND INDIRECT RIGHTS

Contractarian, or contractualist, approaches to morality are generally thought to lend little or no support to the friend of animal rights. Contractarian approaches, it is assumed, are unable to underwrite the granting of *direct* moral status to non-human animals, although they may be compatible with the granting of *indirect* moral status to the extent that non-humans bear certain relations to humans, the bearers of direct moral status. Put in the idiom of rights, it is customary, and important, to distinguish between two sorts of rights, direct and indirect:

Direct rights: An individual I possesses a direct right R to a certain commodity or action if and only if (a) I possesses R, and (b) the possession of R by I does not depend on the existence of rights possessed by any individual distinct from I.

Indirect rights: An individual I possesses an indirect right R to a certain commodity or action if and only if (a) I possesses R, and (b) the possession of R by I does depend on the existence of rights possessed by an individual distinct from I.

The notion of a commodity is construed very broadly here to include such things as life, liberty, education, and so on. The concept of an action is similarly understood.

There are various ways in which this distinction might manifest itself. For example, consider the claim that a dog possesses indirect rights. One way in which this might be so is that if I, as a possessor of direct moral rights, am emotionally attached to my dog so that harm to my dog would upset me in some way, then I might have a *prima facie* right to require that you do not harm my dog. My dog has no right not to be harmed by you, but I have a right that my dog not be harmed by you. And any harm visited upon my dog by you is an infringement not of my dog's direct rights (since he has none) but of mine. In this case, it is correct to speak of the harm done to my dog as an infringement of his indirect rights; rights that he possesses only in virtue of rights that I possess. In this case, then, the violation of my dog's indirect rights derives from the violation of my direct rights.

There is another well-known sense in which a dog might come to be a bearer of indirect rights. There is a view associated with Aquinas and Kant among others according to which a harm such as cruelty inflicted on my dog is wrong not because of the harm it does to my dog, but because of the deleterious effect it has upon the person who inflicts the harm.[1] Cruelty and callousness to non-humans is wrong not in itself but because it tends to make the perpetrators cruel and callous and this can then go on to infect their dealings with other human beings. He who is hard in his dealings with animals becomes hard in his dealings with humans, or so the idea goes. Now, at this point, I am not at all concerned with whether this idea is correct (and, in particular, whether it gets the direction of causation right). The point is simply that this is another version of the indirect rights view. According to this view, my dog possesses indirect rights only in virtue of the existence of a distinct individual – a human – who possesses direct rights. It differs from the first case in that the violation of my dog's indirect rights here does not stem so directly from the violation of another's direct rights. Presumably, the person who is cruel to my dog does not thereby have his rights infringed upon. Nonetheless, what makes the cruelty to my dog wrong, on this view, is the tendency for it to lead to character traits which will extend to the person's inter-actions with humans, and therefore to violations of their direct rights. Ultimately, then, both ways of developing the indirect rights view make the possession of indirect rights by an individual dependent on the possession of direct rights by distinct individuals. Indirect rights can be possessed and violated only in virtue of the possession and violation of direct rights.

It is generally thought that contractarian approaches to morality are not capable of underwriting the attribution of direct rights to non-human animals. The reason for this is that non-human animals are, it is assumed, not rational agents, and contractarian approaches subsume, under the umbrella of moral consideration or concern, only rational agents. Thus, for example, according to Carruthers:

Morality is here [i.e. according to the contractarian approach] pictured as a system of rules to govern the interaction of rational agents within society. It, therefore, seems inevitable, on the face of it, that only rational agents will be assigned direct rights on this approach. Since it is rational agents who are to choose the system of rules, and choose self-interestedly, it is only rational agents who will have their position protected under the rules. There seems no reason why rights should be assigned to non-rational agents. Animals will, therefore, have no moral standing under Rawlsian contractualism, in so far as they do not count as rational agents.[2]

Carruthers, of course, endorses this conclusion and sees it, if anything, as a *strength* of contractarian approaches that they do not assign direct rights to non-humans. However, this view of contractarianism seems to be shared by both foes *and* friends of animal rights. Thus, Tom Regan, by far the most influential defender of the concept of animal rights, claims:

> it [Rawls's contractarianism] systematically denies that we have direct duties to those human beings who do not have a sense of justice – young children, for instance, and many mentally retarded humans.[3]

Regan shares with Carruthers the assumption that contractarianism, as represented by John Rawls, only applies to rational agents. And since many, if not all, non-human animals cannot be regarded as rational agents in the relevant sense, contractarian approaches will fail to assign them direct moral rights.

I think this view can be questioned in several ways. Certainly, the all or nothing manner in which discussions of non-human rationality tend to take place is eminently questionable, on both theoretical and methodological grounds.[4] However, for the purposes of the central moral argument of this book, nothing much turns on whether non-humans should be regarded as rational agents. I shall argue that there is nothing in contractarianism *per se* that requires that the protection afforded by the contract be restricted to rational agents. The fact that the *framers* of the contract must be conceived of as rational agents does not entail that the *recipients* of the protection afforded by the contract must be rational agents. In fact, I shall argue that when contractarianism is properly understood, quite the opposite conclusion turns out to be true. If a contractarian position is consistently applied, the recipients of the protection offered by the contract *must* include not only rational, but also non-rational, individuals.

3. CONTRACTARIANISM AND ANIMAL RIGHTS: THE ORTHODOX VIEW

The first task is to flesh out in a little more detail the reasons contractarianism is thought to be incompatible with the possession, by non-humans, of direct rights. The underlying argument for this incompatibility seems to be of the following form.

P1. According to contractarianism, moral rights and duties are dependent on the existence of an actual or hypothetical contract.

P2. The framers of the contract and the moral rights and duties embodied therein have to be conceived of as rational agents.

P3. Therefore, the contract and its embodied moral rights and duties apply only to rational agents.

P4. Non-human animals are not rational agents.

P5. Therefore, the contract and its embodied rights and duties do not apply to non-human animals.

P6. Direct moral rights are possessed only by those individuals subsumed by the contract and its embodied rights and duties.

C. Therefore, non-human animals do not possess direct moral rights.

This argument, I think, expresses the orthodox understanding of the relation between contractarianism and animal rights. The argument, of course, is compatible with non-humans being the bearers of indirect rights, but not with their possession of direct rights.

The argument is, of course, not deductively valid, and it would be unfair to present it as such and to criticize it for its failure in this regard. Nonetheless, there is still a large jump from P2 to P3. To claim that the framers of a contract must be conceived of as rational agents obviously does not entail that the recipients of the protection afforded by the contract must be similarly conceived. The argument can be rendered plausible, then, only if some justification for the move from P2 to P3 can be provided. And such attempted justification can take several forms.

One form of such justification, for example, is associated with, among others, Thomas Hobbes and, more recently, David Gaulthier, and focuses on the usefulness that a contract would have for us.[5] The idea is that, for us to regard a contract as in any way binding, we have to recognize that it would be a good thing for us if we adhered to the contract. Adhering to the contract involves accepting certain restrictions upon one's freedom, and we will find this acceptable, and hence adhere to the contract, only if these restrictions allow us to obtain a good that outweighs the value of the freedom lost. The sort of good Hobbes had in mind, for example, was common purpose and protection from enemies. Non-human animals, however, don't seem to fit very easily into this contractarian idea. They, being unable to understand the terms of the contract, cannot agree to abide by its principles. Therefore, it is argued, we would agree to accept restrictions on our freedom, but they do not. Therefore, we would lose something in agreeing to abide by the contract, and get nothing in return from them. Therefore, it is argued, non-human animals cannot be included as beings with whom we can meaningfully contract.

What is of interest at present is not the specific content of this justification, but the form it takes. The crucial assumption is that, if the contract idea is to work, then some account must be given of how the contract can be binding on us. Then, it is argued that the contract can be binding only if all the individual contractors agree to be bound in the same sort of way. Thus, any individual who cannot agree to be bound in the way specified by the contract cannot be meaningfully regarded as a contractor; and non-rational agents would provide a paradigm case of individuals who are not capable of being contractors in this sense. It is these assumptions, I think, which underlie the inference from P2 to P3. We might represent these as an extra premise as follows:

P2(a). Any individual who is not a contractor is subject neither to the conditions of the contract nor the protection afforded by the contract.

Therefore, the protection of the contract extends only as far as those individuals who can be meaningfully regarded as contractors. And this, it is argued, excludes non-human animals.

In the remainder of this chapter, I shall argue that the above is only one way of developing the contract idea. This way of developing the idea, in fact, corresponds pretty closely to what, in Chapter 3, was called *Hobbesian contractarianism*. There is, in fact, another, perfectly legitimate, way of developing the contract idea – more *Kantian* in nature – such that it does *not* entail that the protection of the contract extends only as far as the contractors themselves. This alternative development of the contract idea, I shall argue, is capable of explaining the sense in which the contract is binding without presupposing that its scope is thereby limited to the contractors. Moreover, I shall argue that the version of the contract idea to be defended in the sections to follow is, in several key respects, superior to the type of explication given above.

4. RAWLS AND CONTRACTARIANISM

The starting point for the version of contractarianism to be developed in this chapter is provided by the position defended by John Rawls in *A Theory of Justice*, and, more recently, *Political Liberalism*.[6] The reason for starting with Rawls is, of course, that he is (deservedly) the most influential of modern contractarians, and, consequently, any defence of contractarianism must effectively define itself in relation to Rawls's view. At the outset, however, one point of contrast should be noted. Rawls is primarily interested in political philosophy, and his application of contractarianism is used to determine the nature of what he calls the *basic structure of society*, that is 'the way in which the major social institutions distribute fundamental rights and duties and determine the division of advantages from social cooperation'.[7] And by 'major social institutions' Rawls means the political constitution and the principal economic and social arrangements. I propose to use the contractarian idea in a somewhat broader sense as providing a general theory of morality; that is, as providing a framework for the assignation of moral rights and duties in general, and not just political rights of the sort discussed by Rawls. That is, the contractarian idea, as I propose to use it later in the chapter, will be conceived of as, in principle, being capable of providing us with general principles of morality, and not simply principles relating individuals to basic societal structures. While this differs in scope from Rawls's view, this application of the contract idea is, of course, by no means idiosyncratic.

The ideas that form the conceptual heart of Rawls's contractarianism are those of the *original position* and the associated idea of the *veil of ignorance*. For Rawls, the way to think about what would be a just organization of society is to imagine what principles would be agreed to by people who were denied knowledge of certain facts about themselves. The people here find themselves in the original position, and the facts of which they have no knowledge are excluded by the veil of ignorance. The facts excluded by this veil can be divided into two sorts. Firstly, the occupants of the original position do not know their socio-economic position in society, nor do they know their own natural talents or endowments. Secondly, they do not know their own conceptions of the good; that is, given that there are alternative possible sets of beliefs about how one should live one's life, the occupants of the original position do not know which set of beliefs they will hold. The occupants of the original position are conceived of as rational. And while they do not suffer from envy, they are concerned to put themselves in as advantageous a position as possible after the lifting of the veil of ignorance.

Rawls claims that a person put in the original position would choose two principles of distributive justice:

> First principle – Each person is to have an equal right to the most extensive total system of equal basic liberties compatible with a similar system for all.
> Second principle – Social and economic inequalities are to be arranged so that they are both:
> (a) to the greatest benefit of the least advantaged, consistent with the just savings principle, and
> (b) attached to offices and positions open to all under conditions of fair equality of opportunity.[8]

(He also defends various priority rules which are not directly relevant to the concerns of this chapter.)

It is important to realize, however, that the concept of the original position cannot, *by itself*, motivate these two principles. That is, Rawls, in fact, has two essential arguments for these principles of justice and not, as is commonly thought, one.[9] The first argument functions by contrasting his theory with what he takes to be the prevailing ideology concerning distributive justice – namely the ideal of equality of opportunity. The political system that embodies this ideal is referred to by Rawls as the system of *liberal equality*. Rawls argues that his theory (i.e. *democratic equality*) better fits our considered intuitions concerning justice, and that it more consistently spells out the very ideals of fairness that underwrite the prevailing ideology. I propose to call this the *intuitive equality argument*. The second argument defends the principles of justice by showing that they are the principles that would be adopted by rational agents in the original position. I shall refer to this as the *social contract argument*. Rawls has, of course, placed far more emphasis on the social contract argument, and this has led many people to overlook the intuitive equality argument. This, however, constitutes a serious oversight, since, as I shall try to show, the former is crucially dependent on the latter.

Understanding the relation between the intuitive equality argument
and the social contract argument is essential to understanding the way
in which contractarianism can underwrite the attribution of rights to
non-humans.

The Intuitive Equality Argument

In broad outline, the basis of what I have called the *intuitive equality
argument* looks like this:

> P1. If an individual I is not responsible for their possession of prop-
> erty P, then I is not morally entitled to P.
> P2. If I is not morally entitled to P, then I is not morally entitled to
> whatever benefits accrue from their possession of P.
> P3. For any individual I, there will be a certain set of properties
> $S = \{P_1, P_2 \dots P_n\}$ such that I possesses S without being respons-
> ible for possessing S.
>
> ---
>
> C. Therefore, for any individual I, there is a set S of properties such
> that I is not morally entitled to the benefits which accrue from
> possession of S.[10]

In other words, if a property is *undeserved* in the sense that its possessor is not responsible for, or has done nothing to merit, its possession,
then its possessor is not morally entitled to whatever benefits accrue
from that possession. Possession of the property is a morally arbitrary
matter and, therefore, cannot be used to determine the moral entitlements of its possessor. The argument also has a corresponding
negative form, according to which, morally speaking, one should not
be penalized for the possession of a property one has done nothing to
deserve. It doesn't really matter which of the two forms we concen-
trate on. I shall focus on the positive form as described above.

Rawls believes that the above argument underlies the ideal of
equality of opportunity which he identifies with the prevailing liberal
orthodoxy. That is, the principle that *one is not morally entitled to
benefits that accrue from properties one has done nothing to earn* is a
principle which provides a conceptual foundation for the politics of
liberal equality and its embodied ideal of equality of opportunity.
Rawls endorses this principle. His case against the concept of equality of opportunity, as this is usually understood, stems not from a
disagreement with the principle as such, but, rather, centres around
the range of properties that should be regarded as morally arbitrary,

and thus falling within the scope of the principle. It is a commonplace that being born into a certain position in society – in a particular social, racial, economic, or gender group – is an undeserved and, hence, morally arbitrary property. And, therefore, one should be neither benefited from nor penalized by possession of such a property. In other words, economic and social inequalities are undeserved, and, hence, it is unfair for one's fate to be made any better or worse by this sort of undeserved inequality. However, what the concept of equal opportunity, as this concept is understood in contemporary liberal cultures, overlooks is that there are many more properties which are undeserved in the requisite sense. In particular, inequalities in natural talents or capacities are undeserved in precisely the same way as social, racial, economic and gender properties. No one deserves to be born athletically gifted, stunningly handsome or with an IQ of 153, any more than they deserve to be born into a certain privileged class, sex, or race. Therefore, if it is unjust for someone to benefit from possession of undeserved social, racial, economic, or gender properties, then it must be equally unjust for them to benefit from possession of undeserved natural talents.

What is going here is that we have a principle – the principle of equality of opportunity – which is embodied in contemporary liberal ideology, and is broadly accepted within this framework, but is not *consistently* implemented. Thus, Rawls's argument provides a more coherent and theoretically penetrating expression of the very assumptions which underlie the prevailing liberal view. And Rawls's argument turns on the distinction, a distinction which will prove important in the arguments of later sections, between a principle being *embodied* in an ideology, and that principle being *consistently adhered to* by proponents of that ideology. Rawls's point, in part, is that the former does not entail the latter. And where we have a dissonance between the embodiment of a principle and the consistent adherence to that principle, the moral philosopher's job, in part, is to point out, and hopefully rectify, this dissonance.

The Social Contract Argument

Rawls's social contract argument runs as follows. We imagine a so-called *original position* whose occupants are behind a *veil of ignorance*:

No one knows his place in society, his class position or social status, nor does anyone know his fortune in the distribution of natural assets and abilities, his intelligence, strength, and the like. I shall even assume that the parties do not know their conceptions of the good or their special psychological propensities. The principles of justice are chosen behind a veil of ignorance. This ensures that no one is advantaged or disadvantaged in the choice of principles by the outcome of natural chance of the contingency of social circumstances. Since all are similarly situated and no one is able to design principles to favour his particular condition, the principles of justice are the result of a fair agreement of bargain.[11]

The concept of the original position, and the associated idea of the veil of ignorance, will play a central role in this book's defence of the attribution of (direct) rights to non-human animals. Therefore, at this point it is essential to clear up one serious, and actually quite extraordinary, misunderstanding of these concepts that has been prevalent in recent years.

Many communitarian critics of Rawls have objected to the notion of an original position on the grounds that it entails a spurious metaphysical conception of the self. This claim is based on the idea that when the multifarious types of knowledge described above have been bracketed off, as demanded by the veil of ignorance, we are left with nothing but a radically *unencumbered* self. That is, we are left with a self which has its ends only contingently. Communitarians believe this is false view of the self. It ignores the fact that the self is *embedded* or *situated* in existing social practices, and that these, in an important sense, define the self or constitute its identity as the particular self that it is. It makes no sense then, on the communitarian view, to try and imagine a self in the original position. A self which occupied the original position would have had taken away from it precisely those features which constitute its identity; it would therefore have ceased to be a self. An unencumbered self, therefore, is radically unimaginable because the whole idea of a self occupying an original position is incoherent.[12]

This is, of course, not the place to enter into a discussion of communitarianism. Even without such discussion, however, it is not difficult to see that this sort of criticism is misguided. The concepts of the original position and veil of ignorance are neither expressions of, nor do they entail, any metaphysical theory of the person. Rather, they constitute an intuitive test of fairness. Just as we might try to ensure a fair division of a cake by making sure that the person who cuts it does not know what piece he will get, so too we ensure a just distribution of rights by making sure those who are able to influence the selection process in their favour, due to their better position, are unable to do so. The cutter of the cake does not know which piece he will get, therefore he cuts the pieces fairly; the distributor of rights does not know where in the distributive scheme he will fit, therefore he distributes justly. Similarly, the notion of the contract, in Rawls's hands, is not to be confused with any agreement – actual *or* hypothetical – but as a device for teasing out the implications of certain premises concerning people's moral equality. That is, the idea of the original position is used as a heuristic device to model the idea of the moral equality of individuals.

This being so, there is no dubious metaphysical conception of the self embodied in the concept of the original position. Firstly, the concept of the original position does not require that there could actually be a self, or selves, which inhabit the original position. That is, Rawls is not committed to the *metaphysical* possibility of occupants of the original position. Secondly, the concept of the original position does not even entail that it is possible to imagine the nature of occupants of the original position. That is, Rawls is not even committed to the *conceptual* possibility of a self existing behind the veil of ignorance. The reason he is committed to neither of these possibilities is because the original position and veil of ignorance are simply heuristic devices. Even in *A Theory of Justice*, Rawls is quite clear on the heuristic status of these concepts. He writes:

> Some may object that the exclusion of nearly all particular information makes it difficult to grasp what is meant by the original position. Thus, it may be helpful to observe that one or more persons can at any time enter the original position, or perhaps, better, simulate the deliberations of this hypothetical situation, simply by reasoning in accordance with the appropriate restrictions … To say that a certain conception of justice would be chosen in the original position is equivalent to saying that rational deliberation satisfying certain conditions and restrictions would reach a certain conclusion.[13]

And in later works, obviously mindful of the misunderstandings of his work on precisely this issue, Rawls is even more clear on the heuristic status of the concept of the original position. It is simply, as Rawls says, a 'device of representation', which serves as a means of 'public reflection and self-clarification'.[14]

One can 'enter' the original position, then, not by becoming a radically unencumbered self, but by reasoning in accordance with certain restrictions. More precisely, one can put oneself in the original position simply by imagining that one is without a certain attribute that one does in fact have, or without a certain conception of the good that one does in fact hold.[15] And this does not require that we imagine ourselves without *any* attribute or without *any* conception of the good. It simply requires that we be able to bracket these features of ourselves in a one-by-one piecemeal manner. Rawls indicates that he will go on speaking in terms of the original position because such talk is 'economical and suggestive', and brings out certain essential features one might otherwise overlook. Given the frequent and egregious misunderstandings occasioned by Rawls's use of this concept, one may legitimately wonder if this decision was wise. But be that as it may, the important point is that the concept of the original position, and the associated concept of the veil of ignorance, are both heuristic through and through.

In failing to recognize the heuristic status of the concept of the original position, one not only misunderstands Rawls's views, one also, I think, fails to grasp the power and originality of his thinking about justice. Correct understanding of the concept of the original position is so central to the case I shall make for animal rights, that I shall return to the task of clarification in the next section. At present we must move on to consider the relation between the social contract argument and the intuitive equality argument.

The Mutual Dependence of the Arguments

As was mentioned earlier, Rawls has placed much more emphasis on the social contract argument, and this has led many to overlook the intuitive equality argument. To do this, however, would be to fail to understand how Rawls's overall defence of liberalism works. I shall try to show that the social contract argument cannot be understood independently of the intuitive equality argument (and nor, indeed, can the latter ultimately be understood in isolation from the former). The two arguments are, essentially, co-dependent and mutually reinforcing.

Rawls's defence of liberalism has been objected to on the grounds that he rigs the description of the veil of ignorance, and, hence, of the original position, in order to yield the principles of justice he requires (e.g. the difference principle).[16] This sort of objection is, however, misconceived, since Rawls is perfectly willing to admit this. He recognizes that 'for each traditional conception of justice there is an interpretation of the initial situation in which its principles are the preferred solution.'[17] There are many possible descriptions of the original position that are compatible with the goal of creating a fair decision procedure, and the difference principle would not be chosen in all of them. So, in order to determine which principles would be chosen in the original position, we first need to know which description of that position to accept. And, according to Rawls, one of the grounds on which we choose a description of the original position is that it yields principles we find intuitively acceptable. That is, one important way of justifying a description of the original position is that it yields the sort of principles which emerge from the intuitive equality argument. This is so because it is precisely this argument which is based on the principles embodied in our contemporary liberal ideology.

In deciding on the preferred description of the original position, we 'work from both ends'. This means that if the principles that are yielded by a given description of the original position do not match our convictions of justice, as expressed in the intuitive equality argument, then we have a choice:

> We can either modify the account of the initial situation or we can revise our existing judgments, for even the judgments we take provisionally as fixed points are liable to revision. By going back and forth, sometimes altering the conditions of the contractual circumstances, at others withdrawing our judgments and conforming them to principle, I assume that eventually we shall find a description of the initial situation that both expresses reasonable conditions and yields principles which match our considered judgments duly pruned and adjusted. This state of affairs I refer to as reflective equilibrium.[18]

The latter state of affairs is described as an equilibrium because the principles yielded by the original position and the judgements yielded by the intuitive equality argument coincide; and it is reflective since we now know to what principles our intuitive judgements of equality conform.

It is important to realize that Rawls, in this passage, is advocating working from *both* ends. Not only can our description of the original position be modified by our intuitive judgements of equality, but so too can our intuitive judgements of equality be modified by our description of the original position. The relation, in other words, is genuinely dialectical. Failure to appreciate this point can often lead to an ultra-conservative interpretation of Rawls, according to which our description of the original position is wholly at the mercy of our intuitive judgements of equality, themselves seen as not subject to this kind of review or modification. This interpretation of Rawls, I think, robs his position of much of its power and distinctiveness. And, in any event, it is far from Rawls's notion of reflective equilibrium. Indeed, it seems much more akin to what we might call *unreflective* equilibrium. And it is this sort of unreflective equilibrium which often lies at the heart of the view that contractarianism does not provide an adequate foundation for animal rights.[19] And, once again, in deciding when our intuitive but unreflective judgements concerning justice should be overridden, the intuitive equality argument is crucial.

To see this, recall how Rawls was able to override the intuitive but unreflective judgements underlying the politics of liberal equality, identified by Rawls as the prevailing liberal ideology. The prevailing justification for economic distribution in our society is based on the idea of 'equality of opportunity'. Inequalities of income and prestige etc. are assumed to be justified if and only if there was fair competition in the awarding of the offices and positions that yield those benefits. This conflicts with Rawls's theory, for while Rawls also requires equality of opportunity in the allocation of positions, he denies that the people who fill the positions are thereby entitled to a greater share of society's resources. A Rawlsian society may pay such people more than average, but only if it benefits all members of society to do so. Under the difference principle, people only have a claim to a greater share of resources if they can show that it benefits those who have lesser shares. Thus, Rawls's theory conflicts with what passes for common sense in capitalist societies. What motivates this common-sense view is the idea that it is fair for individuals to have unequal shares of social goods if those inequalities are earned and deserved by the individual and, conversely, that it is unfair for individuals to be disadvantaged or privileged by arbitrary and undeserved differences in their social circumstances. As Rawls points out, however, there is another source of undeserved inequality that this argument ignores. While it is true that social inequalities are undeserved, it is also true that inequalities in natural talents are equally undeserved. No one deserves to be born handicapped, or with an IQ of 70, any more than they deserve to be born into a certain under-privileged class, race, or sex. Therefore, distributive shares should not be influenced by these factors either. What is going on here is that Rawls is using the intuitive equality argument to undermine a widely accepted, indeed common-sense, view of just distribution. This common-sense idea of just distribution is no doubt intuitive – after all, many people intuit it – but not sufficiently reflective. And to rely on such a principle and use it to determine the interpretation of the ori-ginal position would not be a case of reflective equilibrium, it would, as we might say, be a case of unreflective equilibrium. Thus, what determines whether an intuition of justice is a reflective intuition or not is the consistent application of the intuitive equality argument. This argument, therefore, plays a central role in determining the correct description of the original position, and, therefore, the prin-ciples of justice which are derived from this.

Later in the chapter, I shall argue that many of the arguments against extending a Rawlsian conception of justice to non-humans, remarks issuing from Rawls as well as others, are based on unreflective intuitions; intuitions not compatible with the consistent application of the intuitive equality argument. Since it is the consistent application of this argument that *should* determine which description of the original position we employ, these unreflective intuitions can play no role in determining this description. Now, however, it is time to see how a Rawlsian version of contractarianism can be used to underwrite the attribution of rights to non-humans. The first essential stage is to return to the task of clarifying the concept of the original position.

5. THE ORIGINAL POSITION REVISITED

In order to understand how the concept of the original position can provide a logical foundation for attribution of rights to non-humans, it is essential to remove certain serious misunderstandings that surround this concept. This will be the task of this section.

The task of clarification began in the previous section when replying to communitarian criticisms of Rawls. I argued that Rawls was not committed to a view of the self as essentially unencumbered. That is, Rawls was committed neither to the metaphysical nor even to the conceptual possibility of an unencumbered self. This is actually part of a wider issue.

The crucial point is this. The concept of the original position, and the associated concept of the veil of ignorance are simply heuristic concepts, or, as Rawls puts it, 'devices of representation'. The original position should *not* be thought of as any kind of state of affairs.

That is, the concept of the original position is not a descriptive concept in the sense that it does not function to describe a situation or state of affairs. And this is true whether the envisaged state of affairs is conceived of as actual *or* as merely logically possible.

It is fairly clear, of course, that the concept of the original position does not function to describe any *actual* situation. Viewed in this way, the function of the concept would be to make an extremely implausible empirical claim; and no one, it seems, would want to suppose that this is indeed its function. However, even though the function of the concept is seen not to be descriptive of an actual state of affairs, many have thought that it is does function to describe another type of situation. That is, many have thought that the function of the concept is to pick out a hypothetical, imaginable or logically possible situation or state of affairs. I want to argue, on the other hand, that the concept does not function to pick out *any* state of affairs, whether actual or logically possible. Therefore, the concept of the original position does not entail that it is possible to *imagine* a radically unencumbered self of the sort that could occupy a hypothetical original position. Nor does it entail the *logical possibility* of a radically unencumbered self occupying an original position. That is, the concept of an original position entails neither the imaginability or logical possibility of an unencumbered self nor the imaginability or logical possibility of a position in which such a self could meaningfully be thought to be.

What the concept of the original position describes is not a possible state of affairs nor an imaginable one, but, rather, a certain type of reasoning process. This process of reasoning looks something like this: 'As a matter of fact, I have property P. But what if I did not have P? What principles of morality would I want adopted if I didn't have P?' One 'enters' the original position, in the only meaningful sense in which one can be said to enter it, when one engages in a reasoning process of this type. And, Rawls's talk of a self occupying an original position is simply a way of adverting to a person who is restricting his or her reasoning about morality in accordance with the above sort of schema. That is, being in the original position is not a matter of being in a logically, metaphysically or physically possible situation. It is simply a matter of allowing one's reasoning about morality to be guided by the above sorts of restrictions. Two important clarifications are in order here.

1. Firstly, given this understanding of the concept of the original position, there is no requirement that to be in this position one must have bracketed *all* one's properties. That is, in order to occupy the

original position, one does *not* need to ask oneself the following sort of question: 'What moral principles would I want adopted if I had none of the properties I now, in fact, know myself to have?' Imagining oneself without any properties would, of course, be tantamount to imagining an unencumbered self. However, this is not required. All that is required is that one be able to bracket, or suspend belief in one's possession of, each individual property in a piecemeal, one-by-one, manner. The process is akin to repairing the Ship of Theseus while still at sea.[20] In order to avoid being partial to a particular distribution of moral principles on the basis of one's possessing a given property, one simply has to imagine not having that property and asking oneself what moral principles one would like to see adopted in that situation. Identification of the most adequate set of moral principles, then, is simply a matter of collating the results from these sort of piecemeal inquiries.

2. Secondly, we need to observe an important distinction between what we can call *imagining that* and *imagining what it would be like*. Suppose our moral reasoner, for example, had the property of being male. In order to 'enter' the original position, he would have to reason in the following sort of way: 'Suppose I didn't have the property of being male. What principles of morality would I like to see adopted in that situation?' Since the person, *ex hypothesi*, has the property of being male, this is a case where he imagines *that* he is not male. However, there is nothing in this procedure which requires him to imagine *what it would be like* to not have the property of being male. Imagining that you don't have a particular property and imagining what it would be like not to have that property are two very different things.

This distinction, of course, derives from a distinction between two different types of knowledge. On the one hand there is factual knowledge, often referred to as knowledge by *description*, i.e. knowledge that a particular description can be applied to (or withheld from) a given object. On the other hand, there is knowledge by *acquaintance*, knowledge which is constituted by direct personal awareness or consciousness of something. The distinction is, of course, familiar from the work of Bertrand Russell.[21]

The crucial category of knowledge/imagination for the purposes of the original position is knowledge or imagination *that*. One needs to be able to imagine that one does not have a particular property one in fact does have; one does not need to be able to imagine what it would be like to not have that property. Firstly, the latter demand would, in many cases, be extremely difficult, if not impossible, to satisfy; I might have no idea what it was like to be female. Secondly, even if the condition was possible to satisfy, there would be severe difficulties in actually determining when one had in fact satisfied it. I, for example, would have no way of knowing if my imaginative exercises had in fact succeeded in yielding to me the awareness of what it is like to be female. And both these objections would hold even if one was willing to allow that the whole concept of there being an experience of what it is like to be something is not irredeemably flawed.

Fortunately, however, being 'in' the original position does not have to involve the ability to imagine what it would be like to lack a given property. In the case of my lacking the property of being male, for example, I do not have to be capable of imagining what it would be like to be female in order to deduce what moral principles I would like adopted in that situation. All that is required is that I know certain pertinent *facts* about women. The relevant facts, here, would include things like preferences and how a hypothetical moral or political arrangement would impact on those preferences. Thus, the fact that a given preference P might be so far removed from the preferences I in fact possess that I find it difficult or impossible to imagine having P does not undermine the validity of the original position. All that is required for me to be in the original position is that I know *that* a person has a given preference, not that I know what it is like to have that preference. This point has fairly obvious implications for the possibility of bringing non-human animals under the scope of the protection afforded by the contract, and the practice of attributing preferences and other types of mental states to non-humans will be discussed at length in the next chapter.

In addition to these clarifications, there is also one important corollary of the above understanding of the concept of the original position. The corollary is this: the original position is not *essentially* an expression of the contract idea, at least, not if this idea is thought to involve distinct individuals contracting with each other. That is, the notion of different agents contracting with each other is not an essential part of the idea of the original position. The original position is perfectly compatible with a construal whereby we imagine various agents contracting with each other behind a veil of ignorance. However, neither the multiplicity of agents nor the notion of contracting is essential to the idea of the original position.

To see this, consider the following scenario. Imagine that *metempsychosis*, transmigration of the soul, is in fact true. And suppose, at some time when you are in between souls, God says to you: 'I am not going to tell who or what you are going to be in your next life. However, I shall allow you to choose what moral principles you would like to see adopted in whatever world it is you are going to inhabit.' Of course, transmigration of the soul is undoubtedly false, and this scenario commits you neither to it nor to an untenable dualist view of the person. The point is simply that this is another way of setting up the original position, and the restrictions on one's reasoning about oneself that effectively constitute this position. The veil of ignorance is, in this case, effected by the fact that you do not occupy a body and God will not tell you which body you are going to occupy next. Thus, whatever restrictions on your knowledge are thought to be involved in Rawls's version of the original position can also be mirrored in this metempsychotic version. The crucial point, of course, is that any possibility of partiality is removed by your ignorance of your position in society; your conception of the good, etc.

When we view the original position in this way, it is fairly clear that the original position can be occupied by one person alone. There is no need to view the position as one in which a multiplicity of rational agents contract or agree among themselves. While it is perfectly consistent to imagine the original position as one in which a collection of distinct individuals contract among themselves in this way, this is not essential to the setting up of the position. One person denied any knowledge of him- or herself satisfies the conditions of the original position in an equally legitimate way. That is, what is crucial to the original position is the idea that an individual is denied all particular knowledge about him- or herself (or whatever subset of particular knowledge is deemed relevant by the intuitive equality argument), and is forced to choose principles of morality on this basis. The idea of distinct individuals denied such knowledge contracting with each other to choose these principles is an additional, and non-essential, element.

There is a clear sense, then, in which the original position is not an essentially contractarian idea, at least not if this involves distinct individuals contracting with each other. Since, however, Rawls is usually thought of – by himself as well as others – as a contractarian, I shall go on speaking of Rawls's position as a contractarian one. And I shall, sometimes, speak of the rules of morality chosen by a person in the original position as a contract. However, in future argument, the use I shall make of the concept of the original position is not an essentially contractarian one, it does not involve the notion of distinct individuals contracting with each other.

6. THE ORIGINAL POSITION AND ANIMAL RIGHTS

When the concept of the original position is properly understood, and when the connection between the description of the original position, the principles derivable from the position, and the intuitive equality argument is properly grasped, there is no reason to think that the bearers of the rights derivable from the original position are restricted to rational agents. The fact that it is (ideally) rational agents who, in the original position, are responsible for formulating the principles of morality does not entail that these principles, there-fore, subsume, or apply to, only rational agents. Indeed, given the nature of the intuitive equality argument, and the dependence of the description of the original position on this argument, it is clear why this claim should be rejected.

To see this, recall, firstly, the intuitive equality argument. The argument, in essence, runs as follows: If a property P is undeserved, in the sense that one is not responsible for possessing it, then it is morally arbitrary and one is not morally entitled to it. If one is not morally entitled to P, then one is also not morally entitled to whatever benefits stem from the possession of P. However, rationality seems to be an undeserved property if any property is. A person plays no role in deciding whether or not she is going to be rational; she either is or she is not. The decision is not hers, but nature's. Therefore, according to the terms of the intuitive equality argument, it is a morally arbitrary property, and one is not morally entitled to its possession. Therefore, also, one is not morally entitled to whatever benefits accrue from its possession. Therefore, to restrict the beneficiaries of the protection afforded by the contract to rational agents would be to contravene the intuitive equality argument. But it is the results of this argument which, in large part, determine the description of the original position, and hence the principles of morality we derive from the original position. Therefore, it is a restriction we cannot legitimately apply.

It is true that we sometimes speak of a person cultivating their rationality, or of endeavouring to do the rational thing in a given situation. And this may lead one to think that possession of rationality is something over which we have control, or even have to earn. However, this is not the sense of rationality that is relevant to the notion of moral consideration. This point is made quite forcefully by Rawls himself. No one, presumably, would want to claim that the more rational a person is, the more rights they have. Rationality, in the only sense possibly relevant to determination of moral rights, is what Rawls calls a *range property.*[22] For example, the property of being on the interior of the unit circle is a range property of points on a plane. All points inside the circle have this property although their coordinates vary within a certain range. And they all have this property equally. It is rationality conceived of as this sort of range property that is employed by Rawls. We all possess rationality, and we all do so equally, even if some of us do better on IQ tests than others. And conceived of in this way, it is clear that our possession of rationality is not something over which we have any control. Our possession of this property depends on nature, and not on our own decisions and actions. It is, therefore, a morally arbitrary property in Rawls's sense.

Therefore, it seems that, given the interdependence on the intuitive equality argument and the social contract argument, it seems that knowledge that one is a rational agent should be bracketed off in the original position. This is what the intuitive equality argument tells us. It is also worth noting that the claim that knowledge of one's own rationality should, in the original position, be bracketed coheres much better with one of Rawls's ways of characterizing the original position as one in which the participants have knowledge of all general principles of psychology, sociology, economics and the like, but *no* particular knowledge about themselves.[23] Since knowledge that one will be a rational agent is an obvious case of particular knowledge of the properties of oneself, it seems that this must be bracketed in the original position. And if one does not know that one will be a rational agent, then, if Rawls is correct, one will, in the original position, inevitably formulate principles that take this into account. And at the very least, this would bring non-rational beings under the scope of the difference principle.

Hence, when the relation between the social contract argument and the intuitive equality argument is correctly understood, it is seen that knowledge of one's own rationality must, for the sake of consistency, be bracketed in the original position. Hence, there is, or at least should be, nothing in Rawls's position which entails that non-rational creatures fall outside the sphere of justice. Similarly, there is nothing in the concept of the original position which entails that non-human animals fall outside the sphere of morality. On the contrary, once it is understood that what moral principles we can deduce from the original position depend on the description we give of that position, and once we understand that what we regard as an adequate description of this position derives from the consistent application of the intuitive equality argument, then we must allow that the principles of morality apply equally to both rational and non-rational individuals.

In fact, once the connection between the intuitive equality argument and the principles derivable from the original position is made clear, it seems that knowledge that one is a human being must also be bracketed in the original position. The property of being human is, again, something over which we have no choice. The property is undeserved in the sense that we are not responsible for possessing it. Therefore, according to the intuitive equality argument, the property is as morally arbitrary as the property of belonging to a given class, race, or gender. It is something over which we have no control. Therefore, according to the intuitive equality argument, we are not morally entitled to whatever benefits accrue from possession of this property. Therefore, given that the considerations underlying the intuitive equality argument are partly constitutive of the description we give of the original position, knowledge of one's human status is knowledge that should be bracketed in the original position. Therefore, if the above arguments are correct, the sphere of morality should not be restricted to human beings.

7. REFLECTIVE AND UNREFLECTIVE INTUITIONS

The central features of the account given so far are the following. Firstly, there are certain ideas, embodied in, broadly speaking, liberal democratic cultures, which can be accorded the status of intuitions on the grounds that many people intuit them, or claim to intuit them. These include the idea that we have no direct duties towards non-human animals and the idea that non-rational agents are not full members of the moral community. However, these intuitions are not consistent with a more basic principle which is arguably constitutive of, or essential to, contemporary liberal ideology. This principle, which underlies the intuitive equality argument, is the idea that possession of a property whose bearer has done nothing to merit, at least by itself, confers no moral entitlements on that bearer. It is this principle, and the intuitive equality argument based upon it, which, in large part, determine the description we are to give of the original position and, crucially, determine which epistemological factors are to be excluded by the veil of ignorance. And it is this description of the original position which will determine the principles of morality that can correctly be derived from it. Therefore, the original intuitions must, on pain of inconsistency, be rejected. Intuitions they may be, but they are not sufficiently *reflective* ones. And we are justified, of course, in rejecting these intuitions and not the intuitive equality argument because the latter is considerably more basic; it is what underlies and lends consistency and coherence to the very idea of contemporary liberal democracy, at least as developed by theorists such as Rawls. We can reject the intuitions concerning non-humans and non-rational agents without damaging the concept of democratic equality; but reject the intuitive equality argument, and the politics of liberal democracy go with it.

Interestingly enough, there are plenty of examples of unreflective intuitions of this sort which are endorsed – if I am right, incorrectly – by Rawls in *A Theory of Justice*. And these give rise to the idea that Rawls himself is committed to denying the moral claims of non-humans. Rawls himself, it is often thought, has ruled out bringing non-humans under the scope of the principles of justice. And, if this is true, how can we expect the suitably extended version of his argument to bring non-human animals under the scope of the principles of morality in general? This interpretation of Rawls is widespread and tenacious, but I think that his actual position is a lot more equivocal. Rawls says that it is *moral persons* who are entitled to equal justice, where,

> Moral persons are distinguished by two features: first they are capable of having (and are assumed to have) a conception of their good (as expressed by a rational plan of life); and second they are capable of having (and are assumed to acquire) a sense of justice, a normally effective desire to apply and to act upon the principles of justice, at least to a certain minimum degree.[24]

Most would agree that non-human animals are not moral persons in this sense. Does this mean that they are not owed justice in Rawls's sense? Only if being a moral person is a *necessary* condition of being owed justice. But, in fact, Rawls is quite clear that being a moral person is only a sufficient condition of falling under the scope of the principles of justice.

> We see, then, that the capacity for moral personality is a sufficient condition for being entitled to equal justice. Nothing beyond the essential minimum is required. *Whether moral personality is also a necessary condition I shall leave aside.*[25]

Unless Rawls is willing to claim that possession of moral personality is both a sufficient *and* necessary condition of being entitled to equal justice, there is nothing in his theory as such which rules out non-humans being entitled to equal justice. Since he is not willing to make this claim (and for good reason I think) we can conclude that there is nothing in Rawls's theory as such which rules out according equal justice to non-humans.

It is true that Rawls, at several points, claims that non-humans are not entitled to equal justice:

> Our conduct towards animals is not regulated by these principles, or so it is generally believed.[26]

> Presumably this excludes animals; they have some protection certainly, but their status is not that of human beings.[27]

> While I have not maintained that the capacity for a sense of justice is necessary in order to be owed the duties of justice, it does seem that we are not required to give strict justice anyway to creatures lacking this capacity.[28]

There is nothing in Rawls's theory as such, however, that entails, or in any way supports, these claims. In fact, if the arguments of earlier sections are correct, then consistent application of the intuitive equality argument would rule out these claims. The consistent application of the intuitive equality argument, that is, entails the negation of these claims. Since it is the consistent application of this argument which determines the correct description of the original position, and since it is the description of the original position which determines what principles of justice are derivable from it, the above claims are not compatible with the correct understanding of Rawls's theory. Rawls is, therefore, not entitled to make them. That is, this is a simple case of Rawls not perceiving all the entailments of his theory.

The hesitation Rawls has in making the above claims is in fact quite evident in the qualifications involved in them: 'or so it is generally believed'; 'presumably'; 'it does seem'. Hardly ringing endorsements. The claims, in fact, seem to have the status of what I earlier referred to as *unreflective intuitions*; intuitions enshrined in common sense, but not compatible with the consistent application of the intuitive equality argument. Since the consistent application of the intuitive equality argument is essential to achieving a state of reflective equilibrium, the above claims are not ones we would accept in a state of reflective equilibrium. That is, they are not *reflective* intuitions. Writing in the intellectual climate of that time, when the concept of animal liberation was not even a twinkle in Peter Singer's eye, one can, perhaps, excuse Rawls for falling victim here. But what one must do now is firmly distinguish the unreflective intuitions apparently endorsed by Rawls, but which are in fact incompatible with his theory, from the genuine entailments of that theory. The comments of Rawls listed above are not genuine entailments of his theory; they are in fact inconsistent with the genuine entailments of his theory.

8. OTHER OBJECTIONS

In the literature there are two further common objections to using contractarianism to underwrite the notion of animal rights.

The first of these runs as follows. Once we start extending the scope of morality to include non-humans, there is, in principle, no limit to this extension. If we are willing to accord moral rights to non-humans, why not accord it to plants, even to inanimate objects? This objection is easily met. The limits of morality are, on the contractarian approach, determined by what occupants of the original position should rationally care about. That is, the scope of morality is restricted to things that an occupant of the original position could rationally worry about being. I can, in the original position, worry about being at least certain sorts of non-human animal since there is something that it is like to be them (at least some of them). That is, non-human animals can, for example, suffer, and if I were one of them I wouldn't want this to happen to me. But if I were told that I was going to be a plant, or a car, then I couldn't care less what happened to me (and rationally so). Plants and cars are not sentient, hence do not suffer. Therefore, in the original position, I would not vote to include these under the scope of the principles of morality just in case I became one. The contractarian position, then, makes sentience the cut-off point for morality. And there is no worry of extending the scope of the principle of morality beyond this limit.[29]

Another objection is raised by Carruthers. According to Carruthers, extension of the contract to non-rational agents would 'destroy the theoretical coherence of Rawlsian contractualism'. He writes:

As Rawls has it, morality is, in fact, a human construction ... Morality is viewed as constructed *by* human beings, in order to facilitate interactions *between* human beings, and in order to make possible a life of co-operative community.[30]

Actually, I think that Rawls really says nothing of the sort. His theory is completely independent of any story concerning the origin of morality. I shall, for the sake of argument, ignore this rather obvious difficulty.

Even if we ignore this, however, the appeal to the origin of morality is rather curious since it automatically leads to a charge of *genetic fallacy*: roughly, the fallacy of confusing the *origin* of morality with the *content* of morality. Carruthers is quick to attempt to head off this charge by emphasizing that he is not claiming that moral statements are really disguised claims about the conditions of survival of the species. This is all very well, but there is, of course, more than one way of committing the genetic fallacy. The basic problem is this. Even if morality were constructed by human beings in order to facilitate inter-actions between human beings, it does not follow that this sort of origin exhausts the present content of morality, nor that it delimits its scope.

This sort of point is well made by Singer.[31] The origin of morality, in fact, might well lie in various mechanisms built in to social animals by a process of natural selection. These mechanisms, in various ways, facilitated social cooperation. If we want to talk about who 'devised' these mechanisms, then the only remotely plausible answer must be *genes*. The mechanisms were 'devised' by genes in order to facilitate the survival of genes through the social cooperation of their gene vehicles (i.e. social animals). Now, I'm not suggesting for a moment that this is true, though it does strike me as substantially more plaus-ible than Carruthers's story. The point is that even if it is true, it does not follow that the scope and content of morality is restricted to genes, the interaction of genes, and the survival of genes. As Singer points out, morality can develop in ways that are quite distinct from, and even incompatible with, its origin. Therefore, to think that the origin of morality determines the scope and content of morality is to commit the genetic fallacy; and Carruthers has committed this fallacy whatever his protestations to the contrary.

One final objection is perhaps worthy of note. It might be argued that it not possible to use a contractarian approach to underwrite the moral claims of animals because it is simply incoherent to suppose that, in the original position, one might not have the property of being human. To suppose that a person in the original position might turn out to have the property of being, say, a cow or a dog, is impossible because it violates every possible criterion of personal identity. You cannot suppose, for example, that you might turn out to be a cow because you could not possibly be the same individual as a cow.

Whatever individual you supposedly imagine you are in this situation, that individual would not, and could not, be you.

The first thing to be said against this objection is that it does not matter whether you suppose yourself to be a non-human animal or another human being. It is still the case that every possible criterion of personal identity will be violated by this supposition. If you were another human being you would have a different body and brain, so body- and brain-based criteria of personal identity would not apply. Also, since you would have a different set of memories and other psychological states, accounts of personal identity based on psychological continuity would also be inapplicable. Therefore, by any standard of personal identity, you could not, in the actual world, be the same person as one in the original position. And this applies whether you turn out to be non-human *or* human.

It might be thought that this renders Rawls's position incoherent. It does not, however, for the simple reason that, as emphasized in previous sections, the original position is not a place where one can be, it is simply a certain type of reasoning process. Therefore, talk of persons being 'in' the original position is metaphorical through and through. And, therefore, questions of the identity of persons in the original position with those outside it simply do not arise. To suppose that such questions do arise is to misunderstand the nature and status of the original position.

9. CONTRACTARIANISM AND VEGETARIANISM

In developing a contractarian account of animal rights, the hard work is defending the claim that non-human animals – and moral patients in general – are recipients of the protection offered by the contract, despite the fact that they are non-rational, and despite the fact that they cannot be regarded as contractors. The task of the preceding sections has been to provide just such a defence. Once this is done, the task of applying the contractarian approach to specific issues involving non-humans is relatively straightforward. Therefore, I do not propose to pursue the question of the application of the contract idea to specific issues in any great depth. Nonetheless, it might be instructive to see how such an application would proceed in the case of one particularly central issue involving non-human animals, namely the moral questions surrounding our raising and killing of non-humans for food.

The original position, it has been argued in this chapter, is a heuristic device that affords us a way of approaching moral problems. In a sense – in the thoroughly heuristic sense explained above – the original position gives us the opportunity to shape – in our minds at least – certain aspects of our world. We can ask ourselves: if I did not know who or what I was, or was going to be, and, therefore, if I did not know what characteristics, powers, aptitudes, needs, and so on I possess, how would I like the world to be? Even in the original position, however, our power to fashion, conceptually speaking, the ideal world is strictly limited. We can shape the moral and political relations that obtain in our ideal world, but we have no say over its natural order. We have to assume the laws of nature as presently given, and we have to assume that the world is, in all natural respects, the same as the world we presently inhabit. Our brief, provided by the original position, concerns the moral and political order, not the natural one.

According to the contractarian approach, in order to determine the morality of our raising and killing non-human animals for food – of engaging in animal husbandry in the broadest sense – we have to put ourselves in the original position. In this position, it has been argued, the veil of ignorance excludes knowledge of one's species, and one's status as a rational or moral agent. From the perspective of the original position, the limits of moral considerability, that is, the limits of what one can be morally concerned with, coincide with the class of individuals one can rationally worry about being. And this class can, for present purposes, be sub-divided into three: (a) human beings, (b) non-humans typically eaten by humans, and (c) non-humans not typically eaten by humans. In the original position, one does not know into which group one will fall. The two possibilities relevant to the question of the moral status of animal husbandry are, of course, that one might fall into (a) and (b). From the contractarian perspective, the morality of our raising and killing animals for food depends on the rationality of the choices we would make from behind the veil of ignorance. And, to determine this, we have to identify what the members of each category stand to gain and lose from such choices.

Consider, first, what humans beings would stand to lose from the widespread adoption of vegetarianism. To choose a world where vegetarianism was morally obligatory for humans would be to choose a world where humans, relative to the actual world, have to give up certain things. The first point to note, however, is that these things do not include life or health. In most environments at least, a healthy life is perfectly possible for a vegetarian, a fact attested to by the existence of millions of healthy vegetarians living in almost all parts of the world. There is no doubt, of course, that meat is a valuable source of nutrition, primarily because it provides all of the amino acids essential for human beings (i.e. amino acids that the human body is not capable of producing on its own). Meat, however, is not essential in this regard since the essential amino acids can also be obtained from suitable combinations of vegetable protein. And while the knowledge necessary for effecting such combinations is, perhaps, not currently widespread – due in large part to the prevalence of meat-eating in our society – this knowledge is in no way abstruse or recondite. The necessary knowledge is, in fact, no more complex than that required to combine suitable amounts of protein, carbohydrate, and fat in one's diet. Vegetarianism, then, does not ordinarily require humans to give up either their life or health.

If vegetarianism were to become widespread, the principal thing that humans would have to give up would be certain pleasures of the palate. Meat, for most people at least, is often delicious. Some vegetarians actually profess to dislike the taste of meat, others, however, having been persuaded by moral considerations, still dream of rump steaks, and of those heady days when pork ribs would be merrily crackling on the barbecue. While meat is undoubtedly tasty, it is perhaps easy to make too much of this. One who does like the taste of meat dishes is not thereby precluded from finding vegetarian dishes equally appetizing. It is not as if vegetarianism and eating palatable food are mutually exclusive options. To suppose that they are is simply to be ignorant of what it is possible to do with the humble vegetable.

Even if vegetarian dishes are less palatable than meat-based dishes, and it is not clear that they are, we have to weigh up humans' loss of certain pleasures of the palate against what the animals we eat have to give up because of our predilection for meat. Most obviously, of course, they have to give up their lives, and all the opportunities for the pursuing of interests and satisfaction of preferences that go with this. For most of the animals we eat, in fact, death may not be the greatest of evils. They are forced to live their short lives in appalling and barbaric conditions, and undergo atrocious treatment. Death for many of these animals is a welcome release.

When you compare what human beings would have to 'suffer' should vegetarianism become a widespread practice with what the animals we eat have to suffer given that it is not, then if one were to make a rational and self-interested choice in the original position, it is clear what this choice would be. If one did not know whether one was going to be a human or an animal preyed on by humans, the rational choice would surely be to opt for a world where vegetarianism was a widespread human practice and where, therefore, there was no animal husbandry industry. What one stands to lose as a human is surely inconsequential compared to what one stands to lose as a cow, or pig, or lamb. After all, how many lamb chops would one be prepared to accept for one's life? Therefore, the rational choice must be to opt for a world where vegetarianism was morally obligatory for humans. And if this is the rational choice in the original position, then, if contractarianism is correct, it is the moral choice in the actual world.

If this conclusion is not immediately obvious, then it can be supported by the following considerations. Suppose it were the case that there were two distinct groups of humans. One group, who we can call the *morlocks*, were cannibals, and they raised and killed another group of humans, the *eloi*, for food, in roughly the same manner in which we now raise and kill non-humans for food. Suppose, also, that like us the morlocks are easily capable of living on vegetable matter alone. The contractarian approach explains why the practice of the morlocks is wrong. In the original position, given that one does not know whether one was going to be a morlock or an eloi, it would be clearly irrational to opt for the above system. If one turned out to be an eloi one would be consigning oneself to a nasty fate, whereas if one turned out to be a morlock one would be perfectly capable of surviving by other means. Therefore, to opt, from behind the veil of ignorance, for the imagined morlock/eloi system would be clearly irrational. Therefore, if the contractarian approach is correct, this system is immoral.

So, in the case of human beings at least, to opt for the system of human husbandry described above would be clearly irrational. However, once we allow that non-humans are entitled to the protection of the contract, it does not matter whether one is considering a system of human husbandry or a system of animal husbandry. That is, if, in the original position, knowledge of one's species is excluded by the veil of ignorance, then it would be just as irrational to opt for a system of animal husbandry as it would be to opt for a system of human husbandry. Therefore, both systems are, from the standpoint of the original position, equally immoral.

In animal liberationist writings it is common to find the following principle being defended: don't do to animals what you wouldn't be prepared to do to similarly endowed humans. One of the virtues of the contractarian approach, I think, is that it shows clearly the basis of this principle. Once it is allowed that knowledge of one's species should be one of those things excluded by the veil of ignorance, it would be just as irrational to opt for a system that permitted harmful or injurious treatment of non-humans as it would be to opt for a system that permitted the same sort of treatment for humans. From the perspective of the original position, both options are equally irrational. Hence, if the contractarian approach is correct, both are equally immoral. The principle, 'Don't do to animals what you wouldn't be prepared to do to similarly endowed humans' is, then, derivable from the original position once we allow that knowledge of species membership should be bracketed by the veil of ignorance. And given that this is so, the principle can be used as a useful rule of thumb by which to judge our dealings with non-humans.

The above argument, at one point, mentioned the suffering undergone by animals involved in the husbandry industry. This may encourage the thought that if we could somehow eliminate this suffering, the original position might yield a contrary conclusion: that meat-eating is morally acceptable if the animals involved were treated well during their lives and then killed painlessly. On this suggestion, then, it is not in the killing of animals *per se* that the wrongness of eating meat consists in, but in the fact that they are treated so abominably when they are alive. On the present suggestion, the practice of factory farming should be firmly contrasted with that of hunting wild animals for food. This latter practice is morally legitimate, so the argument goes, because the animals here live natural, hence relatively satisfactory, lives. So, according to the present suggestion, if we eliminate factory farming and other intensive rearing practices and eat only non-domesticated or genuinely free-range animals, then our practice of eating meat can be defended.

While it is no doubt true that a world in which the human population ate only wild or genuinely free-range animals would be a morally better world than the actual one, it is still not the case that it would be better than a world where all humans were vegetarians. First of all, the suggestion that we should only eat non-domesticated or free-range animals is completely unfeasible given the present human population. This however, is not the main problem with the argument. The main problem concerns the morality of the suggestion, not its feasibility. We have the task of comparing two worlds: World 1, where all humans are vegetarians and world 2, where all humans eat only non-domesticated or free-range animals. To judge the relative moral status of the two worlds, one can return to the original position. There is a possibility that you will be a human, and there is also a possibility that you will be an animal killed and eaten by humans. If the former, then vegetarianism requires you to sacrifice certain pleasures of the palate. If the latter, then the failure of humans to adopt vegetarianism requires that you sacrifice your life. A relatively trivial interest of the human has to be weighed against the vital interest of the non-human. Once again there is no contest. If this is not immediately obvious, consider again the situation of the morlocks and the eloi. In H. G. Wells's *The Time Machine*, the eloi were allowed to lead idyllic lives before they were killed. Since they were killed while in a quasi-hypnotic trance, their deaths were also painless. Nonetheless, it would still surely be irrational to opt, from the original position, for the system of the morlock and eloi. If one turned out to be the latter, one loses one's life. If one turns out to be the former, then one can always survive by other means. Given that it would be irrational to opt for the system of the morlock and eloi, and given that, in the original position one has no knowledge of one's species, it must be equally irrational to opt for a world where animals are eaten by humans, assuming that humans can always survive by other means. And this holds irrespective of the quality of life enjoyed by the animal prior to its being killed and eaten. Therefore, the contractarian position yields the conclusion that vegetarianism is morally obligatory, even if the non-humans we propose to eat are treated well and have happy lives.

Two further consequences of the contractarian position are worthy of note. The first concerns the moral relation between predator and prey. The practice of animal husbandry is often defended, usually more in the popular arena than the philosophical, on the grounds that other animals kill and eat each other. If some animals kill and eat other animals, then why shouldn't we? Or so the argument goes. More precisely, if the lion's preying on the gazelle is not morally wrong, then why should our preying on cows, pigs, or lambs be so? On the other hand, if our preying on cows, pigs and lambs is morally wrong, then why wouldn't the gazelle have a case against the lion?

This sort of objection is often met with the claim that lions, unlike us, are not moral agents. That is, they are unable to morally assess their actions by dispassionately evaluating then in the light of the moral principles they embody, or with which they conflict. Hence the lion cannot be charged with doing anything wrong in killing the gazelle. However, this reply, by itself, will not do the work required of it. For, while the lion might not be doing anything for which it can be morally blamed, we might still have a duty to render assistance to the gazelle in precisely the same way in which we might have a duty to prevent a person being harmed by any innocent threat. If a baby has acquired possession of a loaded gun and is firing it in the direction of passers-by, then the baby, not being a moral agent, is not doing anything for which it can be morally blamed. It is what we can call an innocent threat. Nevertheless, if I am, at fairly minimal risk to myself, able to dispossess the baby, then it seems, *prima facie*, that I have a duty to render assistance to the innocent bystanders by doing so. Similarly, even if the lion cannot be blamed for what it does to the gazelle, we might still have a duty of assistance to the gazelle.

The claim that we have a duty of assistance to prey animals is, I think will be accepted by most, clearly intolerable. Fortunately, however, the contractarian position does not entail that we have such a duty. In the original position, one of things one docs not know is whether one is going to be incarnated as a predatory animal or as a prey animal, as a carnivore or a herbivore. Given that this is so, to opt for any moral principle which entailed that moral agents have duties of assistance to prey animals would be potentially disastrous. It potentially condemns one to a slow death through starvation. Hence, if one does not know whether one is going to be a carnivore or herbivore, it would be irrational to choose a world which contained such a principle. Even if one turned out to be a herbivore, in fact, the principle would almost certainly prove counterproductive. One of the things one would know in the original position – since one is in possession of all laws pertaining to the natural world – is the role predators play in culling the weaker members of any group of prey animals, thus ensuring the continuing health of the group. One would also know that any situation where a prey animal's natural predator has (almost always at the hand of man) been eradicated is a situation in which the number of prey animals explodes so drastically that disease and starvation are the inevitable result. Even if one turns out to be a prey animal, therefore, opting for a world where moral agents have duties to protect one from one's predators is to opt for a world where the likelihood of one's succumbing to disease or starvation is greatly increased. Thus, there is nothing in the contractarian position which entails that moral agents have duties of assistance to prey animals. With regard to the relation between predators and the animals upon which they prey, the contractarian position is this: Let them be!

A second consequence of the contractarian position concerns

certain sorts of human societies living, as we say, on the margins of existence. One important difference between humans and other predators is that humans, typically, are quite capable of surviving without eating meat. This is not, however, true of all humans. There are, of course, certain human societies occupying the margins of existence where eating of meat is essential to survival for the simple reason that supplies of vegetable protein are scarce or non-existent. The *innuit* provide an obvious example. In such cases, the humans involved must be classified as, for all practical purposes, carnivores: creatures unable to survive without eating meat. The original position allows that it is morally acceptable for these people to eat meat. In the original position, to adopt a rule which proscribed this would be irrational; it would be to adopt a rule that potentially sealed one's own fate. More generally, according to the contractarian position, the class of human beings who, for whatever reason, are unable to survive without eating meat should be treated along the same lines as any other carnivore. It is perfectly acceptable for such individuals to eat meat, nor do we have any duties of assistance to the animals upon which they prey.

Perhaps the major argument employed by defenders of the practice of animal husbandry appeals to economic considerations; it focuses on the economic impact that widespread vegetarianism would have, both on those employed in the animal husbandry industry, and on their dependants. The livelihoods of many people – farmers, factory owners, meat packers, transporters, retailers, veterinarians, etc. – are bound up with the success of the animal husbandry industry. Should the industry fail, as it would if vegetarianism became widespread, these people would stand to lose the proverbial shirts off their backs. This would impact not only on those employed in the industry but also on their dependants. Therefore, it can be, and frequently is, argued, the practice of animal husbandry can successfully be defended by appeal to these sorts of considerations.

Indeed, it might be thought that we could frame these considerations to dovetail nicely with the contractarian framework. In the original position, one does not know what place in society one will occupy. It could turn out, therefore, that one is employed in the animal husbandry industry, or is a dependant of someone so employed. Therefore, it would be irrational to opt for any moral principle which had as a consequence that the animal husbandry industry should be prohibited. In opting for such a principle, one is potentially consigning oneself to financial ruin.

Actually, as I shall try to show, the contractarian position has no truck with this sort of appeal to economic considerations. And any suggestion that it does rests, I think, on a serious misunderstanding of what sorts of considerations can be relevantly incorporated into one's deliberations in the original position. In the remainder of this section, I shall, first, sketch what I think the contractarian position is with regard to the appeal to economic considerations, and, secondly, attempt to diagnose the misunderstanding of the notion of the original position which might lead to the perception that economic considerations are morally relevant.

According to the contractarian position, the appeal to economic considerations is, in the above case, illegitimate. The morality of the practice of raising and killing animals for food should be decided from the original position, and, in that position, the only relevant considerations are what humans and the animals upon which they prey stand to lose from the abandonment or continuation of the practice. But, for reasons which will become clear, economic losses (or gains) cannot legitimately be included as relevant factors in this. The contractarian position, here, can perhaps best be understood in relation to its position on the practice of slavery.

The contractarian position on slavery is that the institution is unjust and, hence, cannot be legitimately defended by appeal to the economic benefits that may accompany it. One cannot legitimately defend an unjust institution by appealing to economic benefits that it may bring. Thus, the abolition of slavery in, for example, the southern United States was the morally correct course of action, even though it had a devastating impact on the livelihoods of those employed in the cotton industry and on their dependants. In fact, abolition undoubtedly had a calamitous impact on the economy of the South a whole, leaving the region in a desperate economic slump from which, arguably, it is still recovering today. Nevertheless, according to the contractarian pos-ition, since slavery was an unjust institution, abolishing it was the correct thing to do. And it would not be legitimate to attempt to defend slavery by appealing to the desirable economic consequences of its retention. This is not to say that economic considerations can never be morally relevant factors; clearly they can. However, they can be employed as morally relevant considerations only when the institutions they are used to evaluate satisfy certain standards of justice. Slavery does not do so, and therefore cannot be defended by appeal to economic considerations. According to the contractarian position defended here, the same attitude should be

taken with regard to the animal husbandry industry. The institution as
a whole is unjust, and, therefore, cannot be defended by appeal to
economic factors.

The contractarian position in this regard can be made clearer by
contrast with that of utilitarianism. All forms of utilitarianism would
have to include economic considerations as morally relevant. And, for
utilitarianism, whether or not an institution such as slavery counts as
just or not is something that can only be decided after all these
considerations have been taken into account. For the contractarian,
on the other hand, there is a prior standard of justice, and economic
considerations will be morally relevant to the evaluation of an institution only if it meets this standard. And the standard is provided by
someone in the original position reasoning in accordance with his or
her own best interests.

That is the attitude that, I think, the contractarian position takes
with regard to the practice of raising and killing non-humans for
food, and to any appeal to economic considerations in defence of that
practice. What now needs to be shown is exactly *why* the appeal to
economic considerations is, from the contractarian perspective,
illegitimate. To see why this is so, consider the following two situations. In scenario 1, you and three others are sat at a table and you
are informed by a fifth person that he is going to distribute
£1 000 000 between you. You are further told that one of you will
receive £999 999.97 while the other three will receive one penny each.
None of you knows, let us suppose, which one will get the fortune.
Scenario 2 is importantly different. In scenario 2, you are again sat
at a table with three others and you are informed that you are, collectively, to receive £1 000 000. However, in this scenario, you are
required to divide the money into four sums; and prior to this division, you do not know who will receive which sum. The difference
between the two cases, then, is that in the former you have no control
over the distribution of money; it is something outside your control,
a brute fact with which you are simply presented. In the second case,
however, the distribution of the money is something which is, so to
speak, up for grabs; something to be fixed by negotiation amongst
yourselves.

It is important to realize that it is only the second situation that
corresponds to the original position. The point of the original position is for you to effect a distribution of, among other things,
economic resources and relations, and not to simply be presented
with an already existing distribution of such things. So, a situation

constituted by (i) an already existing distribution of economic resources and relations, and (ii) a decision that you have to make on the basis of this pre-existing distribution, is not an instance of the original position. The distribution of economic resources and relations is precisely one of the things that is up for grabs in the original position. The claim that economic considerations can legitimately be included in the original, then, depends on seeing the position as setting the following question: 'Given that economic resources are directed towards the animal husbandry industry in such a way that the individuals employed therein, and their dependants, will suffer serious financial hardship should the industry fail, what moral rules would you like to see adopted?' This, however, is emphatically not the question the original position sets us. The question of whether economic resources should be directed in such a way is precisely one of the things that is up for negotiation in the original position. In other words, the economic arguments against vegetarianism would work only if the original position functioned in the manner of scenario 1; that is, against a background of antecedently assumed economic relations. It does not function in this way however. The direction of economic resources and the resulting character of economic relations are themselves open to negotiation in the original position.

Once this is understood, it becomes evident that the economic arguments against vegetarianism have no force. In the original position, you are able to opt for a world where there is an animal husbandry industry, and you are also able to opt for a world where there is no animal husbandry industry. The relative moral status of the two worlds depends on the rationality of the choice one makes. Given that you don't know whether you will be human or non-human, eater or eaten, and given that you cannot assume any antecedent economic circumstances, it is fairly clear that to opt for the latter world – the world without an animal husbandry industry – would be the rational choice. And it is this fact, if the contractarian position is correct, which makes the practice of raising and killing animals for food morally wrong.

10. CONCLUSION

This chapter has been concerned with a contractarian approach to morality in general, and with its application to the concept of animal rights. The approach developed here has been based on the position developed by Rawls, but is, I think, sufficiently distinct from Rawls's position to be dubbed *neo-Rawlsianism*. The approach developed here is not restricted to the development of principles of justice, conceived of as governing interactions between individuals and the basic structures of society, but concerns the delineation of principles of morality in general. In addition, several key Rawlsian concepts have been reinterpreted. I have argued that a contractarian approach of this neo-Rawlsian sort can provide a sound theoretical foundation for the attribution of rights to non-human animals. The key to this is understanding how two central aspects of Rawls's pos-ition converge. The social contract argument depends on the intuitive equality argu-ment in the sense that the latter determines the acceptability of the description of the original position, and this determines which prin-ciples of morality we shall accept. Consistent application of the intuitive equality argument, I have claimed, will yield a certain sort of description of the original position. This description of the original position will, in turn, yield principles of morality which apply not only to human beings (i.e. rational agents) but also to many sorts of non-human animals. The final section looked at one application of this general framework: the moral case for vegetarianism.

7 Animal Minds

1. INTRODUCTION: MORALITY AND MENTALITY

The contractarian defence of animal rights, defended in the previous chapter, requires that non-human animals possess at least some sorts of mental states. According to the contractarian position, the limits of moral consideration are determined by what, from the perspective of the original position, one could rationally worry about being. That is, the boundaries of moral considerability coincide with those of *sentience*. Therefore, in order for the contractarian defence to work, we must at least be able to attribute conscious states to non-human animals.

It is common to distinguish broadly between two categories of mental states: *sensations* and *propositional attitudes*.[1] The category of sensations incorporates two quite different sorts of state. On the one hand, sensations include bodily feelings like pains, tickles, orgasms, and nausea. On the other, they also include perceptual or quasi-perceptual experiences like seeming to see a pink cadillac or a pink elephant, hearing a loud trumpet or a mellow sax, tasting a sweet strawberry or a bitter lemon. Experiences of this latter sort are distinguished from bodily feelings in that they are *about* something; each of them has what is known as an *intentional object*. The reason both bodily feelings and perceptual (or quasi-perceptual) experiences are classified together as sensations is because they share a crucial common feature: they are both defined by their *phenomenology*, that is by how they seem to their subjects. What it is to undergo a sensation, in this broad sense, is a matter of what it is like for the subject of a sensation. Sensations, that is, are essentially conscious states: to have a certain sensation is simply to be in a particular conscious state. Therefore, attribution of conscious states to animals presupposes, at the very least, that they can be bearers of sensations.

The connection between propositional attitudes and consciousness is not quite so direct. Propositional attitudes are mental states that have what is known as *content*. That is, they are states whose ascription to a person involves the use of a 'that'-clause, as in 'Jones believes that the sky is blue'. The class of propositional attitudes includes not only cognitive states like beliefs, but also conative and

159

affective states – desiring, hoping, fearing, anticipating, dreading, etc. Propositional attitudes, unlike sensations, are not defined by a distinctive phenomenology. Believing that one is the owner of a pink cadillac, for example, is compatible with a variety of different feelings: pride, embarrassment, remorse, etc. Moreover, propositional attitudes are not essentially conscious states. One's belief, for example, that Ouagadougou was the capital of (what used to be) the Upper Volta presumably manifests itself only rarely on the conscious stage.[2] Nonetheless, one can still have this belief even if one is only seldom aware that one has it. Propositional attitudes are what are known as *dispositional* states: whether or not one has a propositional attitude is a matter of one's behaviour, typically one's dispositional behaviour. Thus, for example, if someone asked me if I believed that Ouagadougou was the capital of what used to be the Upper Volta, I would reply in the affirmative. Nevertheless, while propositional attitudes are not essentially conscious states, it is usually thought that they are essentially states that can, in appropriate circumstances, be made conscious. This may sometimes be easy, and if theorists such as Freud are correct, it may sometimes be extremely difficult. Nonetheless, it is usually thought that propositional attitudes can, at least in principle, be made conscious. And, their capacity for becoming conscious is a property they have essentially; nothing can count as a propositional attitude unless it is, at least potentially, conscious.

Whether or not this latter claim is true, there are good reasons for thinking that the contractarian defence of animal rights requires the attribution of propositional attitudes to animals. From the perspective of the original position, in order to decide how one would like the moral and social world to be if one were a member of species S, one must have some idea of the *preferences* of typical members of S. And preference is a propositional attitude. In fact, preference is a certain type of desire: a desire that a particular alternative or situation should obtain as opposed to others. Moreover, it is plausible to suppose that possession of desires by an organism entails that it also possesses beliefs. It is difficult to see, for example, how one can desire a book (or, more precisely, desire that one have the book) without believing that one does not presently have the book. Possession of a certain desire, entails possession of certain associated beliefs. And, so, if the contractarian defence requires attribution of desires to non-humans, it also requires attribution of beliefs.

Therefore, I shall assume that if the contractarian approach is genuinely applicable to the case of non-human animals, it must be possible to attribute both sensations and propositional attitudes beyond the merely human sphere. There is, in fact, nothing particularly idiosyncratic about the contractarian approach in this regard. Most, if not all, attempts to bring non-human animals into the moral sphere presuppose, at least implicitly, that they are the possessors of mental states of both categories. As we have seen, Peter Singer's argument for animal liberation derives from his preference utilitarianism, and its application to non-humans presupposes that they are the bearers of preferences. Tom Regan's defence of animal rights depends essentially on the claim that certain sorts of non-humans are subjects-of-a-life, where an individual is a subject-of-a-life only if it has beliefs, desires, perceptions, memories, etc. and a sense of the future, including its own future. Therefore, a sound defence of the practice of ascribing mental states to non-human animals can quite plausibly be regarded as a cornerstone of the attempt to bring them under the umbrella of moral considerability.

The most direct way, therefore, of blocking the inclusion of non-humans under the moral umbrella would be by denying that they have a mental life. At one time, such a denial was widely accepted, and inspired by such notable philosophers as Descartes and Malebranche. In present times, however, any blanket denial of the mental life of animals strikes us as patently absurd. That is, it is now widely accepted that many sorts of non-human animals are possessors of sensations. All the evidence – behavioural, evolutionary, neurophysiological and anecdotal – points unequivocally in this direction. And the attribution of sensations to non-humans is no longer a serious issue.

It is often thought that the attribution of propositional attitudes to non-humans is more problematic. Contemporary efforts to exclude non-humans from the sphere of morality by excluding them from the sphere of mentality focus on the attribution of propositional attitudes. If a conceptual line in the sand is to be drawn, it is argued, then beliefs, desires and propositional mental states provide us with the necessary stick. Accordingly, it is with the attribution of propositional attitudes to non-humans that this chapter is concerned.

2. THE HOLISM OF THE MENTAL

The case against the possibility of attributing propositional attitudes to non-humans has been developed by several authors, most notably

Donald Davidson and Stephen Stich. All these arguments, however, clearly tend to converge on a single Ur-argument. And the conceptual centrepiece of this argument is a principle sometimes referred to as the *holism of the mental*. Davidson develops his case as follows.

Suppose we watch a dog chase a cat who runs up an oak tree, and then disappears from sight. The dog remains barking at the foot of the tree, looks upward, etc. It seems plausible to suppose that the dog believes that the cat is up the tree (and that the dog desires to catch the cat). However, Davidson argues that this supposition is problematic. He writes:

> Can the dog believe of an object that it is a tree? This would seem impossible unless we suppose the dog has many general beliefs about trees: that they are growing things, that they need soil and water, that they have leaves or needles, that they burn. There is no fixed list of things someone with the concept of a tree must believe, but without many general beliefs there would be no reason to identify a belief as a belief about a tree, much less an oak tree. Similar considerations apply to the dog's supposed thinking about the cat.[3]

The moral, according to Davidson, is this:

> We identify thoughts, distinguish between them, describe them for what they are, only as they can be located within a dense network of related beliefs. If we really can intelligibly ascribe single beliefs to a dog, we must be able to imagine how we would decide whether the dog has many other beliefs of the kind necessary for making sense of the first.[4]

But this creates a problem:

> It seems to me that no matter where we start, we very soon come to beliefs such that we have no idea at all how to tell whether a dog has them, and yet such that, without them, our confident first attribution looks shaky.[5]

The principle assumed in these passages is the principle of the holism of the mental which, following Davidson, I shall understand as primarily a principle governing the *attribution* of beliefs (and other propositional attitudes) to individuals. The principle can be stated as follows:

> *Holism of the mental*: the attribution of a single belief or other propositional attitude to an individual requires, and only makes

sense in terms of, the attribution of a network or system of related beliefs (or other propositional attitudes).[6]

As the first passage makes clear, Davidson's worries in this regard ultimately stem from concerns about the possibility of attributing content to the supposed belief of the dog. This is reflected in the fact that the principle of the holism of the mental, a principle governing the attribution of beliefs to individuals, derives from a distinct thesis, one which concerns the identity of the content, or meaning, that beliefs possess. We can refer to this latter thesis as the principle of *content holism*:

> *Content holism*: the content of a belief (or other propositional attitude) possessed by an individual is determined by the relations which that content bears to the contents of all other beliefs (or other propositional attitudes) possessed by that individual.[7]

Thus, we cannot attribute content to the alleged belief of the dog (i.e. that the cat is up the tree) because content is fixed by the content of other beliefs; such as the claim that trees are growing things, that they need soil and water, etc. Therefore, we cannot attribute the requisite content to the dog since the surrounding beliefs that are constitutive of that content are missing. Content, however, is essential to any belief. A belief is, at least in part, identified by way of its content. The belief that the cat is in the tree, for example, is distinguished from the belief that the cat is in the house by way of the distinct contents of the beliefs. Therefore, since content is essential to beliefs, if we cannot attribute the content, we cannot attribute the belief. Therefore, we cannot attribute to the dog the belief that the cat is up the tree.

A similar line of argument is developed by Stich. Stich also sees the crucial difficulty in attributing beliefs to non-humans as deriving from a problem in identifying their content. In 'Do Animals Have Beliefs?', Stich argues that the question of what content can be ascribed to non-humans is moot.[8] The question has no answer. In his later book, *From Folk Psychology to Cognitive Science*, he takes a somewhat more conciliatory stance when he claims that the question is hopelessly *context-relative*. In some conversational contexts, ascription of content based states to a non-human animal would be correct, but in other contexts, ascription of the same content based state to the same animal at the same time would be incorrect.[9]

Stich's argument is based on his analysis of the concept of belief, and the corresponding notion of belief content. According to Stich, the relation of content-identity is, in fact, a similarity relation. The notion of the content of a belief can be factored into three elements: causal-pattern similarity, ideological similarity, and reference similarity.

A pair of beliefs count as similar along the dimension of *causal-pattern similarity* if they have similar patterns of potential causal interaction with other beliefs and with (actual or possible) stimuli. In addition to *global* causal-pattern similarity, there are various dimensions along which a pair of beliefs can be *partially* causal-pattern similar. For example, a pair of beliefs may interact similarly with other beliefs in inference, but may have different links with stimuli. These beliefs would count as similar when the context focuses on inferential connections, but as rather dissimilar when the context focuses interest on the connections between belief and perception. Causal-pattern similarity is the feature that is focused upon by classical functionalist accounts of content.

The second sort of feature used to assess similarity of beliefs is what Stich calls *ideological similarity*. The ideological similarity of a pair of beliefs is a function of the extent to which the beliefs are embedded in similar networks of belief. Ideological similarity measures the 'doxastic neighbourhood' in which a given pair of belief states find themselves. As in the case of causal-pattern similarity, partial ideological similarity is often more important than global ideological similarity. Since belief states are compound entities, ideological similarity can be assessed separately for the several concepts that compose a belief. And context can determine which concepts are salient in the situation at hand. For example, suppose the context focuses on 'bourgeois'. Then if Jack and Jill both say, 'Abstract art is bourgeois', we may count them as having similar beliefs if their other beliefs invoking the bourgeois concept are similar, even if they have notably different beliefs invoking their abstract art concept. But if the difference in their conceptions of abstract art looms large in the context, our judgement will be reversed, and they will not count as having similar beliefs.

The third sort of feature used in assessing belief state similarity is *reference similarity*. According to Stich, a pair of beliefs count as reference similar if the *terms* the subjects use to express the beliefs are identical in reference. What actually fixes reference is not an easy matter to decide. One prime candidate is the causal history of the term, a causal chain stretching back through the user's concept, through the concept of the person from whom he acquired the term, and so on back to the person or stuff denoted. A second candidate, defended by Wittgenstein, Burge, and others, is the use of the term in the speaker's linguistic community. Neither of these accounts is free from difficulties. And Stich does not wish to adjudicate between these accounts. He does say, however, that in his view context is an important determinant of reference.

According to Stich, therefore, the notion of sameness of content, hence the notion of sameness of belief, is a complex concept which straddles all three features of causal-pattern, ideological, and reference similarity. Depending on the context of discussion, one or more of these factors can assume primary importance.

When we attribute content to an individual, either human or non-human, therefore, our attribution is carried by one or more of these three factors. Stich, however, claims that reference similarity is inapplicable to non-humans. The reason is that, according to Stich, a pair of beliefs count as reference similar if the *terms* the subjects use to express the beliefs are identical. This characterization, of course, automatically makes the concept of reference similarity inapplicable to non-language using creatures. Therefore, reference similarity can play no role in determining the content of the beliefs of non-linguistic creatures. Determination of the content of such beliefs, therefore, is solely a matter of the causal pattern and ideological network in which the beliefs are embedded. But this entails that there are strongly holistic constraints on the concept of content-identity. If causal-pattern and ideological similarity are the only determinants of the content of a belief, then such content will be solely a function of the causal and ideological relations that the belief bears to other beliefs. However, it is very implausible to suppose that the causal-pattern and ideological networks of beliefs present in non-human animals will be in any way similar to those present in humans. And, therefore, Stich claims, since this is all we have to go on in the case of non-humans, we are unable to attribute content to non-human animals. But, since content is essential to beliefs and other propositional attitudes, this means that we are unable to attribute these states to them also. The prospect of attributing propositional attitudes to non-humans founders on the impossibility of attributing content to them.

Therefore, Stich, like Davidson, identifies the problem of attributing beliefs and other propositional attitudes to non-humans as deriving from the problem of attributing content to such creatures. And, in both cases, the problem in attributing content to them, derives from the holism, and the constraints it imposes, that is constitutive of content. In fact, in both Davidson and Stich, we find essentially the following argument.

(1) We can attribute a belief (or other propositional attitude) to a non-human animal only if we can attribute content to that belief.

(2) We can attribute content to the belief of a non-human animal only if it possesses a broad network of related beliefs that is largely similar to our own.

(3) Non-human animals do not possess a broad network of beliefs that is largely similar to our own.

(4) Therefore, we cannot attribute content to the beliefs of non-human animals.

(5) Therefore, we cannot attribute beliefs to non-human animals.

The same argument applies, *mutatis mutandis*, to all propositional attitudes. This is by far the most important argument against attributing mental states to animals. Indeed, I think that ultimately it is the only remotely plausible argument against doing so. Fortunately, at least for the moral claims of animals, the argument fails. The remainder of the chapter will be concerned with explaining exactly why it does so.

3. AN UNSUCCESSFUL REFUTATION

At this point it may be worthwhile to pause and consider Regan's attempt to meet the challenge provided by the holism of the mental.[10] As I shall try to show, Regan's challenge fails, but its failure is, I think, nonetheless instructive.

Regan begins by distinguishing two conceptions of what is involved in possessing a concept of a given object x (e.g. a tree). The first of these is what he calls the *all-or-nothing view*. According to this view, the concept of x, possessed by an individual, is constituted by *all* the beliefs held by that individual regarding x. Thus, if two individuals differ with regard to the beliefs they hold about x, then they have distinct concepts of x. Thus, since the beliefs I have about trees differ from the beliefs had by our imagined dog, we possess distinct concepts of a tree. Thus, it is not possible to attribute to the dog the belief that the cat is up the tree. The dog does not possess the concept of a tree and, therefore, cannot possess any beliefs about trees.

As Regan points out, there are serious problems with the all-or-nothing view. It is implausible to suppose that any of us share precisely the same beliefs about anything. And, if the all-or-nothing view were correct, this fact would preclude us from sharing any concepts. If every belief we might have about trees is relevant to the determination of the concept of a tree, then, it seems overwhelmingly likely that each one of us, or at least most of us, will have distinct concepts of a tree. But this would render communication about trees impossible. If the all-or-nothing view of concepts were correct, it is not communication, but equivocation, which would be the rule. And the possibility of attributing beliefs to anyone, not only dogs, would be undermined.

Regan contrasts the all-or-nothing view with what he calls the *more-or-less* view. According to this view, concept possession is a matter of degree. The more beliefs two individuals share about x, the more they share the same concept of x. Children, for example, who know that trees are growing things, that they need soil and water, but not that they produce the energy they require by photosynthesis share, to some extent, our concept of a tree. The more-or-less view has distinct advantages over the all-or-nothing view. Primarily, it allows us to make sense of the attribution of concepts, and hence beliefs, to normal adult members of our own culture (something the all-or-nothing view was hard pressed to do) and also to children, to members of different cultures, to the mentally enfeebled, and so on (something the all-or-nothing view could certainly not do).

Assuming that the more-or-less view of concepts is preferable to the all-or-nothing view, Regan then attempts to use it to establish the validity of attributing content to non-humans. In this context, Regan introduces the idea of a *preference-belief*. Let us call our imagined dog 'Brenin', and give him a bone (perhaps to make up for the disappointment of missing out on the cat). Can Brenin have the belief that we are giving him a bone? Given the arguments of Davidson and Stich, this will depend on whether Brenin possesses the concept of a bone, and this, in turn, will depend on whether he has the requisite beliefs about bones. But, as Regan points out, we can be reasonably sure that Brenin possesses at least one belief about bones: he believes that bones satisfy certain desires and are to be chosen to satisfy those desires. That is, he believes that the bone will satisfy his desire for a particular flavour and should be chosen if he wishes to satisfy that desire.

Thus, Brenin's behaviour surely licenses attribution to him of at least this preference-belief. But, Regan argues, this is one of the beliefs that define the content of our concept of a bone. Therefore, given the more-or-less view of content possession, we can say that Brenin possesses our concept of a bone, at least more-or-less.

This attempt to enfranchise Brenin is certainly ingenious. Unfortunately, it too possesses serious problems. Firstly, it is not clear that the switch to the more-or-less view solves the problem of communication afflicting the all-or-nothing view. Vastly different sorts of information can, on the more-or-less view be associated with possession of the same concept. But if we assume that it is information that gets transmitted in communication, the problem of equivocation still looms large. Secondly, it is at least arguable that the plausibility of the more-or-less view stems from its confusing two quite different senses of 'more-or-less believing that p'. On the one hand there is the relatively innocuous idea that agents can differ in their *epistemic commitment* to p (I will nail my flag to p; you grant p only your provisional assent). This idea is not at issue. On the other hand there is the idea that *content identity* is a matter of degree. There is a big difference between the claim that one can more or less believe that p, and the claim that what one believes is more or less p. And it is the second claim that is at issue here. The idea that there might be something that is almost, but not quite, the proposition that there is a bone buried in the yard seems to make little sense.

Third, and most importantly, however, even though Davidson and Stich clearly reject the all-or-nothing view of concept possession, they would still not accept Regan's premise that possession of a single belief is sufficient for possession of a concept, even to a degree. Davidson, for example, writes:

> There is no fixed list of things someone with the concept of a tree must believe, but without many general beliefs there would be no reason to identify a belief as a belief about a tree, much less an oak tree.[11]

Possession of a concept does not require possession of any fixed list of beliefs; hence the all-or-nothing view should be rejected. However, it does require a certain threshold number of beliefs. Possession of a single preference belief about a bone, for example, is presumably not sufficient for possession of the concept of a bone. What Regan has presented us with, in effect, is a false dilemma. We are not forced to choose between an all-or-nothing view of concept possession which makes communication between distinct individuals a practical impossibility, and a more-or-less view which entails that possession of even a single belief is sufficient for possession of a concept. Davidson and

Stich adopt a third alternative: possession of many beliefs about x is required for possession of the concept of x, but possession of any fixed list of beliefs is not. We might call this a *cluster theory* of concept possession.

Therefore, I think we should conclude that Regan's attempt to psychologically enfranchise animals fails. At this point we may encounter a temptation to which many defenders of non-human mentality have succumbed. As DeGrazia, for example, points out, there is no straightforward inference from the claim that the content of animal beliefs is inexpressible by us to the claim that, therefore, they possess no content.[12] There is no reason to suppose, that is, that content must be expressible by us humans in order to count as content. This claim is quite correct, but tempts us into yielding too much to the argument from holism. The temptation is to simply yield and allow that while non-humans may possess beliefs and other propositional attitudes, the content of those attitudes is forever inexpressible by us. They have beliefs, but we can never know what those beliefs are. I think that this grants far too much to the arguments of Davidson and Stich. It is, in fact, perfectly possible to make accurate and determinate attributions of content, and hence of content-based states, to non-human animals. In the remainder of this chapter, I shall try to show why.

4. ATTRIBUTING CONTENT

The argument to be developed in the remainder of the chapter runs as follows. First, I shall argue that the content of any belief is constituted by two factors. On the one hand there is the *mode of representation* of the belief, that is, the way or manner in which the belief represents what is known as its intentional object, that is, the thing that the belief is about. On the other, there is the reference of the belief; the object that the belief takes as its intentional object. The content of the belief supervenes on, or is determined by, both factors taken together. Secondly, and in consequence, the attribution of a belief to an individual can be carried by, or based on, either of these factors. Sometimes, our attribution of a belief to an individual will be based on the way or manner in which that belief represents its intentional object; sometimes it will be carried by the intentional object itself and not its mode of representation. Thus, attribution of a belief can, in different contexts, be sensitive to distinct and non-reducible factors, and this affects our conception of the beliefs thus attributed. Third, attributions of belief based on, or sensitive to, the referent of the belief, and not its mode of representation, are not constrained by the sorts of holistic considerations adduced by Davidson and Stich. That is, an attribution of a belief to an individual that is sensitive to the object of the belief, and not the mode of representation of that object, does not depend on, or in any way require, that the belief be embedded in a network of beliefs. Fourth, and finally, attribution of beliefs to non-humans can therefore be carried, and justified, on the basis of knowledge of the reference of those beliefs; knowledge of the mode of representation of the beliefs is not necessary.

Content and Reference

The content of any belief (or other propositional attitude) is constituted by two distinct and non-reducible factors. The content of any belief depends on its intentional object, that is, on the object the belief is a belief about. Part of the content here derives from what is known as the *mode of representation* of the object; that is, the way in which the object is represented. But part of the content derives from the object itself, and not from its mode of representation. This point was brought to prominence by now classic thought experiments developed by Hilary Putnam and Tyler Burge.[13] Here is Putnam's version. The basic idea is now well known, so I shall be brief.

We are to conceive of a near duplicate of our planet: twin-earth. Not only are the physical environments of earth and twin-earth largely identical, but many inhabitants of earth have duplicate counterparts on twin-earth. These counterparts are type-identical with their corresponding earthlings with respect to physical constitution, and also with respect to experiential and dispositional histories, where these are specified non-intentionally. The key difference between the two planets is that the liquid on twin-earth that runs in rivers and taps, although qualitatively identical with the liquid that we, on earth, refer to with the term 'water', is not in fact water, but, rather, a distinct substance. Thus, although the twin earthlings refer to this substance with the term 'water', it is not water since it is not a substance with a chemical structure made up of two parts of hydrogen to one part of oxygen but, instead, has a complex chemical structure – XYZ. Let us call this substance *retaw*. Now, if $Herbert_1$ is an English speaker of earth, and $Herbert_2$ is his twin-earth counterpart, then it is fairly clear that when $Herbert_1$ says 'water is wet', and $Herbert_2$ produces an utterance of the same phonetic form, they say something different. Their utterances have distinct meanings. And this is true even though, *ex hypothesi*, what is going on in their heads is identical. Meanings, as Putnam points out, are not in the head. Moreover, these differences go on to effect oblique occurrences of these sentences that specify the content of the respective Herbert's beliefs. Thus, Herbert$_1$ believes that water is wet. But Herbert$_2$ cannot have this belief. Herbert$_2$ believes that retaw is wet (even though he would express this belief by an utterance of the form 'water is wet'). Thus, the content of the two Herberts' beliefs differ, and thus their beliefs differ, even though what is going on in their heads is the same.

Putnam's thought experiment works by driving a wedge between the two factors that determine the content of belief. The beliefs of Herbert$_1$ and Herbert$_2$ have the same mode of representation of their objects. That is, they represent water and retaw in precisely the same way – as colourless, odourless, drinkable, etc. liquids. Nonetheless, the contents of the beliefs, and hence the beliefs themselves, differ. And this shows that the content of a belief cannot be entirely determined by its mode of representation of an object. Content is, in part, constituted by the referential properties of beliefs.

We are now in a position to see just what a crucial move was Stich's refusal to apply the concept of reference similarity to non-human animals. Stich, remember, thinks that the notion of content-identity is a similarity relation which can be factored into three components: causal-pattern similarity, ideological similarity, and reference similarity. But Stich also thinks that the relation of reference similarity is inapplicable to non-human animals: since they have no language, reference similarity is out of the question. This follows from his characterization of reference similarity as a relation holding between the terms of a language and the world. However, Stich gives no justification or defence of this characterization. Stich does allow that some sort of derivative reference relation might obtain between the representations possessed by non-human animals and the world. But he does not regard this as important enough to warrant the inclusion of reference similarity as a determinant of the content of animal belief states. In my view, this is to get the order of primacy reversed. Reference is a relation which holds *primarily* between internal states of creatures and the world, or between the behaviour of creatures and the world, and *derivatively* between terms or expressions and the world. And this claim will be defended later in the chapter. For now, it is sufficient to point out that in excluding the relation of reference from the factors involved in attributing beliefs to non-humans, Stich is excluding an important constituent of the content of beliefs. No wonder he regards the attribution of beliefs to non-humans as problematic.

Reference and Transparency

The fact that the content of any belief depends on two distinct factors means that an attribution of a belief to an individual can be made on the basis of either factor. Our attributions of belief, that is, answer to two distinct interests we have in such attributions. When the context, for example, calls for us to be interested in the way in which an individual represents an object, our attribution will typically be carried by, and hence sensitive to, the mode of representation of that object. Thus, if, for example, we were interested in the respective behaviours of the two Herberts, how they interact with water or retaw, whether they will drink it, wash in it, etc., then our attribution of belief to them would be based on, and carried by, the mode of representation of water or retaw. Other contexts, however, might require sensitivity to the referential constituent of the content. Questions of truth and falsity, for example, require sensitivity to this latter constituent.

Putnam's example, in effect, shows that there are two distinct ways of looking at, or individuating, the content of any belief, hence two distinct ways of looking at, or individuating, that belief. Contents of beliefs, hence beliefs themselves, can be individuated *narrowly* or *broadly*. A belief narrowly individuated comprises the mode of representation of the intentional object of that belief. It is the belief narrowly individuated that plays a causal-explanatory role in the agent's psychology. That is, it is not the relation to the referent that is causally or explanatorily relevant to the agent's behaviour but the way in which that referent is represented internally. It is not *what* is represented that matters to causal or explanatory role but *the way in which* it is represented. On the other hand, it seems undeniable that beliefs have representational or semantic properties – for they have truth-conditions – and these properties exert a pull in the individu-ation of beliefs by content. The belief individuated by way of its referential or semantic properties is a belief broadly individuated. Putnam's thought experiment thus shows that these two ways of individuating beliefs are not equivalent and, in certain circumstances, can come apart. Thus, the two Herberts are identical in point of their beliefs narrowly individuated but distinct in point of their beliefs broadly individuated. And, therefore, we must recognize that belief content is essentially a hybrid of conceptually disparate elements, *both* of which inform our conception of belief and its individuation.[14]

Because the same belief can, in different contexts, be subject to distinct standards of individuation, our attribution of beliefs and other propositional attitudes to individuals is fundamentally ambiguous. In certain cases, the attribution will be carried by the mode of representation of the object of the belief. In certain other contexts, however, the attribution will be carried by the referential properties of the belief; that is, it will be based on the intentional or represented object of the belief, and not the manner in which this object is represented. There is no question of which attribution is the correct one; both are equally legitimate. And which sort of attribution we make is, in any particular case, largely a function of our interests underlying this attribution.

There is, in fact, a familiar linguistic device we use to record the fact that distinct standards of individuation can be applicable to, and hence govern the attribution of, the same belief. There are what is known as *transparent* attributions of a belief, and there are *opaque* attributions of that belief. An opaque attribution of a belief is an attribution of a belief individuated narrowly, a belief individuated by way of its mode of representation of its object. A transparent attribution of a belief is an attribution of a belief individuated broadly, individuated by way of its semantic or referential properties. Put in these terms, in Putnam's twin-earth case, the two Herberts are subject to the same opaque attributions of belief but distinct transparent attributions of belief. Similarly, if I believe, to use one of Quine's examples, that Jones is a spy, and if, unbeknownst to me, the tallest man in the room is Jones, then I am subject to the opaque attribution of the belief that Jones is a spy and subject to the transparent (but not the opaque) attribution of the belief that the tallest man in the room is a spy.

Both opaque and transparent attributions of belief are equally legitimate, but they are driven by different interests, governed by distinct standards of individuation for beliefs, and appropriate in different contexts.

Transparency and Holism

Suppose an explorer comes across a hitherto undiscovered primitive tribe. The tribespeople, let us suppose, are terrified of his camera. Since they have never seen a camera before, and since they are manifestly terrified of it, it is clear that their concept of a camera occupies a place in a vastly different causal and ideological network of beliefs than our own. Nevertheless, it would surely be misguided to insist that therefore, they can possess no beliefs or other propositional attitudes towards the camera. And it would be equally misguided to claim that it is not possible to specify the content of their beliefs. Indeed, adequately explaining their behaviour would require both postulation of belief and of a determinate content. Thus, for example, we might explain their terror by hypothesizing that they believe the camera will take their soul. Unless one was in the grip of a theory, one would surely allow that the tribespeople can bear this sort of belief about the camera.

What grounds our confidence here is the possibility of transparent attributions of belief? That is, it is correct to say of a tribesman that he believes of the camera that it will take his soul. And such an attribution does not require that the tribesman possesses a concept of the camera whose content is individuated by its place in a network of beliefs. The tribesman, let us suppose, does possess a network of beliefs about the camera, and this network is very different from our own. As a result, he possesses a concept, narrowly individuated, of a camera that is very different from our own. However, the transparent attribution of beliefs about the camera is in no way affected by this fact. The transparent attribution of the belief, in this case, is sensitive to, and carried by, the camera itself, and not the mode of representation of the camera. It is only when the content of a belief is individuated narrowly, by its mode of representation, that attribution of a belief is subject to the sort of holistic constraints that concern Davidson and Stich. When the content of a belief is individuated broadly, in terms of the belief's object itself and not its mode of representation, then attribution of this belief is not subject to these constraints. And this is why it is possible to legitimately attribute beliefs and other content bearing states to individuals who possess vastly different causal and ideological networks than our own.

The arguments of Davidson and Stich, then, even if correct, can have application only to situations in which the attribution of beliefs and other propositional attitudes is opaque. Transparent attributions of beliefs are not affected by the sorts of holistic constraints identified by Davidson and Stich.

Attributing Content to Animals

Precisely the same principles apply in the case of non-human animals. A dog's concept of a tree, it is plausible to suppose, occupies a place in a vastly different system of beliefs and other propositional attitudes than does our corresponding concept. The dog, presumably does not know that trees are growing things, that they require soil and water, that they drop leaves and needles, that they burn, etc. And this, it is argued, is grounds for denying the dog the concept of a tree. Hence it is grounds for denying the dog any beliefs about trees, including the belief that the cat is up the tree.

This argument, however, will work only in the case of opaque attributions of belief. In such attribution, belief content is individuated narrowly, in terms of the mode of representation of the intentional object of the belief. Such attributions are, therefore, sensitive to, and carried by, the mode of representation of the belief's object, since an object's mode of representation in a belief does depend on other beliefs possessed by a subject. Transparent ascriptions, on the other hand, depend on individuating belief content broadly, by reference to the intentional object of the belief itself and not that object's mode of representation. Since the identity of the belief's intentional object is not determined by its mode of representation, such attributions are not in any way dependent on this mode of representation. And, therefore, transparent attributions of belief are not subject to the sort of holistic constraints that govern opaque attributions.

Therefore, the fact that a dog such as Brenin lacks many, or even all, of the beliefs about trees that humans typically possess can, at most, impact on the possibility of making opaque attributions of belief to him. Transparent attributions, on the other hand, are not affected by this deficit. Therefore, to argue that Brenin cannot have the belief that there is a cat up the tree because it would be impossible to specify the content of any such alleged belief ultimately rests on a failure to adequately recognize that there are two distinct ways of individuating the content of a belief, hence two distinct ways of individuating beliefs, and therefore, two distinct ways in which beliefs can be attributed. The fact that any belief had by Brenin about trees would occupy a place in a radically different causal and ideological network than the corresponding belief of a human can, at most, impact only on the narrowly individuated content of his belief. It cannot affect the content of his belief when that content is broadly individuated. Hence, the fact leaves unaffected the possibility of a transparent attribution of belief to Brenin.

This defence of attributing beliefs and other propositional attitudes to animals is anticipated by Davidson. He writes:

Someone may suggest that the position occupied by the expression 'that oak tree' in the sentence 'The dog thinks the cat went up that oak tree' is, in Quine's terminology, transparent. The right way to put the dog's belief (the suggestion continues) is 'The dog thinks, with respect to that oak tree, that the cat went up it' or 'That oak tree is the one the dog thinks the cat went up.'[15]

According to Davidson, however, the problem with this suggestion is that:

> such constructions, while they may relieve the attributer of the need to produce a description of the object that the believer would accept, nevertheless imply that there is some such description; the *de re* description picks out an object the believer could somehow pick out.[16]

Here, however, we must be careful to distinguish two importantly distinct claims: (i) the possibility of making a transparent attribution of a belief to an individual depends on there being a narrowly individuated content possessed by that belief, and (ii) the possibility of making a transparent attribution of a belief to an individual depends on our knowing what the narrowly individuated content of that belief is. The defence of attributing beliefs to non-humans developed in the above pages arguably entails (i). Unless one is prepared to accept the somewhat implausible claim that narrow and broad content can come apart to the extent that it possible for the latter to exist without the former, one should accept that the transparent attribution of a belief to an individual presupposes the existence of a narrowly individuated content possessed by that belief. Hence the possibility of making a transparent attribution of a belief to an individual arguably entails the possibility *in principle* of making a corresponding opaque attribution of a belief to that individual. However, this does not entail that, in order to make a transparent attribution of a belief to an individual one must know what the narrowly individuated content of that belief is. All that is required for us to make a transparent attribution of a belief to an individual is that the belief picks out an object under a particular mode of representation. It does not entail that we know what that mode of representation is. Transparent attributions of belief do not entail the possibility *in practice* of corresponding opaque attributions.

The correct reply to Davidson, then, is to simply accept that we are unable to make opaque attributions of belief to non-humans. This is not because such attributions are intrinsically impossible, but they may be impossible for us. Even this point is, I think, far from certain. The fact that we might be unable, in practice, to make opaque attributions of belief to, for example, Brenin does not mean that we are unable to develop the expertise necessary to do so. Presumably such expertise would require a detailed investigation of the structure and evolutionary history of that part of Brenin's brain responsible for representing the world coupled with a detailed ethological investigation of the ways in which Brenin and other dogs behave with respect to trees. But there is no evidence to suggest that such studies, or the knowledge that results from them, is beyond our grasp. However, more importantly, even if opaque attributions of belief to Brenin were forever beyond our grasp, this would not entail that such attributions were in principle impossible, nor does it entail that Brenin's belief possesses no narrowly individuated content.

Whatever the ultimate status of our knowledge of the way in which Brenin represents trees, all that is required for a transparent attribution to Brenin of a belief about a tree is that (i) there is such a mode of representation, and (ii) we know what the intentional object of his belief is. And condition (ii), crucially, is not affected by the sorts of holistic constraints identified by Davidson and Stich. Thus, we can make transparent attributions of belief without being able to make opaque attributions of belief. And this, ultimately, is why it is legitimate to attribute content, hence attribute beliefs and other propositional attitudes to non-humans. We can attribute to Brenin the belief that the cat is up the tree for precisely the same reason as we could attribute the belief that the camera is a stealer of souls to the primitive tribesman. In both cases, the attribution is transparent.

5. HOW ANIMALS CAN REFER

I have argued that, in arguments over whether it is possible to ascribe propositional attitudes to non-human animals, we must be careful to observe the distinction between opaque and transparent attributions. An opaque attribution of a propositional attitude to an individual depends essentially on the mode of presentation of the intentional object of the attitude; that is, on the way in which that object is represented to the individual. A transparent attribution, on the other hand, depends only on the identity of the intentional object, and not on the way in which that objected is represented. Opaque attributions, being dependent on the mode of representation of intentional objects, are crucially dependent on the causal and ideological networks of beliefs in which the attributed attitude is embedded, since these are partial determinants of the mode of presentation of the attitude's intentional object. Transparent attributions, however, are not similarly dependent on such networks of attitudes, since it is not generally true that the mode of representation of an intentional object determines the identity of that object. Therefore, while opaque attributions of propositional attitudes to non-humans might be undermined by the fact that non-human minds are constituted by vastly different networks of beliefs than our own, transparent attributions are not undermined by this fact. The arguments of Davidson and Stich, then, can, at most, jeopardize opaque attributions of propositional attitudes to non-humans; they in no way undermine transparent attributions of such attitudes.

We are now in a position to see just what a crucial move was Stich's refusal to apply the concept of reference similarity to non-human animals. Stich, remember, thinks that the notion of content-identity is a similarity relation which can be factored into three components: causal-pattern similarity, ideological similarity, and reference similarity. But Stich also thinks that the relation of reference similarity is inapplicable to non-human animals. This follows from his characterization of reference similarity as a relation holding between the terms of a language and the world. However, Stich gives no justification or defence of this characterization. Stich does allow that some sort of derivative reference relation might obtain between the representations possessed by non-human animals and the world. But he does not regard this as important enough to warrant the inclusion of reference similarity as a determinant of the content of animal beliefs and other propositional attitudes. Stich, however, is definitely swimming against the current on this point. The orthodox view is that reference is a relation which holds *primarily* between internal states of individuals and the world and only *derivatively* between terms or expressions and the world. And this is, ultimately, why it is possible to make transparent attributions of propositional attitudes to individuals, both human and otherwise. The remainder of this chapter will be concerned with explaining how the internal representations of non-human animals might be able to refer to, or represent, the world.

One of the principal projects of recent philosophy of mind has been the attempt to provide an account of the relation of representation. This has been particularly important insofar as the notion of representation has been seen as the basis of the relation of intentionality. The intentionality of mental states, at least acccording to one prominent account, derives from the representational relations holding between internal states and the world. The account of representation I shall now consider is by no means the only possible account; and it does have its opponents. However, it is, in my view, the best philosophical account currently available. It is worth noting that even if the following should prove an inadequate account of representation, all competing accounts construe representation as a natural relation holding primarily between internal states of individuals and the world. Thus, even if the following account turns out to be wrong, all competing accounts are compatible with the claim that the notion of reference is applicable to non-language using animals. Thus, they are all compatible with the practice of making transparent attributions of propositional attitudes to animals. The account I favour has been developed most fully by Ruth Millikan, and is known as the *teleological theory*.[17]

A teleological theory of mental representation will employ, as a pivotal concept, what Millikan calls *relational proper function*. The proper function of some mechanism, trait, or process is what it is *supposed* to do, what it has been *designed* to do, what it *ought* to do. The concept of proper function is a normative concept. Proper functions can come about either through the intentions of a designer, or through a mindless process such as natural selection. A hammer has the proper function of knocking in nails in virtue of the intentions of its designers, makers, and users. A heart, on the other hand, has the proper function of pumping blood in virtue of various pressures of natural selection.

The proper function of an item is defined in terms of what that item *should* do, not what it actually does or is disposed to do. The concept of proper function, being normative, cannot be defined causally or dispositionally. What something does, or is disposed to do, is not always what it is supposed to do. To use a flagship example of Millikan's, the proper function of a sperm cell is to fertilize the ovum. The vast majority of sperm cells, however, do not accomplish this task. The proper function of an item is its *Normal* function, where, following Millikan, the capitalized 'N' indicates that this is a normative sense of normal as opposed to a causal or dispositional one.

The Normal function of many evolved items is *relational* in character. In the case of evolved organisms, function is ultimately relative to gene reproduction; that is, the function of many evolved characteristics is ultimately to enhance reproductive capacity. Generally this means that the characteristic is to enable the organism (the gene vehicle) to cope with its environment: to locate food, evade predators, protect itself against heat and cold, and so on. It is here that the relationality of Normal or proper function arises. Normal functions are often defined relatively to some environmental object or feature: the function of the chameleon's skin is to make the chameleon the same colour as its immediate environment; the function of the lion's curved claws is to catch and hold on to prey; the function of the bee's dance is to help other bees locate nectar, and so on. In each case, the function of the characteristic is specified in terms of a relation to an environmental item. And the reason for this is that the very reason the characteristic in question exists is that it has evolved to meet certain environmental pressures.

The core idea of the teleological theory of mental representation is that the mechanisms responsible for mental representations are evolutionary products also. As such, they will have relational proper functions. The idea, then, is that the representational features of a given cognitive mechanism derive from the environmental objects, properties or relations that are incorporated into that mechanism's relational proper function. That is, if a cognitive mechanism M has evolved in order to detect environmental feature E, then this is what makes an appropriate state S of M about E; this is what gives the state S the content that E. In this way, the representational content of cognitive state S derives from the relational proper function of mechanism M that produces S.

This account requires a clear distinction to be drawn between a cognitive state and a cognitive mechanism. Roughly, the distinction will be implemented in the following way. An organism's cognitive state tokens are (often) caused by events occurring in that organism's environment. And there are mechanisms, typically neuronal, that mediate those causal transactions. Each of these mechanisms will, presumably, have an evolutionary history and, therefore, will possess a proper function. And, it is plausible to suppose, this proper function will be precisely to mediate the tokenings of cognitive states. That is, on the teleological view, there are various neural mechanisms whose proper or normal function is to produce tokenings of cognitive states in environmentally appropriate circumstances. According to the teleological theory, the content of these cognitive states derives from the environmental features that are incorporated into the proper functions of the mechanisms that produce these states. Thus, if cognitive state S is produced by mechanism M, and if the proper function of M is to produce S in environmental circumstances E, then, according to the teleological theory, S represents, or is about, E. In this way, the content of a cognitive state derives from the relational proper function of the mechanism that produces it.

There is nothing in this story that requires cognitive states – beliefs, desires, etc. – to themselves have proper functions. It is perfectly consistent to claim that the content of a cognitive state derives from relational proper function while denying that the cognitive state itself has that proper function. And this is good for the teleological account, because the claim that cognitive states such as beliefs and desires have proper functions is notoriously difficult to defend.

The teleological theory does not purport to provide a complete theory of *content*. If it did, it would attract the obvious objection that mechanisms and structures of organisms can have relational proper functions and yet not have propositional content. It does not seem appropriate, for example, to assign semantic content to hearts, despite their relational proper function. Rather, the teleological theory is advanced as a theory of the referential component of representation. It does not try to explain why a state might represent an organism in a particular way. It does try to explain why a state can represent, in the sense of refer to, denote, or pick out, a particular object. The teleological theory only purports to be a theory of a part of content: that part of content that is constituted by the referential component of the representational relation.

This being so, the teleological theory is best viewed within the framework of the two-factor account of propositional attitudes developed earlier. As we have seen, our intuitive conception of content is constituted by two distinct factors. On the one hand there is a mode of presentation of the intentional object of a belief; on the other, there is the intentional object itself. The content of the belief is constituted both by the mode of presentation of the object, and by the representational relation the belief bears to the object itself, independently of its mode of presentation. Consequently, there are two distinct ways in which a propositional attitude might be attributed: opaquely or transparently. Transparent attributions of belief and other propositional attitudes do not require detailed knowledge of the mode of presentation of the intentional objects of belief; they merely require that we know *which* objects are the intentional objects of beliefs. Transparent attributions of beliefs to non-human animals, therefore, will be legitimate as long as we have some reason for thinking that non-human animals have internal states that function to represent, or pick out, environmental (or bodily) items. This is where the teleological theory comes in. If we understand representation in the way suggested by the teleological theory, then it becomes essentially a biological phenomenon. Internal states can represent environmental items in virtue of the fact that the mechanisms which produce such states have evolved to produce them in circumstances where a given environmental item is present. The representational properties of the state derive from the evolutionarily determined relational proper function of the biological mechanisms that produce them. Representation, therefore, is ultimately a biological notion. And, given that non-human animals clearly do have internal mechanisms which have evolved to detect certain environmental features, it is perfectly appropriate, at least in principle, to make transparent attributions of beliefs and other propositional attitudes to them.

Therefore, for example, when you arrive home and your dog on the inside scratches at the door while you, on the other side, are fumbling for your key, it is perfectly legitimate to ascribe to the dog the belief that you are on the other side of the door. We don't have to know how the dog represents you, that is we don't have to know under what mode of presentation the dog subsumes you. And presumably the dog's mode of presentation of you is radically different from that mode of presentation whereby you represent yourself to yourself, or whereby you are represented by others. All we need to know, in order to make the transparent attribution of this belief to him, is that he detects *you*. What initially grounds our confidence that he detects you, as opposed to anyone else, is the difference in his behaviour when another person approaches the door (the tone and cadence of the bark changes, etc.). And what justifies our confidence that there is some sort of detection going on here is, ultimately, evolutionary theory. We know, on evolutionary grounds, that dogs are going to have evolved mechanisms to detect friends from foes, familiar from strange animals, pack members from outsiders. Thus, if the teleological theory is true, we know on evolutionary grounds that some sort of representation is going on here. And we know from careful observation of behaviour, what the object of the representation is. And this is all we need to know in order to make a transparent attribution of belief.

6. CONCLUSION

I have argued that the worries raised by Davidson and Stich presuppose that our attributions of belief and other propositional attitudes to non-human animals are exclusively opaque attributions. If this were so, the practice of making such attributions might be undermined by the fact that any alleged beliefs of non-human animals would occupy a place in a radically different causal and ideological network than those of humans. This would undermine our ability to identify the content of such beliefs, and, hence our ability to attribute beliefs in the first place. However, difference in doxastic networks surrounding a given belief has no impact on the transparent ascription of beliefs to animals. All that is required to make such ascriptions is to identify the referential properties of the belief; and this will require, above all else, identifying to which objects in the world the animal is referring. Stich ruled out the possibility of the content of animal beliefs being, in part, constituted by referential properties by defining the relation of reference as holding between the terms of a language and the world. However, this move is unjustified. There are excellent reasons for thinking that representational relations obtain primarily between internal states of animals and the world, and derivatively between terms of a language and the world. The teleological theory provides one, but by no means the only, expression of just this sort of view. Therefore, there are excellent reasons for believing that non-human animals are capable of referring. And this is all that is required for transparent ascriptions of propositional attitudes to non-human animals to be justified. Therefore, there is every reason to think that our transparent attributions of propositional attitudes to non-humans are justified.

There is a tendency in certain circles to view attribution of propositional attitudes to non-human animals as a form of crude anthropomorphism or misguided sentimentalism. In fact it is not. In the case of non-human animals (as well as in the case of many humans) propositional attitude ascription is transparent ascription. And all that is required to make such ascriptions is the belief that animals are capable of referring to, or picking out, objects in their environment. And the reasons for thinking this stem neither from anthropomorphism nor from sentimentalism, but simply from good old-fashioned, down to earth, evolutionary biology.

Notes

1. ANIMAL RIGHTS: A CONTRACTARIAN DEFENCE

1. Peter Singer, *Animal Liberation* (New York: *The New York Review of Books*, 1975). Reprinted by Thorsons (1991). All references are to the latter.
2. *Practical Ethics* (Cambridge: Cambridge University Press, 1980). 'Utilitarianism and Vegetarianism', *Philosophy and Public Affairs*, 9, 8 (1980). 'Animals and the Value of Life', in *Matters of Life and Death*, ed. Tom Regan (New York: Random House, 1980). 'Killing Humans and Killing Animals', *Inquiry*, 22 (1979). 'All Animals are Equal', *Philosophical Exchange*, 1, 5 (1974).
3. Tom Regan, *The Case for Animal Rights* (Berkeley: University of California Press, 1984). Reprinted by Routledge (1988). All references are to the latter.
4. Deserving of mention here are the following (in no particular order) S. F. Sapontzis, *Morals, Reasons, and Animals* (Philadelphia: Temple University Press, 1987); Mary Midgeley, *Animals and Why They Matter* (Harmondsworth: Penguin, 1984); James Rachels, *Created from Animals: The Moral Implications of Darwinism* (Oxford: Oxford University Press, 1990); David DeGrazia, *Taking Animals Seriously* (Cambridge: Cambridge University Press, 1996); Stephen Clark, *The Moral Status of Animals* (Oxford: Oxford University Press, 1977).
5. Peter Carruthers, *The Animals Issue: Moral Theory in Practice* (Cambridge: Cambridge University Press, 1992).
6. Tom Regan, *The Case for Animal Rights* pp. 163–74.
7. I borrow the terminology of *Hobbesian* and *Kantian* contractarianism from Will Kymlicka's essay 'Contractarianism', in Peter Singer (ed.), *A Companion to Ethics* (Oxford: Basil Blackwell, 1989). Kymlicka is very clear on the difference between the two forms.
8. John Rawls, *A Theory of Justice* (Oxford: Oxford University Press, 1971).
9. See Kymlicka, 'Contractarianism'.
10. John Rawls, *A Theory of Justice*, p. 121.

2. ARGUING FOR ONE'S SPECIES

1. A somewhat similar scenario is to be found in Colin McGinn's example of the vampires who are capable of living on orange juice. See his *Moral Literacy, or How to do the Right Thing* (Cambridge: Hackett, 1992), pp. 21–2.
2. The story is taken from Dave Foreman's 'Foreword' to *Wild Earth*, 1, 3 (1991).

3. LIBERALISM AND THE EXPANDING CIRCLE

1. Peter Singer, *Animal Liberation*, p. 15.
2. The priority of the right over the good is a formulation of liberalism associated with John Rawls. See his *A Theory of Justice*.
3. John Locke, *Essay on the Law of Nature*, ed. W. Von Leyden (Oxford: Oxford University Press, 1965), p. 111.
4. John Locke, *The Reasonableness of Christianity*, ed. G. Ewing (Washington D.C.: Regency Gateway, 1965), p. 162.
5. John Locke, *Essay on the Law of Nature*, p. 187.
6. Ibid., p. 185.
7. See also John Locke, *Two Treatises of Government*, ed. P. Laslett (Cambridge: Cambridge University Press, 1963), p. 427. Also, John Locke, 'A Letter Concerning Toleration' in his *The Second Treatise of Civil Government and A Letter Concerning Toleration*, ed. J. Gough (Oxford: Basil Blackwell, 1947).
8. John Locke, *An Essay Concerning Human Understanding*, ed. P. Nidditch (Oxford: Oxford University Press, 1975), 1.2.12.
9. Ibid., 2.28.5.
10. David Gauthier, 'Why Ought One Obey God? Reflections on Hobbes and Locke', *Canadian Journal of Philosophy*, 7, 2 (1977).
11. This point is made by Bernard Williams in his *Morality: An Introduction to Ethics* (New York: Harper and Row, 1972), p. 64.
12. Ibid., p. 65.
13. Ibid., p. 65.
14. John Stuart Mill, *On Liberty*, ed. Elizabeth Rapaport (Cambridge: Hackett, 1978). Also, John Stuart Mill, *Utilitarianism, Liberty, Representative Government*, ed. A. D. Lindsay (London: J. M. Dent and Sons, 1968).
15. This interpretation of Mill is defended by John Gray, *Mill on Liberty: A Defence* (London: Routledge and Kegan Paul, 1983).
16. The two forms of contractarianism are clearly distinguished by Will Kymlicka in his 'Contractarianism'.
17. The terminology is borrowed from Kymlicka's 'Contractarianism'.
18. The expression is again borrowed from Kymlicka's 'Contractarianism'.
19. John Rawls, *A Theory of Justice*, p. 121.

4. UTILITARIANISM AND ANIMALS: PETER SINGER'S CASE FOR ANIMAL LIBERATION

1. Peter Singer, *Animal Liberation*, pp. 2–23.
2. See especially, Peter Singer, 'Utilitarianism and Vegetarianism'.
3. J. J. C. Smart, 'An Outline of a System of Utilitarian Ethics', in J. J. C. Smart and B. Williams (eds.), *Utilitarianism: For and Against* (Cambridge: Cambridge University Press, 1973), pp. 18–21.
4. I sometimes think philosophers, being necessarily a cerebral lot, often tend to be somewhat out of touch with those more somatically inclined. It seems to me, having conducted a completely unscientific survey of

some of my more hedonistically oriented friends, that many people in fact would volunteer to be hooked up to the machine. Hence, I do not endorse these criticisms, I merely outline them.

5. Smart, in fact, describes the machine in this more general way. I have distinguished the pleasure machine from the more general experience machine simply for expository purposes.
6. John Rawls, *A Theory of Justice*, p. 24.
7. Tom Regan, *The Case for Animal Rights*, pp. 208–11.
8. G. E. Moore, *Ethics* (Oxford: Oxford University Press, 1912).
9. John Rawls, *A Theory of Justice*, pp. 23ff.
10. Tom Regan, *The Case for Animal Rights*, pp. 208ff.
11. J. S. Mill, *Utilitarianism, Liberty, Representative Government*, ed. A. D. Lindsay (London: J. M. Dent and Sons, 1968). R. M. Hare, 'Rights, Utility, and Universalization: Reply to J. L. Mackie', in R. G. Frey (ed.), *Utility and Rights* (Minneapolis: University of Minnesota Press, 1984). J. Harsanyi, *Essays on Ethics, Social Behaviour, and Scientific Explanation* (Dordrecht: Reidel, 1976). J. Griffin, *Well Being: Its Meaning, Measurement, and Moral Importance* (Oxford: Oxford University Press, 1986).
12. R. M. Hare, 'Rights, Utility, and Universalization: A Reply to J. L. Mackie', p. 106.
13. Ronald Dworkin, *Taking Rights Seriously* (London: Duckworth, 1977), p. 234.
14. Will Kymlicka, *Contemporary Political Philosophy* (Oxford: Oxford University Press, 1990), p. 40.
15. John Rawls, *A Theory of Justice* pp. 31, 450, 564.
16. Peter Singer, 'All Animals are Equal', p. 155.
17. Tom Regan, *The Case for Animal Rights* pp. 220ff.

5. TOM REGAN: ANIMAL RIGHTS AS NATURAL RIGHTS

1. Tom Regan, *The Case for Animal Rights* p. 243.
2. Regan regards utilitarianism as an essentially teleological theory, in the sense explained in the previous chapter.
3. Tom Regan, *The Case for Animal Rights* pp. 326–7.
4. Ibid., 267–73.
5. Ibid., p. 272.
6. Ibid., pp. 284–5.
7. Ibid., p. 305.
8. Ibid., p. 298.
9. Ibid., p. 308.
10. Ibid., p. 331.
11. Ibid., p. 333.
12. It is worth noting that it is not possible to derive the worse-off principle from the contractarian position I shall develop in the next chapter. The contractarian position, that is, does not license a blanket 'save the ones made worse-off' claim. What also has to be factored in to contractarian considerations is the likelihood of oneself being one of the

worse-off, or one of the better off. This, I think, is a strength of the contractarian position.

6. CONTRACTARIANISM AND ANIMAL RIGHTS

1. Immanuel Kant, 'Duties to Animals and Spirits', in his *Lectures on Ethics*, trans. Louis Infield (New York: Harper & Row, 1963).
2. Peter Carruthers, *The Animals Issue* (Cambridge: Cambridge University Press, 1992), pp. 98–9.
3. Tom Regan, 'The Case for Animal Rights', in Peter Singer (ed.), *In Defence of Animals* (Oxford: Basil Blackwell, 1985), p. 17.
4. For a much more balanced discussion, see David DeGrazia, *Taking Animals Seriously* (Cambridge: Cambridge University Press, 1996), pp. 166–210.
5. David Gauthier, *Morals by Agreement* (Oxford: Oxford University Press, 1986).
6. John Rawls, *A Theory of Justice* (Oxford: Oxford University Press, 1971). *Political Liberalism* (Oxford: Oxford University Press, 1993).
7. John Rawls, *A Theory of Justice* pp. 7–11.
8. Ibid., pp. 302–3.
9. This point is made with admirable clarity by Will Kymlicka, *Contemporary Political Philosophy* (Oxford: Oxford University Press, 1990), p. 55.
10. John Rawls, *A Theory of Justice* pp. 100–8.
11. Ibid., p. 12.
12. Michael Sandel, *Liberalism and the Limits of Justice* (Cambridge: Cambridge University Press, 1982).
13. John Rawls, *A Theory of Justice*, p. 138.
14. See especially 'Justice as Fairness: Political not Metaphysical', *Philosophy and Public Affairs*, 14, 3 (1985), pp. 223–51.
15. It is this crucial point which seems to be continually overlooked by communitarian critics of Rawls.
16. See, for example, R. M. Hare, 'Rawls' Theory of Justice', in N. Daniels (ed.), *Reading Rawls* (New York: Basic Books, 1975). Brian Barry, *The Liberal Theory of Justice* (Oxford: Oxford University Press, 1973).
17. John Rawls, *A Theory of Justice*, p. 121.
18. Ibid., p. 20.
19. This point applies in particular, I think, to Peter Carruthers, *The Animals Issue*.
20. The analogy is due to Simon Caney, 'Liberalism and Communitarianism: A Misconceived Debate', *Political Studies*, 40, 2 (1992) p. 277.
21. See his *Problems of Philosophy* (Oxford: Oxford University Press, 1912), chapter 5.
22. John Rawls, *A Theory of Justice*, p. 508.
23. Ibid., p. 131.
24. Ibid., p. 505.
25. Ibid., pp. 505–6.

26. Ibid., p. 504.
27. Ibid., p. 505.
28. Ibid., p. 512.
29. I say 'no worry', but this is tendentious. Those concerned with the environment, for example, might want to extend the scope of morality in precisely the way that I have argued contractarianism rules out. I think, in fact, that contractarian approaches can yield a genuine environmental ethic. However, the rights they will accord the non-animate environment will necessarily be indirect ones.
30. Peter Carruthers, *The Animals Issue*, p. 102.
31. Peter Singer, *The Expanding Circle: Ethics and Sociobiology* (Oxford: Oxford University Press, 1981).

7. ANIMAL MINDS

1. The distinction is originally due to Bertrand Russell.
2. The example is borrowed from Stephen Stich, *From Folk Psychology to Cognitive Science* (Massachusetts: MIT Press, 1983), p. 5.
3. Donald Davidson, 'Rational Animals', in E. LePore and B. McLaughlin (eds.), *Actions and Events: Perspectives on the Philosophy of Donald Davidson* (Oxford: Basil Blackwell, 1985), pp. 473–80, 475. See also Davidson's 'Thought and Talk', in S. Guttenplan (ed.), *Mind and Language* (Oxford: Oxford University Press, 1975), pp. 7–23.
4. Donald Davidson, 'Rational Animals', p. 475.
5. Ibid., p. 475.
6. See Donald Davidson, 'Mental Events', in his *Essays on Actions and Events* (Oxford: Oxford University Press, 1980), pp. 207–25.
7. Content holism has played a central role in Davidson's writings in the philosophy of language. See his *Inquiries into Truth and Interpretation* (Oxford: Oxford University Press, 1984).
8. Stephen Stich, 'Do Animals have Beliefs?', *Australasian Journal of Philosophy*, 57 (1979), pp. 15–28.
9. Stephen Stich, *From Folk Psychology to Cognitive Science*, pp. 104–6.
10. Tom Regan, *The Case for Animal Rights*, pp. 49–60.
11. Donald Davidson, 'Rational Animals', p. 475.
12. David DeGrazia, *Taking Animals Seriously: Mental Life and Moral Status* (Cambridge: Cambridge University Press, 1996). DeGrazia himself falls victim to the temptation described here.
13. Hilary Putnam, 'The Meaning of "Meaning"', in K. Gunderson (ed.), *Language, Mind and Knowledge: Minnesota Studies in the Philosophy of Science*, 7 (Minneapolis: University of Minnesota Press, 1975). Tyler Burge, 'Individualism and the Mental', *Midwest Studies in Philosophy*, 4 (1979). See also Burge's 'Individualism and Psychology', *Philosophical Review*, 95 (1986), pp. 3–45.
14. Colin McGinn, 'The Structure of Content', in A. Woodfield (ed.), *Thought and Object* (Oxford: Oxford University Press, 1982), pp. 207–58.
15. Donald Davidson 'Rational Animals', p. 475.

16. Ibid., p. 475.
17. Ruth Millikan, *Language, Thought and Other Biological Categories* (Massachusetts: MIT Press, 1984).

Index